Learning Python Network Programming

Utilize Python 3 to get network applications up and running quickly and easily

Dr. M. O. Faruque Sarker

Sam Washington

BIRMINGHAM - MUMBAI

Learning Python Network Programming

First published: June 2015

Production reference: 1100615

Published by Packt Publishing Ltd.
Livery Place
35 Livery Street
Birmingham B3 2PB, UK.

ISBN 978-1-78439-600-8

www.packtpub.com

Credits

About the Authors

Dr. M. O. Faruque Sarker is a software architect based in London, UK, where he has been shaping various Linux and open source software solutions, mainly on cloud computing platforms, for commercial companies, educational institutions, and multinational consultancies. Over the past 10 years, he has been leading a number of Python software development and cloud infrastructure automation projects. In 2009, he started using Python, where he was responsible for shepherding a fleet of miniature E-puck robots at the University of South Wales, Newport, UK. Later, he honed his Python skills, and he was invited to work on the Google Summer of Code (2009/2010) programs for contributing to the BlueZ and Tahoe-LAFS open source projects. He is the author of *Python Network Programming Cookbook, Packt Publishing*.

He received his PhD in multirobot systems from the University of South Wales. He is currently working at University College London. He takes an active interest in cloud computing, software security, intelligent systems, and child-centric education. He lives in East London with his wife, Shahinur, and daughter, Ayesha.

All praises and thanks to Allah, the God who is the Merciful and the Beneficent. I would not be able to finish this book without the help of God. I would like to thank Packt Publishing's entire team and my coauthor, Sam, who were very friendly and cooperative in this long journey. I would also like to thank my family and friends for their sacrifice of time, encouraging words, and smiles.

Sam Washington currently works at University College London as a member of its Learning and Teaching Applications team, developing and supporting the University's Moodle virtual learning environment, its wikis and blogs, and its online media services. Prior to this, he was a system administrator for UCL's several museums. He has working experience of managing the demands of varied web applications, and deploying and supporting Windows, Linux, and TCP/IP networks. He has been using Python for professional and personal projects for over 7 years.

I would like to thank the team at Packt for their encouragement and input throughout this project, especially Rebecca, Rohit, Saurabh, Trishla, and Akshay. I would also like to thank the reviewers for all their insights and corrections, Anhad Jai Singh, Ben Tasker, Grzegorz Gwóźdź, Ilja Zegars, Tom Stephens, Vishrut Mehta, Konstantin Manchev, and Andrew Armitage. I would like to express my immense respect and gratitude to the entire Python community for creating such a great programming language and ecosystem, and thanks to Faruque for giving me this opportunity to give a little in return. And Christina, thank you for still being here. You can have me back now.

About the Reviewers

Konstantin Manchev Manchev is a technical support professional, who has more than 15 years of experience in a wide range of operating systems, database services, scripting, networking, and security in the mobile telecommunication systems. He actively participates in the adaption of various vendor equipment projects to live mobile operator networks.

He has worked on the following technologies:

- Mobile systems such as GSM, UMTS, 3G, and WiFi
- Vendors such as Cisco, ALU, NSN, RedHat, and Canonical
- Network elements such as MSC, VLR, HLR, MSCS, OCS, NGIN, and PCRF
- Network protocol suites such as SS#7 and TCP/IP
- Webpage technologies such as HTTP, XML, HTML, SOAP, and REST
- Operating systems such as Linux (Debian, Ubuntu, RHEL, and CentOS), Windows, and Unix
- Virtualisation and Cloud technologies such as EC2, OpenStack, VMware, VirtualBox, and so on
- Programming languages such as Perl, Python, awk, bash, C, Delphi, Java, and so on
- Databases such as MongoDB, InfluxDB, MySQL, MS SQL, Oracle, and so on
- Monitoring systems such as Nagios, Grafana, Zabbix, and so on

He specializes in IT and Telecom services support, installation, configuration, maintenance, and implementation of the latest market technology solutions. He is a Linux enthusiast.

I would like to thank my wife, Nadya Valcheva-Mancheva, my kids, Elena Mancheva and Daniel Manchev, and colleagues, Attila Sovak, Ketan Delhiwala, Jerzy Sczudlowski, Aneesh Kannankara, Devrim Kucuk, Peter De Vriendt, Peyo Chernev, Andrey Royatchki, Tzvetan Balabanov, Vasil Zgurev, Ludmil Panov, Plamen Georgiev, Ivailo Pavlov, Mitko Bagrev, and Milen Cholakov for their support.

Vishrut Mehta is a student of IIIT Hyderabad, who is pursuing his masters in the field of cloud computing and software-defined networks. He has participated in the Google Summer of Code 2013 program under Sahana Software Foundation, and he was also the administrator for Google Code-In. He also did his research internship at INRIA, France, for 3 months under Dr. Nikos Parlavantzas in the field of automating multi-cloud applications.

He has worked on *Untangle Network Security* and *Python Network Programming Cookbook,* both by *Packt Publishing.*

I would like to thank my advisors, Dr. Vasudeva Varma and Dr. Reddy Raja, for helping me in my work and constantly supporting me with my research.

Anhad Jai Singh is a computer science graduate from IIIT Hyderabad. He's a part-time system administrator and has worked as a Python developer in the past. He's a two-time release engineering intern at Mozilla, as well as a Google Summer of Code participant. In his free time, he plays with networks and distributed systems. You can find him lurking around IRC networks under the alias of "ffledgling."

Ben Tasker is a Linux systems administrator, penetration tester, and software developer based in Suffolk, UK.

Having initially interacted with Linux at an early age, he's been configuring, scripting, and managing systems ever since. He maintains a blog and documentation archive (`www.bentasker.co.uk`) that attempts to cater to both technical and nontechnical audiences. He is currently active on a number of varied projects and loves every challenge they bring.

Thanks to Claire, my love, for not mentioning the time I've dedicated to this and other projects. I would also like to thank my son, Toby, who's similarly had to share me. The Sanity checks provided by Ben, Dean, and Neil were also very greatly appreciated.

Ilja Zegars is a networking specialist with over 7 years of experience in the networking field. He became a professional Python programmer and Python programming teacher, while studying for his bachelor's degree. Over the years, he mastered his skills in coding and networking. Currently, he is working as a networking specialist and data analyst at AD-net Technology and FiberBit Technology.

He is the author of the book *Colour Measurement Using Mobile Phone Camera*.

I want to thank my dear, Danhua, for supporting and believing in me.

www.PacktPub.com

Support files, eBooks, discount offers, and more

For support files and downloads related to your book, please visit www.PacktPub.com.

Did you know that Packt offers eBook versions of every book published, with PDF and ePub files available? You can upgrade to the eBook version at www.PacktPub.com and as a print book customer, you are entitled to a discount on the eBook copy. Get in touch with us at service@packtpub.com for more details.

At www.PacktPub.com, you can also read a collection of free technical articles, sign up for a range of free newsletters and receive exclusive discounts and offers on Packt books and eBooks.

https://www2.packtpub.com/books/subscription/packtlib

Do you need instant solutions to your IT questions? PacktLib is Packt's online digital book library. Here, you can search, access, and read Packt's entire library of books.

Why subscribe?

- Fully searchable across every book published by Packt
- Copy and paste, print, and bookmark content
- On demand and accessible via a web browser

Free access for Packt account holders

If you have an account with Packt at www.PacktPub.com, you can use this to access PacktLib today and view 9 entirely free books. Simply use your login credentials for immediate access.

Table of Contents

Preface

Welcome to the world of network programming with Python. Python is a full-featured object-oriented programming language with a standard library that includes everything needed to rapidly build powerful network applications. In addition, it has a multitude of third-party libraries and packages that extend Python to every sphere of network programming. Combined with the fun of using Python, with this book, we hope to get you started on your journey so that you master these tools and produce some great networking code.

In this book, we are squarely targeting Python 3. Although Python 3 is still establishing itself as the successor to Python 2, version 3 is the future of the language, and we want to demonstrate that it is ready for network programming prime time. It offers many improvements over the previous version, many of which improve the network programming experience, with enhanced standard library modules and new additions.

We hope you enjoy this introduction to network programming with Python.

What this book covers

Chapter 1, Network Programming and Python, introduces core networking concepts for readers that are new to networking, and also covers how network programming is approached in Python.

Chapter 2, HTTP and Working with the Web, introduces you to the HTTP protocol and covers how we can retrieve and manipulate web content using Python as an HTTP client. We also take a look at the standard library urllib and third-party Requests modules.

Chapter 3, APIs in Action, introduces you to working with web APIs using HTTP. We also cover the XML and JSON data formats, and walk you through developing applications using the Amazon Web Services Simple Storage Service (S3) and Twitter APIs.

Chapter 4, Engaging with E-mails, covers the principle protocols used in sending and receiving e-mails, such as SMTP, POP3, and IMAP, and how to work with them in Python 3.

Chapter 5, Interacting with Remote Systems, guides you through the ways of using Python to connect to servers and performing common administrative tasks, including the execution of shell commands through SSH, file transfers with FTP and SMB, authentication with LDAP, and to monitor systems with SNMP.

Chapter 6, IP and DNS, discusses the details of the Internet Protocol (IP), ways of working with IP in Python, and how to use DNS to resolve hostnames.

Chapter 7, Programming with Sockets, covers using TCP and UDP sockets from Python for writing low-level network applications. We also cover HTTPS and TLS for secure data transport.

Chapter 8, Client and Server Applications, looks at writing client and server programs for socket-based communication. By writing an echo application and a chat application we look at developing basic protocols, framing network data, and compare the multithreading and event-based server architectures.

Chapter 9, Applications for the Web, introduces you to writing web applications in Python. We cover the main approaches, methods of hosting Python web applications, and develop an example application in the Flask microframework.

Appendix, Working with Wireshark, covers packet sniffers, the installation of Wireshark, and how to capture and filter packets using the Wireshark application.

What you need for this book

This book is aimed at Python 3. While many of the examples will work in Python 2, you'll get the best experience working through this book with a recent version of Python 3. At the time of writing, the latest version is 3.4.3, and the examples were tested against this.

Though Python 3.4 is the preferred version, all the examples should run on Python 3.1 or later, except for the following:

- The `asyncio` example in *Chapter 8, Client and Server Applications*, as the `asyncio` module was only included in Version 3.4
- The Flask example in *Chapter 9, Applications for the Web*, which requires Python 3.3 or later

We're also targeting the Linux operating system, and the assumption is made that you are working on a Linux OS. The examples have been tested on Windows though, and we'll make a note of where there may be differences in the requirements or outcomes.

Virtual environments

It is highly recommended that you use Python virtual environments, or "**venvs**", when you work with this book, and in fact, when doing any work with Python. A venv is an isolated copy of the Python executable and associated files, which provides a separate environment for installing Python modules, independent from the system Python installation. You can have as many venvs as you need, which means that you can have multiple module configurations set up, and you can switch between them easily.

From version 3.3, Python includes a `venv` module, which provides this functionality. The documentation and examples are available at `https://docs.python.org/3/using/scripts.html`. There is also a standalone tool available for earlier versions, which can be found at `https://virtualenv.pypa.io/en/latest/`.

Installing Python 3

Most major Linux distributions come preinstalled with Python 2. When installing Python 3 on such a system, it is important to note that we're not replacing the installation of Python 2. Many distributions use Python 2 for core system operations, and these will be tuned for the major version of the system Python. Replacing the system Python can have severe consequences for the running of the OS. Instead, when we install Python 3, it is installed side by side with Python 2. After installing Python 3, it is invoked using the `python3.x` executable, where x is replaced with the corresponding installed minor version. Most packages also provide a `symlink` to this executable called `python3`, which can be run instead.

Packages to install Python 3.4 are available for most recent distributions, we'll go through the major ones here. If packages are not available, there are still some options that you can use to install a working Python 3.4 environment.

Ubuntu and Debian

Ubuntu 15.04 and 14.04 come with Python 3.4 already installed; so if you're running these versions, you're already good to go. Note that there is a bug in 14.04, which means pip must be installed manually in any venvs created using the bundled `venv` module. You can find information on working around this at `http://askubuntu.com/questions/488529/pyvenv-3-4-error-returned-non-zero-exit-status-1`.

For earlier versions of Ubuntu, Felix Krull maintains a repository of up-to-date Python installations for Ubuntu. The complete details can be found at `https://launchpad.net/~fkrull/+archive/ubuntu/deadsnakes`.

On Debian, Jessie has a Python 3.4 package (`python3.4`), which can be installed directly with `apt-get`. Wheezy has a package for 3.2 (`python3.2`), and Squeeze has `python3.1`, which can be installed similarly. In order to get working Python 3.4 installations on these latter two, it's easiest to use Felix Krull's repositories for Ubuntu.

RHEL, CentOS, Scientific Linux

These distributions don't provide up-to-date Python 3 packages, so we need to use a third-party repository. For Red Hat Enterprise Linux, CentOS, and Scientific Linux, Python 3 can be obtained from the community supported Software Collections (SCL) repository. Instructions on using this repository can be found at `https://www.softwarecollections.org/en/scls/rhscl/python33/`. At the time of writing, Python 3.3 is the latest available version.

Python 3.4 is available from another repository, the IUS Community repository, sponsored by Rackspace. Instructions on the installation can be found at `https://iuscommunity.org/pages/IUSClientUsageGuide.html`.

Fedora

Fedora 21 and 22 provide Python 3.4 with the `python3` package:

```
$ yum install python3
```

For earlier versions of Fedora, use the repositories listed in the preceding Red Hat section.

Alternative installation methods

If you're working on a system, which isn't one of the systems mentioned earlier, and you can't find packages for your system to install an up-to-date Python 3, there are still other ways of getting it installed. We'll discuss two methods, Pythonz and JuJu.

Pythonz

Pythonz is a program that manages the compilation of Python interpreters from source code. It downloads and compiles Python from source and installs the compiled Python interpreters in your home directory. These binaries can then be used to create venvs. The only limitation with this installation method is that you need a build environment (that is, a C compiler and supporting packages) installed on your system, and dependencies to compile Python. If this doesn't come with your distribution, you will need root access to install this initially. The complete instructions can be found at https://github.com/saghul/pythonz.

JuJu

JuJu can be used as a last resort, it allows a working Python 3.4 installation on any system without needing root access. It works by creating a tiny Arch Linux installation in a folder, in your home folder and provides tools that allow us to switch to this installation and run commands in it. Using this, we can install Arch's Python 3.4 package, and you can run Python programs using this. The Arch environment even shares your home folder with your system, so sharing files between environments is easy. The JuJu home page is available at https://github.com/fsquillace/juju.

JuJu should work on any distribution. To install it we need to do this:

```
$ mkdir ~/.juju
$ curl https:// bitbucket.org/fsquillace/juju-repo/raw/master/juju-
  x86_64.tar.gz | tar -xz -C ~/.juju
```

This downloads and extracts the JuJu image to ~/.juju. You'll need to replace the x86_64 with x86 if you're running on a 32-bit system. Next, set up PATH to pick up the JuJu commands:

```
$ export PATH=~/.juju/opt/juju/bin:$PATH
```

It's a good idea to add this to your .bashrc, so you don't need to run it every time you log in. Next, we install Python in the JuJu environment, we only need to do this once:

```
$ juju -f
$ pacman --sync refresh
$ pacman --sync --sysupgrade
$ pacman --sync python3
$ exit
```

These commands first activate the JuJu environment as root, then use the pacman Arch Linux package manager to update the system and install Python 3.4. The final exit command exits the JuJu environment. Finally, we can access the JuJu environment as a regular user:

```
$ juju
```

We can then start using the installed Python 3:

```
$ python3
Python 3.4.3 (default, Apr 28 2015, 19:59:08)
[GCC 4.7.2] on linux
Type "help", "copyright", "credits" or "license" for more information.
>>>
```

Windows

Compared to some of the older Linux distributions, installing Python 3.4 on Windows is relatively easy; just download the Python 3.4 installer from http://www.python.org and run it. The only hitch is that it requires administrator privileges to do so, so if you're on a locked down machine, things are trickier. The best solution at the moment is WinPython, which is available at http://winpython.github.io.

Other requirements

We assume that you have a working Internet connection. Several chapters use Internet resources extensively, and there is no real way to emulate these offline. Having a second computer is also useful to explore some networking concepts, and for trying out network applications across a real network.

We also use the Wireshark packet sniffer in several chapters. This will require a machine where you have root access (or administrator access in Windows). Wireshark installers and installation instructions are available at `https://www.wireshark.org`. An introduction to using Wireshark can be found in the *Appendix, Working with Wireshark*.

Who this book is for

If you're a Python developer, or system administrator with Python experience, and you're looking forward to take your first step in network programming, then this book is for you. Whether you're working with networks for the first time or looking to enhance your existing networking and Python skills, you will find this book very useful.

Conventions

In this book, you will find a number of text styles that distinguish between different kinds of information. Here are some examples of these styles and an explanation of their meaning.

Code words in text, database table names, folder names, filenames, file extensions, pathnames, dummy URLs, user input, and Twitter handles are shown as follows: "IP addresses have been assigned to your computer by running the `ip addr` or `ipconfig /all` command on Windows."

A block of code is set as follows:

```python
import sys, urllib.request

try:
    rfc_number = int(sys.argv[1])
except (IndexError, ValueError):
    print('Must supply an RFC number as first argument')
    sys.exit(2)

template = 'http://www.ietf.org/rfc/rfc{}.txt'
url = template.format(rfc_number)
rfc_raw = urllib.request.urlopen(url).read()
rfc = rfc_raw.decode()
print(rfc)
```

When we wish to draw your attention to a particular part of a code block, the relevant lines or items are highlighted:

```
<body>
...
<div id="content">
<h1>Debian &ldquo;jessie&rdquo; Release Information</h1>
<p>Debian 8.0 was
released October 18th, 2014.
The release included many major
changes, described in
...
```

Any command-line input or output is written as follows:

```
$ python RFC_downloader.py 2324 | less
```

New terms and **important words** are shown in bold. Words that you see on the screen, for example, in menus or dialog boxes, appear in the text like this: "We can see there's a list of interfaces below the **Start** button."

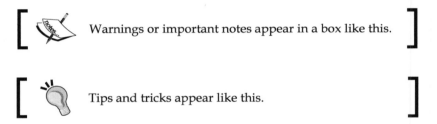

Warnings or important notes appear in a box like this.

Tips and tricks appear like this.

We follow PEP 8 as closely as we can, but we also follow the principle that practicality beats purity, and do deviate in a few areas. Imports are often performed on a single line to save space, and we may not strictly adhere to wrapping conventions do to the nature of printed media; we aim for "readability counts".

We have also chosen to focus on the procedural programming style rather than use object-oriented examples. The reason for this is that it is generally easier for someone familiar with object oriented programming to rework procedural examples into an object oriented format than it is for someone unfamiliar with OOP to do the reverse.

Reader feedback

Feedback from our readers is always welcome. Let us know what you think about this book—what you liked or disliked. Reader feedback is important for us as it helps us develop titles that you will really get the most out of.

To send us general feedback, simply e-mail feedback@packtpub.com, and mention the book's title in the subject of your message.

If there is a topic that you have expertise in and you are interested in either writing or contributing to a book, see our author guide at www.packtpub.com/authors.

Customer support

Now that you are the proud owner of a Packt book, we have a number of things to help you to get the most from your purchase.

Downloading the example code

You can download the example code files from your account at http://www.packtpub.com for all the Packt Publishing books you have purchased. If you purchased this book elsewhere, you can visit http://www.packtpub.com/support and register to have the files e-mailed directly to you.

Errata

Although we have taken every care to ensure the accuracy of our content, mistakes do happen. If you find a mistake in one of our books — maybe a mistake in the text or the code — we would be grateful if you could report this to us. By doing so, you can save other readers from frustration and help us improve subsequent versions of this book. If you find any errata, please report them by visiting http://www.packtpub.com/submit-errata, selecting your book, clicking on the **Errata Submission Form** link, and entering the details of your errata. Once your errata are verified, your submission will be accepted and the errata will be uploaded to our website or added to any list of existing errata under the Errata section of that title.

To view the previously submitted errata, go to https://www.packtpub.com/books/content/support and enter the name of the book in the search field. The required information will appear under the **Errata** section.

Piracy

Piracy of copyrighted material on the Internet is an ongoing problem across all media. At Packt, we take the protection of our copyright and licenses very seriously. If you come across any illegal copies of our works in any form on the Internet, please provide us with the location address or website name immediately so that we can pursue a remedy.

Please contact us at copyright@packtpub.com with a link to the suspected pirated material.

We appreciate your help in protecting our authors and our ability to bring you valuable content.

Questions

If you have a problem with any aspect of this book, you can contact us at questions@packtpub.com, and we will do our best to address the problem.

1
Network Programming and Python

This book will focus on writing programs for networks that use the Internet protocol suite. Why have we chosen to do this? Well, of the sets of protocols supported by the Python standard library, the TCP/IP protocol is by far the most widely employable. It contains the principle protocols used by the Internet. By learning to program for TCP/IP, you'll be learning how to potentially communicate with just about every device that is connected to this great tangle of network cables and electromagnetic waves.

In this chapter, we will be looking at some concepts and methods around networks and network programming in Python, which we'll be using throughout this book.

This chapter has two sections. The first section, *An introduction to TCP/IP networks*, offers an introduction to essential networking concepts, with a strong focus on the TCP/IP stack. We'll be looking at what comprises a network, how the **Internet Protocol (IP)** allows data transfer across and between networks, and how TCP/IP provides us with services that help us to develop network applications. This section is intended to provide a grounding in these essential areas and to act as a point of reference for them. If you're already comfortable with concepts such as IP addresses, routing, TCP and UDP, and protocol stack layers, then you may wish to skip to second part, *Network programming with Python*.

In the second part, we'll look at the way in which network programming is approached with Python. We'll be introducing the main standard library modules, looking at some examples to see how they relate to the TCP/IP stack, and then we will be discussing a general approach for finding and employing modules that meet our networking needs. We'll also be taking a look at a couple of general issues that we may encounter, when writing applications that communicate over TCP/IP networks.

An introduction to TCP/IP networks

The Internet protocol suite, often referred to as TCP/IP, is a set of protocols designed to work together to provide end-to-end transmission of messages across interconnected networks.

The following discussion is based on **Internet Protocol version 4 (IPv4)**. Since the Internet has run out of IPv4 addresses, a new version, IPv6, has been developed, which is intended to resolve this situation. However, although IPv6 is being used in a few areas, its deployment is progressing slowly and a majority of the Internet will likely be using IPv4 for a while longer. We'll focus on IPv4 in this section, and then we will discuss the relevant changes in IPv6 in second part of this chapter.

TCP/IP is specified in documents called **Requests for Comment (RFCs)** which are published by the **Internet Engineering Task Force (IETF)**. RFCs cover a wide range of standards and TCP/IP is just one of these. They are freely available on the IETF's website, which can be found at www.ietf.org/rfc.html. Each RFC has a number, IPv4 is documented by RFC 791, and other relevant RFCs will be mentioned as we progress.

Note that you won't learn how to set up your own network in this chapter because that's a big topic and unfortunately, somewhat beyond the scope of this book. But, it should enable you at least to have a meaningful conversation with your network support people!

IP addresses

So, let's get started with something you're likely to be familiar with, that is, IP addresses. They typically look something like this:

```
203.0.113.12
```

They are actually a single 32-bit number, though they are usually written just like the number shown in the preceding example; they are written in the form of four decimal numbers that are separated by dots. The numbers are sometimes called **octets** or bytes because each one represents 8-bits of the 32-bit number. As such, each octet can only take values from 0 to 255, so valid IP addresses range from 0.0.0.0 to 255.255.255.255. This way of writing IP addresses is called **dot-decimal notation.**

IP addresses perform two main functions. They are as follows:

- They uniquely address each device that is connected to a network
- They help the traffic to be routed between networks

You may have noticed that the network-connected devices that you use have IP addresses assigned to them. Each IP address that is assigned to a network device is unique and no two devices can share an IP address.

Network interfaces

You can find out what IP addresses have been assigned to your computer by running `ip addr` (or `ipconfig /all` on Windows) on a terminal. In *Chapter 6, IP and DNS*, we'll see how to do this when using Python.

If we run one of these commands, then we can see that the IP addresses are assigned to our device's network interfaces. On Linux, these will have names, such as `eth0`; on Windows these will have phrases, such as `Ethernet adapter Local Area Connection`.

You will get the following output when you run the `ip addr` command on Linux:

```
$ ip addr
1: lo: <LOOPBACK,UP,LOWER_UP> mtu 65536 qdisc noqueue state UNKNOWN
    link/loopback 00:00:00:00:00:00 brd 00:00:00:00:00:00
    inet 127.0.0.1/8 scope host lo
       valid_lft forever preferred_lft forever
2: eth0: <BROADCAST,MULTICAST,UP,LOWER_UP> mtu 1500 qdisc pfifo_fast
    state UP qlen 1000
    link/ether b8:27:eb:5d:7f:ae brd ff:ff:ff:ff:ff:ff
    inet 192.168.0.4/24 brd 192.168.0.255 scope global eth0
       valid_lft forever preferred_lft forever
```

In the preceding example, the IP addresses for the interfaces appear after the word `inet`.

An interface is a device's physical connection to its network media. It could be a network card that connects to a network cable, or a radio that uses a specific wireless technology. A desktop computer may only have a single interface for a network cable, whereas a Smartphone is likely to have at least two interfaces, one for connecting to Wi-Fi networks and one for connecting to mobile networks that use 4G or other technologies.

An interface is usually assigned only one IP address, and each interface in a device has a different IP address. So, going back to the purposes of IP addresses discussed in the preceding section, we can now more accurately say that their first main function is to uniquely address each device's connection to a network.

Every device has a virtual interface called the **loopback interface**, which you can see in the preceding listing as interface 1. This interface doesn't actually connect to anything outside the device, and only the device itself can communicate with it. While this may sound a little redundant, it's actually very useful when it comes to local network application testing, and it can also be used as a means of inter-process communication. The loopback interface is often referred to as **localhost**, and it is almost always assigned the IP address 127.0.0.1.

Assigning IP addresses

IP addresses can be assigned to a device by a network administrator in one of two ways: statically, where the device's operating system is manually configured with the IP address, or dynamically, where the device's operating system is configured by using the **Dynamic Host Configuration Protocol (DHCP)**.

When using DHCP, as soon as the device first connects to a network, it is automatically allocated an address by a DHCP server from a predefined pool. Some network devices, such as home broadband routers provide a DHCP server service out-of-the-box, otherwise a DHCP server must be set up by a network administrator. DHCP is widely deployed, and it is particularly useful for networks where different devices may frequently connect and disconnect, such as public Wi-Fi hotspots or mobile networks.

IP addresses on the Internet

The Internet is a huge IP network, and every device that sends data over it is assigned an IP address.

The IP address space is managed by an organization called the **Internet Assigned Numbers Authority (IANA)**. IANA decides the global allocation of the IP address ranges and assigns blocks of addresses to **Regional Internet Registries (RIRs)** worldwide, who then allocate address blocks to countries and organizations. The receiving organizations have the freedom to allocate the addresses from their assigned blocks as they like within their own networks.

There are some special IP address ranges. IANA has defined ranges of **private addresses**. These ranges will never be assigned to any organization, and as such these are available for anyone to use for their networks. The private address ranges are as follows:

- 10.0.0.0 to 10.255.255.255
- 172.16.0.0 to 172.31.255.255
- 192.168.0.0 to 192.168.255.255

You may be thinking that if anybody can use them, then would'nt that mean that devices on the Internet will end up using the same addresses, thereby breaking IP's unique addressing property? This is a good question, and this problem has been avoided by forbidding traffic from private addresses from being routed over the public Internet. Wherever a network using private addresses needs to communicate with the public Internet, a technique called **Network Address Translation (NAT)** is used, which essentially makes the traffic from the private network appear to be coming from a single valid public Internet address, and this effectively hides the private addresses from the Internet. We'll discuss NAT later on.

If you inspect the output of `ip addr` or `ipconfig /all` on your home network, then you will find that your devices are using private range addresses, which would have been assigned to them by your broadband router through DHCP.

Packets

We'll be talking about network traffic in the following sections, so let's get an idea of what it is.

Many protocols, including the principle protocols in the Internet protocol suite, employ a technique called **packetization** to help manage data while it's being transmitted across a network.

When a packetizing protocol is given some data to transmit, it breaks it up into small units — sequences of bytes, typically a few thousand bytes long and then it prefixes each unit with some protocol-specific information. The prefix is called a **header,** and the prefix and data together form a **packet**. The data within a packet is often called its **payload**.

What a packet contains is shown in the following figure:

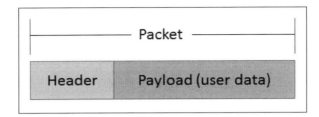

Some protocols use alternative terms for packets, such as frames, but we'll stick with the term packets for now. The header includes all the information that the protocol implementation running on another device needs to be able to interpret what the packet is and how to handle it. For example, the information in an IP packet header includes the source IP address, the destination IP address, the total length of the packet, and the checksum of the data in the header.

Once created, the packets are sent onto the network, where they are independently routed to their destination. Sending the data in packets has several advantages, including multiplexing (where more than one device can send data over the network at once), rapid notification of errors that may occur on the network, congestion control, and dynamic re-routing.

Protocols may call upon other protocols to handle their packets for them; passing their packets to the second protocol for delivery. When both the protocols employ packetization, nested packets result, as shown in the following figure:

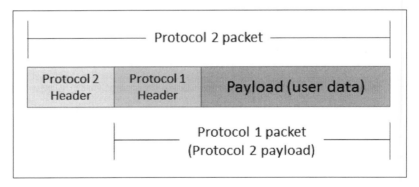

This is called **encapsulation**, and as we'll see shortly, it is a powerful mechanism for structuring network traffic.

Networks

A network is a discrete collection of connected network devices. Networks can vary greatly in scale, and they can be made up of smaller networks. Your network-connected devices at home or the network-connected computers in a large office building are examples of networks.

There are quite a few ways of defining a network, some loose, some very specific. Depending on the context, networks can be defined by physical boundaries, administrative boundaries, institutional boundaries, or network technology boundaries.

For this section, we're going to start with a simplified definition of a network, and then work toward a more specific definition, in the form of IP subnets.

So for our simplified definition, our common defining feature of a network will be that all devices on the network share a single point of connection to the rest of the Internet. In some large or specialized networks, you will find that there is more than one point of connection, but for the sake of simplicity we'll stick to a single connection here.

This connection point is called a **gateway,** and usually it takes the form of a special network device called a **router**. The job of a router is to direct traffic between networks. It sits between two or more networks and is said to sit at the boundary of these networks. It always has two or more network interfaces; one for each network it is attached to. A router contains a set of rules called a **routing table,** which tells it how to direct the packets that are passing through it onwards, based on the packets' destination IP addresses.

The gateway forwards the packets to another router, which is said to be **upstream**, and is usually located at the network's **Internet Service Provider (ISP)**. The ISP's router falls into a second category of routers, that is, it sits outside the networks described earlier, and routes traffic between network gateways. These routers are run by ISPs and other communications entities. They are generally arranged in tiers, and the upper regional tiers route the traffic for some large sections of countries or continents and form the Internet's backbone.

Because these routers can sit between many networks, their routing tables can become very extensive and they need to be updated continuously. A simplified illustration is shown in the following diagram:

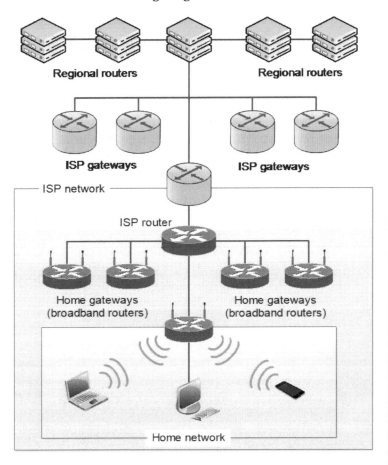

The preceding diagram gives us an idea of the arrangement. Each ISP gateway connects an ISP network to the regional routers, and each home broadband router has a home network connected to it. In the real world, this arrangement gets more complicated as one goes toward the top. ISPs will often have more than one gateway connecting them to the regional routers, and some of these will also themselves be acting as regional routers. Regional routers also have more tiers than shown here, and they have many connections between one another, which are in arrangements that are much more complicated than this simple hierarchy. A rendering of a section of the Internet from data gathered in 2005 provides a beautiful illustration of just how complex this becomes, it can be found at http://en.wikipedia.org/wiki/Internet_backbone#/media/File:Internet_map_1024.jpg.

Routing with IP

We mentioned that routers are able to route traffic toward a destination network, and implied that this is somehow done by using IP addresses and routing tables. But what's really going on here?

One perhaps obvious method for routers to determine the correct router to forward traffic to would be to program every router's routing table with a route for every IP address. However, in practice, with 4 billion plus IP addresses and constantly changing network routes, this turns out to be a completely infeasible method.

So, how is routing done? The answer lies in another property of IP addresses. An IP address can be interpreted as being made up of two logical parts: a **network prefix** and a **host identifier**. The network prefix uniquely identifies the network a device is on, and the device can use this to determine how to handle traffic that it generates, or receives for forwarding. The network prefix is the first n bits of the IP address when it's written out in binary (remember an IP address is really just a 32-bit number). The n bits are supplied by the network administrator as a part of a device's network configuration at the same time that it is given its IP address.

You'll see that n is written in one of two ways. It can simply be appended to the IP address, separated by a slash, as follows:

```
192.168.0.186/24
```

This is called **CIDR notation**. Alternatively, it can be written as a **subnet mask**, which is sometimes just called a **netmask**. This is the way in which you will usually see n being specified in a device's network configuration. A subnet mask is a 32-bit number written in dot-decimal notation, just like an IP address.

```
255.255.255.0
```

This subnet mask is equivalent to /24. We get n from it by looking at it in binary. A few examples are as follows:

```
255.0.0.0       = 11111111 00000000 00000000 00000000 = /8
255.192.0.0     = 11111111 11000000 00000000 00000000 = /10
255.255.255.0   = 11111111 11111111 11111111 00000000 = /24
255.255.255.240 = 11111111 11111111 11111111 11110000 = /28
```

n is simply the number of 1 bits in the subnet mask. (It's always the leftmost bits that are set to 1 because this allows us to quickly get the Network prefix in binary by doing a bitwise AND operation on the IP address and the subnet mask).

So, how does this help in routing? When a network device generates network traffic that needs to be sent across a network, it first compares the destination's IP address with its own network prefix. If the destination IP address has the same network prefix as that of the sending device, then the sending device will recognise that the destination device is on the same network and, therefore, it can then send the traffic directly to it. If the network prefixes differ, then it will send the message to its default gateway, which will forward it on towards the receiving device.

When a router receives traffic that has to be forwarded, it first checks whether the destination IP address matches the network prefix of any of the networks that it's connected to. If that is the case, then it will send the message directly to the destination device on that network. If not, it will consult its routing table. If it finds a matching rule, then it sends the message to the router that it found listed, and if there are no explicit rules defined, then it will send the traffic to its own default gateway.

When we create a network with a given network prefix, in the 32-bits of the IP address, the digits to the right of the network prefix are available for assignment to the network devices. We can calculate the number of the available addresses by raising 2 to the power of the number of available bits. For example, in a /28 network prefix, we have 4 bits left, which means that 16 addresses are available. In reality, we are able to assign fewer addresses, since two of the addresses in the calculated range are always reserved. These are: the first address in the range, which is called the **network address** and the last address in the range, which is called the **broadcast address**.

This range of addresses, which is identified by its network prefix, is called a **subnet**. Subnets are the basic unit of assignment when IANA, an RIR or an ISP allocates IP address blocks to organizations. Organizations assign subnets to their various networks.

Organizations can further partition their addresses into subnets simply by employing a longer network prefix than the one they had been assigned. They might do this either to make more efficient use of their addresses or to create a hierarchy of networks, which can be delegated across the organization.

DNS

We've discussed connecting to network devices by using IP addresses. However, unless you work with networks or in systems administration, it is unlikely that you will get to see an IP address very often, even though many of us use the Internet every day. When we browse the web or send an e-mail, we usually connect to servers using host names or domain names. These must somehow map to the servers' IP addresses. But how is this done?

Documented as RFC 1035, the **Domain Name System (DNS)** is a globally distributed database of mappings between hostnames and IP addresses. It is an open and hierarchical system with many organizations choosing to run their own DNS servers. DNS is also a protocol, which devices use to query DNS servers for resolving hostnames to IP addresses (and vice-versa).

The `nslookup` tool comes with most Linux and Windows systems and it lets us query DNS on the command line, as follows:

```
$ nslookup python.org
Server:          192.168.0.4
Address:         192.168.0.4#53


Non-authoritative answer:
Name:    python.org
Address: 104.130.43.121
```

Here, we determined that the `python.org` host has the IP address `104.130.42.121`. DNS distributes the work of looking up hostnames by using an hierarchical system of caching servers. When connecting to a network, your network device will be given a local DNS server through either DHCP or manually, and it will query this local server when doing DNS lookups. If that server doesn't know the IP address, then it will query its own configured higher tier server, and so on until an answer can be found. ISPs run their own DNS caching servers, and broadband routers often act as caching servers as well. In this example, my device's local server is `192.168.0.4`.

A device's operating system usually handles DNS, and it provides a programming interface, which applications use to ask it to resolve hostnames and IP addresses. Python provides an interface for this, which we'll discuss in *Chapter 6, IP and DNS*.

The protocol stack or why the Internet is like a cake

The Internet Protocol is a member of the set of protocols that make up the Internet protocol suite. Each protocol in the suite has been designed to solve specific problems in networking. We just saw how IP solves the problems of addressing and routing.

The core protocols in the suite are designed to work together within a stack. That is, each protocol occupies a layer within the stack, and the other protocols are situated above and below that layer. So, it is layered just like a cake. Each layer provides a specific service to the layers above it, while hiding the complexity of its own operation from them, following the principle of encapsulation. Ideally, each layer only interfaces with the layer below it in order to benefit from the entire range of the problem solving powers of all the layers below.

Python provides modules for interfacing with different protocols. As the protocols employ encapsulation, we typically only need to work with one module to leverage the power of the underlying stack, thus avoiding the complexity of the lower layers.

The TCP/IP Suite defines four layers, although five layers are often used for clarity. These are given in the following table:

Layer	Name	Example protocols
5	Application layer	HTTP, SMTP, IMAP
4	Transport layer	TCP, UDP
3	Network layer	IP
2	Data-link layer	Ethernet, PPP, FDDI
1	Physical layer	-

Layers 1 and 2 correspond to the first layer of the TCP/IP suite. These two bottom layers deal with the low level network infrastructure and services.

Layer 1 corresponds to the physical media of the network, such as a cable or a Wi-Fi radio. Layer 2 provides the service of getting the data from one network device to another, directly connected network device. This layer can employ all sorts of layer 2 protocols, such as Ethernet or PPP, as long as the Internet Protocol in layer 3 can ask it to get the data to the next device in the network by using any type of available physical medium.

We don't need to concern ourselves with the two lowest layers, since we will rarely need to interface with them when using Python. Their operation is almost always handled by the operating system and the network hardware.

Layer 3 is variously called the Network layer and the Internet layer. It exclusively employs the Internet Protocol. As we have already seen, it has been tasked primarily with internetwork addressing and routing. Again, we don't typically directly interface with this layer in Python.

Layers 4 and 5 are more interesting for our purposes.

Layer 4 – TCP and UDP

Layer 4 is the first layer that we may want to work with in Python. This layer can employ one of two protocols: the **Transmission Control Protocol (TCP)** and the **User Datagram Protocol (UDP)**. Both of these provide the common service of end-to-end transportation of data between applications on different network devices.

Network ports

Although IP facilitates the transport of data from one network device to another, it doesn't provide us with a way of letting the destination device know what it should do with the data once it receives it. One possible solution to this would be to program every process running on the destination device to check all of the incoming data to see if they are interested in it, but this would quickly lead to obvious performance and security problems.

TCP and UDP provide the answer by introducing the concept of **ports**. A port is an endpoint, which is attached to one of the IP addresses assigned to the network device. Ports are claimed by a process running on the device, and the process is then said to be **listening** on that port. Ports are represented by a 16-bit number, so that each IP address on a device has 65,535 possible ports that the processes can claim (port number 0 is reserved). Ports can only be claimed by one process at a time, even though a process can claim more than one port at a time.

When a message is sent over the network through TCP or UDP, the sending application sets the destination port number in the header of the TCP or UDP packet. When the message arrives at the destination, the TCP or UDP protocol implementation running on the receiving device reads the port number and then delivers the message payload to the process that is listening on that port.

Port numbers need to be known before the messages are sent. The main mechanism for this is convention. In addition to managing the IP address space, it is also the responsibility of IANA to manage the assignment of port numbers to network services.

A service is a class of application, for example a web server, or a DNS server, which is usually tied to an application protocol. Ports are assigned to services rather than specific applications, because it gives service providers the flexibility to choose what kind of software they want to use to provide a service, without having to worry about the users who would need to look up and connect to a new port number simply because the server has started using Apache instead of IIS, for example.

Most operating systems contain a copy of this list of services and their assigned port numbers. On Linux, this is usually found at /etc/services, and on Windows this is usually found at c:\windows\system32\drivers\etc\services. The complete list can also be viewed online at http://www.iana.org/assignments/port-numbers.

TCP and UDP packet headers may also include a **source port** number. This is optional for UDP, but mandatory for TCP. The source port number tells the receiving application on the server where it should send replies to when sending data back to the client. Applications can specify the source port that they wish to use, or if a source port has not been specified for TCP, then one is assigned randomly by the operating system when the packet is sent. Once the OS has a source port number, it assigns it to the calling application and starts listening on it for a reply. If a reply is received on that port, then the received data is passed to the sending application.

So, both TCP and UCP provide an end-to-end transport for the application data through the provision of ports, and both of them employ the Internet Protocol to get the data to the destination device. Now, let's look at their features.

UDP

UDP is documented as RFC 768. It is deliberately uncomplicated: it provides no services other than those that we described in the previous section. It just takes the data that we want to send, packetizes it with the destination port number (and optional source port number), and hands it off to the local Internet Protocol implementation for delivery. Applications on the receiving end see the data in the same discrete chunks in which it was packetized.

Both IP and UDP are what are called connectionless protocols. This means that they attempt to deliver their packets on a best effort basis, but if something goes wrong, then they will just shrug their metaphorical shoulders and move on to delivering the next packet. There is no guarantee that our packets will reach their destinations, and no error notification if a delivery fails. If the packets do make it, then there is no guarantee that they will do so in the same order as they were sent. It's up to a higher layer protocol or the sending application to determine if the packets have arrived and whether to handle any problems. These are protocols in the fire-and-forget style.

The typical applications of UDP are internet telephony and video streaming. DNS queries are also transported using UDP.

We'll now look at UDP's more dependable sibling, TCP, and then discuss the differences, and why applications may choose to use one or the other.

TCP

The Transmission Control Protocol is documented as RFC 761. As opposed to UDP, TCP is a connection based protocol. In such a protocol, no data is sent until the server and the client have performed an initial exchange of control packets. This exchange is called a **handshake**. This establishes a connection, and from then on data can be sent. Each data packet that is received is acknowledged by the receiving party, and it does so by sending a packet called an **ACK**. As such, TCP always requires that the packets include a source port number, because it depends on the continual two-way exchange of messages.

From an application's point of view, the key difference between UDP and TCP is that the application no longer sees the data in discrete chunks; the TCP connection presents the data to the application as a continuous, seamless stream of bytes. This makes things much simpler if we are sending messages that are larger than a typical packet, however it means that we need to start thinking about *framing* our messages. While with UDP, we can rely on its packetization to provide a means of doing this, with TCP we must decide a mechanism for unambiguously determining where our messages start and end. We'll see more about this in *Chapter 8, Client and Server Applications*.

TCP provides the following services:

- In-order delivery
- Receipt acknowledgment
- Error detection
- Flow and congestion control

Data sent through TCP is guaranteed to get delivered to the receiving application in the order that it was sent in. The receiving TCP implementation buffers the received packets on the receiving device and then waits until it can deliver them in the correct order before passing them to the application.

Because the data packets are acknowledged, sending applications can be sure that the data is arriving and that it is okay to continue sending the data. If an ACK is not received for a sent packet, then within a set time period the packet will be resent. If there's still no response, then TCP will keep resending the packet at increasing intervals, until a second, longer timeout period expires. At this point, it will give up and notify the calling application that it has encountered a problem.

The TCP header includes a checksum of the header data and the payload. This allows the receiver to verify whether a packet's contents have been modified during the transmission.

TCP also includes algorithms which ensure that traffic is not sent too quickly for the receiving device to process, and these algorithms also infer network conditions and regulate the transmission rate to avoid network congestion.

Together these services provide a robust and reliable transport system for application data. This is one of the reasons many popular higher level protocols, such as HTTP, SMTP, SSH, and IMAP, depend on TCP.

UDP versus TCP

Given the features of TCP, you may be wondering what the use of a connectionless protocol like UDP is. Well, the Internet is still a pretty reliable network, and most of the packets do get delivered. The connectionless protocols are useful where the minimum transfer overhead is required, and where the occasional dropped packet is not a big deal. TCP's reliability and congestion control comes at the cost of needing additional packets and round-trips, and the introduction of deliberate delays when packets are lost in order to prevent congestion. These can drastically increase latency, which is the arch-nemesis of real-time services, while not providing any real benefit for them. A few dropped packets might result in a transient glitch or a drop in signal quality in a media stream, but as long as the packets keep coming, the stream can usually recover.

UDP is also the main protocol that is used for DNS, which is interesting because most DNS queries fit inside a single packet, so TCP's streaming abilities aren't generally needed. DNS is also usually configured such that it does not depend upon a reliable connection. Most devices are configured with multiple DNS servers, and it's usually quicker to resend a query to a second server after a short timeout rather than wait for a TCP back-off period to expire.

The choice between UDP and TCP comes down to the message size, whether latency is an issue, and how much of TCP's functionality the application wants to perform itself.

Layer 5 – The application layer

Finally we come to the top of the stack. The application layer is deliberately left open in the IP protocol suite, and it's really a catch-all for any protocol that is developed by application developers on top of TCP or UDP (or even IP, though these are rarer). Application layer protocols include HTTP, SMTP, IMAP, DNS, and FTP.

Protocols may even become their own layers, where an application protocol is built on top of another application protocol. An example of this is the **Simple Object Access Protocol (SOAP)**, which defines an XML-based protocol that can be used over almost any transport, including HTTP and SMTP.

Python has standard library modules for many application layer protocols and third-party modules for many more. If we write low-level server applications, then we will be more likely to be interested in TCP and UDP, but if not, then application layer protocols are the ones we'll be working with, and we'll be looking at some of them in detail over the next few chapters.

On to Python!

Well, that's it for our rundown of the TCP/IP stack. We'll move on to the next section of this chapter, where we'll look at how to start using Python and how to work with some of the topics we've just covered.

Network programming with Python

In this section, we're going to look at the general approach to network programming in Python. We'll look at how Python lets us interface with the network stack, how to track down useful modules, and cover some general network programming tips.

Breaking a few eggs

The power of the layer model of network protocols is that a higher layer can easily build on the services provided by the lower layers and this enables them to add new services to the network. Python provides modules for interfacing with protocols at different levels in the network stack, and modules that support higher-layer protocols follow the aforementioned principle by using the interfaces supplied by the lower level protocols. How can we visualize this?

Well, sometimes a good way to see inside something like this is by breaking it. So, let's break Python's network stack. Or, more specifically, let's generate a traceback.

Yes, this means that the first piece of Python that we're going to write is going to generate an exception. But, it will be a good exception. We'll learn from it. So, fire up your Python shell and run the following command:

```
>>> import smtplib
>>> smtplib.SMTP('127.0.0.1', port=66000)
```

What are we doing here? We are importing `smtplib`, which is Python's standard library for working with the SMTP protocol. SMTP is an application layer protocol, which is used for sending e-mails. We will then try to open an SMTP connection by instantiating an SMTP object. We want the connection to fail and that is why we've specified the port number 66000, which is an invalid port. We will specify the local host for the connection, as this will cause it to fail quickly, rather than make it wait for a network timeout.

On running the preceding command, you should get the following traceback:

```
Traceback (most recent call last):
  File "<stdin>", line 1, in <module>
  File "/usr/lib/python3.4/smtplib.py", line 242, in __init__
    (code, msg) = self.connect(host, port)
  File "/usr/lib/python3.4/smtplib.py", line 321, in connect
    self.sock = self._get_socket(host, port, self.timeout)
  File "/usr/lib/python3.4/smtplib.py", line 292, in _get_socket
    self.source_address)
  File "/usr/lib/python3.4/socket.py", line 509, in
create_connection
    raise err
  File "/usr/lib/python3.4/socket.py", line 500, in
create_connection
    sock.connect(sa)
ConnectionRefusedError: [Errno 111] Connection refused
```

This was generated by using Python 3.4.1 on a Debian 7 machine. The final error message will be slightly different from this if you run this on Windows, but the stack trace will remain the same.

Inspecting it will reveal how the Python network modules act as a stack. We can see that the call stack starts in `smtplib.py`, and then as we go down, it moves into `socket.py`. The `socket` module is Python's standard interface for the transport layer, and it provides the functions for interacting with TCP and UDP as well as for looking up hostnames through DNS. We'll learn much more about this in *Chapter 7, Programming with Sockets*, and *Chapter 8, Client and Server Applications*.

From the preceding program, it's clear that the `smtplib` module calls into the `socket` module. The application layer protocol has employed a transport layer protocol (which in this case is TCP).

Right at the bottom of the traceback, we can see the exception itself and the `Errno` `111`. This is an error message from the operating system. You can verify this by going through `/usr/include/asm-generic/errno.h` (`asm/errno.h` on some systems) for the error message number 111 (on Windows the error will be a WinError, so you can see that it has clearly been generated by the OS). From this error message we can see that the `socket` module is calling down yet again and asking the operating system to manage the TCP connection for it.

Python's network modules are working as the protocol stack designers intended them to. They call on the lower levels in the stack to employ their services to perform the network tasks. We can work by using simple calls made to the application layer protocol, which in this case is SMTP, without having to worry about the underlying network layers. This is network encapsulation in action, and we want to make as much use of this as we can in our applications.

Taking it from the top

Before we start writing code for a new network application, we want to make sure that we're taking as much advantage of the existing stack as possible. This means finding a module that provides an interface to the services that we want to use, and that is as high up the stack as we can find. If we're lucky, someone has already written a module that provides an interface that provides the exact service we need.

Let's use an example to illustrate this process. Let's write a tool for downloading **Request for Comments (RFC)** documents from IETF, and then display them on screen.

Let's keep the RFC downloader simple. We'll make it a command-line program that just accepts an RFC number, downloads the RFC in text format, and then prints it to `stdout`.

Now, it's possible that somebody has already written a module for doing this, so let's see if we can find anything.

The first place we look should always be the Python standard library. The modules in the library are well maintained, and well documented. When we use a standard library module, the users of your application won't need to install any additional dependencies for running it.

A look through the *Library Reference* at `https://docs.python.org` doesn't seem to show anything directly relevant to our requirement. This is not entirely surprising!

So, next we will turn to third-party modules. The Python package index, which can be found at `https://pypi.python.org`, is the place where we should look for these. Here as well, running a few searches around the theme of RFC client and RFC download doesn't seem to reveal anything useful. The next place to look will be Google, though again, the searches don't reveal anything promising. This is slightly disappointing, but this is why we're learning network programming, to fill these gaps!

There are other ways in which we may be able to find out about useful third-party modules, including mailing lists, Python user groups, the programming Q&A site `http://stackoverflow.com`, and programming textbooks.

For now, let's assume that we really can't find a module for downloading RFCs. What next? Well, we need to think lower in the network stack. This means that we need to identify the network protocol that we'll need to use for getting hold of the RFCs in text format by ourselves.

The IETF landing page for RFCs is `http://www.ietf.org/rfc.html`, and reading through it tell us exactly what we want to know. We can access a text version of an RFC using a URL of the form `http://www.ietf.org/rfc/rfc741.txt`. The RFC number in this case is 741. So, we can get text format of RFCs using HTTP.

Now, we need a module that can speak HTTP for us. We should look at the standard library again. You will notice that there is, in fact, a module called `http`. Sounds promising, though looking at its documentation will tell us that it's a low level library and that something called `urllib` will prove to be more useful.

Now, looking at the `urllib` documentation, we find that it does indeed do what we need. It downloads the target of a URL through a straightforward API. We've found our protocol module.

Downloading an RFC

Now we can write our program. For this, create a text file called `RFC_downloader.py` and save the following code to it:

```
import sys, urllib.request

try:
    rfc_number = int(sys.argv[1])
```

```
except (IndexError, ValueError):
    print('Must supply an RFC number as first argument')
    sys.exit(2)

template = 'http://www.ietf.org/rfc/rfc{}.txt'
url = template.format(rfc_number)
rfc_raw = urllib.request.urlopen(url).read()
rfc = rfc_raw.decode()
print(rfc)
```

We can run the preceding code by using the following command:

```
$ python RFC_downloader.py 2324 | less
```

On Windows, you'll need to use `more` instead of `less`. RFCs can run to many pages, hence we use a pager here. If you try this, then you should see some useful information on the remote control of coffee pots.

Let's go through our code and look at what we've done so far.

First, we import our modules and check whether an RFC number has been supplied on the command line. Then, we construct our URL by substituting the supplied RFC number. Next, the main activity, the `urlopen()` call will construct an HTTP request for our URL, and then it will contact the IETF web server over the Internet and download the RFC text. Next, we decode the text to Unicode, and finally we print it out to screen.

So, we can easily view any RFC that we like from the command line. In retrospect, it's not entirely surprising that there isn't a module for this, because we can use `urllib` to do most of the hard work!

Looking deeper

But, what if HTTP was brand new and there were no modules, such as `urllib`, which we could use to speak HTTP for us? Well, then we would have to step down the stack again and use TCP for our purposes. Let's modify our program according to this scenario, as follows:

```
import sys, socket

try:
    rfc_number = int(sys.argv[1])
except (IndexError, ValueError):
```

```
        print('Must supply an RFC number as first argument')
        sys.exit(2)

host = 'www.ietf.org'
port = 80
sock = socket.create_connection((host, port))

req = (
    'GET /rfc/rfc{rfcnum}.txt HTTP/1.1\r\n'
    'Host: {host}:{port}\r\n'
    'User-Agent: Python {version}\r\n'
    'Connection: close\r\n'
    '\r\n'
)
req = req.format(
    rfcnum=rfc_number,
    host=host,
    port=port,
    version=sys.version_info[0]
)
sock.sendall(req.encode('ascii'))
rfc_raw = bytearray()
while True:
    buf = sock.recv(4096)
    if not len(buf):
        break
    rfc_raw += buf
rfc = rfc_raw.decode('utf-8')
print(rfc)
```

The first noticeable change is that we have used socket instead of urllib. Socket is Python's interface for the operating system's TCP and UDP implementation. The command-line check remains the same, but then we will see that we now need to handle some of the things that urllib was doing for us before.

We have to tell socket which transport layer protocol that we want to use. We do this by using the socket.create_connection() convenience function. This function will always create a TCP connection. You'll notice that we have to explicitly supply the TCP port number that socket should use to establish the connection as well. Why 80? 80 is the standard port number for web services over HTTP. We've also had to separate the host from the URL, since socket has no understanding of URLs.

The request string that we create to send to the server is also much more complicated than the URL that we used before: it's a full HTTP request. In the next chapter, we'll be looking at these in detail.

Next, we deal with the network communication over the TCP connection. We send the entire request string to the server using the `sendall()` call. The data sent through TCP must be in raw bytes, so we have to encode the request text as ASCII before sending it.

Then, we piece together the server's response as it arrives in the `while` loop. Bytes that are sent to us through a TCP socket are presented to our application in a continuous stream. So, like any stream of unknown length, we have to read it iteratively. The `recv()` call will return the empty string after the server sends all its data and closes the connection. Hence, we can use this as a condition for breaking out and printing the response.

Our program is clearly more complicated. Compared to our previous one, this is not good in terms of maintenance. Also, if you run the program and look at the start of the output RFC text, then you'll notice that there are some extra lines at the beginning, and these are as follows:

```
HTTP/1.1 200 OK
Date: Thu, 07 Aug 2014 15:47:13 GMT
Content-Type: text/plain
Transfer-Encoding: chunked
Connection: close
Set-Cookie: __cfduid=d1983ad4f7…
Last-Modified: Fri, 27 Mar 1998 22:45:31 GMT
ETag: W/"8982977-4c9a-32a651f0ad8c0"
```

Because we're now dealing with a raw HTTP protocol exchange, we're seeing the extra header data that HTTP includes in a response. This has a similar purpose to the lower-level packet headers. The HTTP header contains HTTP-specific metadata about the response that tells the client how to interpret it. Before, `urllib` parsed this for us, added the data as attributes to the response object, and removed the header data from the output data. We would need to add code to do this as well to make this program as capable as our first one.

What can't immediately be seen from the code is that we're also missing out on the `urllib` module's error checking and handling. Although low-level network errors will still generate exceptions, we will no longer catch any problems in the HTTP layer, which `urllib` would have done.

The 200 value in the first line of the aforementioned headers is an HTTP **status code,** which tells us whether there were any problems with the HTTP request or response. 200 means that everything went well, but other codes, such as the infamous 404 'not found' can mean something went wrong. The urllib module would check these for us and raise an exception. But here, we need to handle these ourselves.

So, there are clear benefits of using modules as far up the stack as possible. Our resulting programs will be less complicated, which will make them quicker to write, and easier to maintain. It also means that their error handling will be more robust, and we will benefit from the expertise of the modules' developers. Also, we benefit from the testing that the module would have undergone for catching unexpected and tricky edge-case problems. Over the next few chapters, we'll be discussing more modules and protocols that live at the top of the stack.

Programming for TCP/IP networks

To round up, we're going to look at a few frequently encountered aspects of TCP/IP networks that can cause a lot of head-scratching for application developers who haven't encountered them before. These are: firewalls, Network Address Translation, and some of the differences between IPv4 and IPv6.

Firewalls

A firewall is a piece of hardware or software that inspects the network packets that flow through it and, based on the packet's properties, it filters what it lets through. It is a security mechanism for preventing unwanted traffic from moving from one part of a network to another. Firewalls can sit at network boundaries or can be run as applications on network clients and servers. For example, iptables is the de facto firewall software for Linux. You'll often find a firewall built into desktop anti-virus programs.

The filtering rules can be based on any property of the network traffic. The commonly used properties are: the transport layer protocol (that is, whether traffic uses TCP or UDP), the source and destination IP addresses, and the source and destination port numbers.

A common filtering strategy is to deny all inbound traffic and only allow traffic that matches very specific parameters. For example, a company might have a web server it wants to allow access to from the Internet, but it wants to block all traffic from the Internet that is directed towards any of the other devices on its network. To do so, it would put a firewall directly in front of or behind its gateway, and then configure it to block all incoming traffic, except TCP traffic with the destination IP address of the web server, and the destination port number 80 (since port 80 is the standard port number for the HTTP service).

Firewalls can also block outbound traffic. This may be done to stop malicious software that finds its way onto internal network devices from calling home or sending spam e-mail.

Because firewalls block network traffic, they can cause obvious problems for network applications. When testing our applications over a network, we need to be sure that the firewalls that exist between our devices are configured such that they let our application's traffic through. Usually, this means that we need to make sure that the ports which we need are open on the firewall for the traffic between the source and the destination IP addresses to flow freely. This may take some negotiating with an IT support team or two, and maybe looking at our operating system's and local network router's documentation. Also, we need to make sure that our application users are aware of any firewall configuration that they need to perform in their own environments in order to make use of our program.

Network Address Translation

Earlier, we discussed private IP address ranges. While they are potentially very useful, they come with a small catch. Packets with source or destination addresses in the private ranges are forbidden from being routed over the public Internet! So, without some help, devices using private range addresses can't talk to devices using addresses on the public Internet. However, with **Network Address Translation (NAT)**, we can solve this. Since most home networks use private range addresses, NAT is likely to be something that you'll encounter.

Although NAT can be used in other circumstances, it is most commonly performed by a gateway at the boundary of the public Internet and a network that is using private range IP addresses. To enable the packets from the gateway's network to be routed on the public Internet as the gateway receives packets from the network that are destined for the Internet, it rewrites the packets' headers and replaces the private range source IP addresses with its own public range IP address. If the packets contain TCP or UDP packets, and these contain a source port, then it may also open up a new source port for listening on its external interface and rewrite the source port number in the packets to match this new number.

As it does these rewrites, it records the mapping between the newly opened source port and the source device on the internal network. If it receives a reply to the new source port, then it reverses the translation process and sends the received packets to the original device on the internal network. The originating network device shouldn't be made aware of the fact that its traffic is undergoing NAT.

There are several benefits of using NAT. The internal network devices are shielded from malicious traffic directed toward the network from the Internet, devices which use NAT devices are provided with a layer of privacy since their private addresses are hidden, and the number of network devices that need to be assigned precious public IP addresses is reduced. It's actually the heavy use of NAT that allows the Internet to continue functioning despite having run out of IPv4 addresses.

NAT can cause some problems for network's applications, if it is not taken into consideration at design time.

If the transmitted application data includes information about a device's network configuration and that device is behind a NAT router, then problems can occur if the receiving device acts on the assumption that the application data matches the IP and the TCP/UDP header data. NAT routers will rewrite the IP and TCP/UDP header data, but not the application data. This is a well known problem in the FTP protocol.

Another problem that FTP has with NAT is that in FTP active mode, a part of the protocol operation involves the client opening a port for listening on, and the server creating a new TCP connection to that port (as opposed to just a regular reply). This fails when the client is behind a NAT router because the router doesn't know what to do with the server's connection attempt. So, be careful about assuming that servers can create new connections to clients, since they may be blocked by a NAT router, or firewall. In general, it's best to program under the assumption that it's not possible for a server to establish a new connection to a client.

IPv6

We mentioned that the earlier discussion is based on IPv4, but that there is a new version called IPv6. IPv6 is ultimately designed to replace IPv4, but this process is unlikely to be completed for a while yet.

Since most Python standard library modules have now been updated to support IPv6 and to accept IPv6 addresses, moving to IPv6 in Python shouldn't have much impact on our applications. However, there are a few small glitches to watch out for.

The main difference that you'll notice in IPv6 is that the address format has been changed. One of the main design goals of the new protocol was to alleviate the global shortage of IPv4 addresses and to prevent it from happening again the IETF quadrupled the length of an address, to 128 bits, creating a large enough address space to give each human on the planet a billion times as many addresses as there are in the entire IPv4 address space.

The new format IP addresses are written differently, they look like this:

```
2001:0db8:85a3:0000:0000:b81a:63d6:135b
```

Note the use of colons and hexadecimal format.

There are rules for writing IPv6 addresses in more compact forms as well. This is principally done by omitting runs of consecutive zeros. For example, the address in the preceding example could be shortened to:

```
2001:db8:85a3::b81a:63d6:135b
```

If a program needs to compare or parse text-formatted IPv6 addresses, then it will need to be made aware of these compacting rules, as a single IPv6 address can be represented in more than one way. Details of these rules can be found in RFC 4291, which is available at `http://www.ietf.org/rfc/rfc4291.txt`.

Since colons may cause conflicts when used in URIs, IPv6 addresses need to be enclosed in square brackets when they are used in this manner, for example:

```
http://[2001:db8:85a3::b81a:63d6:135b]/index.html
```

Also, in IPv6, it is now standard practice for network interfaces to have multiple IP addresses assigned to them. IPv6 addresses are classified by what scope they are valid in. The scopes include the global scope (that is, the public Internet) and the link-local scope, which is only valid for the local subnet. An IP address's scope can be determined by inspecting its high-order bits. If we enumerate the IP addresses of local interfaces to use for a certain purpose, then we need to check if we have used the correct address for the scope that we intend to work with. There are more details in RFC 4291.

Finally, with the mind-boggling cornucopia of addresses that are available in IPv6, the idea is that every device (and component, and bacterium) can be given a globally unique public IP address, and NAT will become a thing of the past. Though it sounds great in theory, some concerns have been raised about the implications that this has for issues like user privacy. As such, additions designed for alleviating these concerns have been made to the protocol (`http://www.ietf.org/rfc/rfc3041.txt`). This is a welcome progression; however, it can cause problems for some applications. So reading through the RFC is worth your while, if you're planning for your program to employ IPv6.

Summary

In the first part of this chapter, we looked at the essentials of networking with TCP/IP. We discussed the concept of network stacks, and looked at the principle protocols of the Internet protocol suite. We saw how IP solves the problem of sending messages between devices on different networks, and how TCP and UDP provide end-to-end transport between applications.

In the second section, we looked at how network programming is generally approached when using Python. We discussed the general principle of using modules that interface with services as far up the network stack as we can manage. We also discussed where we might find those modules. We looked at examples of employing modules that interface with the network stack at different layers to accomplish a simple network task.

Finally, we discussed some common pitfalls of programming for TCP/IP networks and some steps that may be taken to avoid them.

This chapter has been heavy on the networking theory side of things. But, now it's time to get stuck into Python and put some application layer protocols to work for us.

2
HTTP and Working with the Web

The **Hypertext Transfer Protocol (HTTP)** is probably the most widely-used application layer protocol. It was originally developed to allow academics to share HTML documents. Nowadays, it is used as the core protocol of innumerable applications across the Internet, and it is the principle protocol of the World Wide Web.

In this chapter, we will cover the following topics:

- The HTTP protocol structure
- Using Python for talking to services through HTTP
- Downloading files
- HTTP capabilities, such as compression and cookies
- Handling errors
- URLs
- The Python standard library `urllib` package
- Kenneth Reitz's third-party `Requests` package

The `urllib` package is the recommended Python standard library package for HTTP tasks. The standard library also has a low-level module called `http`. Although this offers access to almost all aspects of the protocol, it has not been designed for everyday use. The `urllib` package has a simpler interface, and it deals with everything that we are going to cover in this chapter.

The third-party `Requests` package is a very popular alternative to `urllib`. It has an elegant interface and a powerful featureset, and it is a great tool for streamlining HTTP workflows. We'll be discussing how it can be used in place of `urllib` at the end of the chapter.

Request and response

HTTP is an application layer protocol, and it is almost always used on top of TCP. The HTTP protocol has been deliberately defined to use a human-readable message format, but it can still be used for transporting arbitrary bytes data.

An HTTP exchange consists of two elements. A **request** made by the client, which asks the server for a particular resource specified by a URL, and a **response**, sent by the server, which supplies the resource that the client has asked for. If the server can't provide the resource that the client has requested, then the response will contain information about the failure.

This order of events is fixed in HTTP. All interactions are initiated by the client. The server never sends anything to the client without the client explicitly asking for it.

This chapter will teach you how to use Python as an HTTP client. We will learn how to make requests to servers and then interpret their responses. We will look at writing server-side applications in *Chapter 9, Applications for the Web*.

By far, the most widely used version of HTTP is 1.1, defined in RFCs 7230 to 7235. HTTP 2 is the latest version, which was officially ratified just as this book was going to press. Most of the semantics and syntax remain the same between versions 1.1 and 2, the main changes are in how the TCP connections are utilised. As of now, HTTP 2 isn't widely supported, so we will focus on version 1.1 in this book. If you do want to know more, HTTP 2 is documented in RFCs 7540 and 7541.

HTTP version 1.0, documented in RFC 1945, is still used by some older softwares. Version 1.1 is backwards-compatible with 1.0 though, and the `urllib` package and `Requests` both support HTTP 1.1, so when we're writing a client with Python we don't need to worry about whether we're connecting to an HTTP 1.0 server. It's just that some more advanced features are not available. Almost all services nowadays use version 1.1, so we won't go into the differences here. The stack overflow question is, a good starting point, if you need further information: `http://stackoverflow.com/questions/246859/http-1-0-vs-1-1`.

Requests with urllib

We have already seen some examples of HTTP exchanges while discussing the RFC downloaders in *Chapter 1, Network Programming and Python*. The urllib package is broken into several submodules for dealing with the different tasks that we may need to perform when working with HTTP. For making requests and receiving responses, we employ the urllib.request module.

Retrieving the contents of a URL is a straightforward process when done using urllib. Load your Python interpreter and do the following:

```
>>> from urllib.request import urlopen
>>> response = urlopen('http://www.debian.org')
>>> response
<http.client.HTTPResponse object at 0x7fa3c53059b0>
>>> response.readline()
b'<!DOCTYPE HTML PUBLIC "-//W3C//DTD HTML 4.01//EN"
  "http://www.w3.org/TR/html4/strict.dtd">\n'
```

We use the urllib.request.urlopen() function for sending a request and receiving a response for the resource at http://www.debian.org, in this case an HTML page. We will then print out the first line of the HTML we receive.

Response objects

Let's take a closer look at our response object. We can see from the preceding example that urlopen() returns an http.client.HTTPResponse instance. The response object gives us access to the data of the requested resource, and the properties and the metadata of the response. To view the URL for the response that we received in the previous section, do this:

```
>>> response.url
'http://www.debian.org'
```

We get the data of the requested resource through a file-like interface using the readline() and read() methods. We saw the readline() method in the previous section. This is how we use the read() method:

```
>>> response = urlopen('http://www.debian.org')
>>> response.read(50)
b'g="en">\n<head>\n  <meta http-equiv="Content-Type" c'
```

The `read()` method returns the specified number of bytes from the data. Here it's the first 50 bytes. A call to the `read()` method with no argument will return all the data in one go.

The file-like interface is limited. Once the data has been read, it's not possible to go back and re-read it by using either of the aforementioned functions. To demonstrate this, try doing the following:

```
>>> response = urlopen('http://www.debian.org')
>>> response.read()
b'<!DOCTYPE HTML PUBLIC "-//W3C//DTD HTML 4.01//EN"
  "http://www.w3.org/TR/html4/strict.dtd">\n<html
  lang="en">\n<head>\n  <meta http-equiv
...
>>> response.read()
b''
```

We can see that when we call the `read()` function a second time it returns an empty string. There are no `seek()` or `rewind()` methods, so we cannot reset the position. Hence, it's best to capture the `read()` output in a variable.

Both `readline()` and `read()` functions return bytes objects, and neither `http` nor `urllib` will make any effort to decode the data that they receive to Unicode. Later on in the chapter, we'll be looking at a way in which we can handle this with the help of the `Requests` library.

Status codes

What if we wanted to know whether anything unexpected had happened to our request? Or what if we wanted to know whether our response contained any data before we read the data out? Maybe we're expecting a large response, and we want to quickly see if our request has been successful without reading the whole response.

HTTP responses provide a means for us to do this through **status codes**. We can read the status code of a response by using its `status` attribute.

```
>>> response.status
200
```

Status codes are integers that tell us how the request went. The `200` code informs us that everything went fine.

There are a number of codes, and each one conveys a different meaning. According to their first digit, status codes are classified into the following groups:

- 100: Informational
- 200: Success
- 300: Redirection
- 400: Client error
- 500: Server error

A few of the more frequently encountered codes and their messages are as follows:

- `200: OK`
- `404: Not Found`
- `500: Internal Server Error`

The official list of status codes is maintained by IANA and it can be found at `https://www.iana.org/assignments/http-status-codes`. We'll be looking at various codes in this chapter.

Handling problems

Status codes help us to see whether our response was successful or not. Any code in the 200 range indicates a success, whereas any code in either the 400 range or the 500 range indicates failure.

Status codes should always be checked so that our program can respond appropriately if something goes wrong. The `urllib` package helps us in checking the status codes by raising an exception if it encounters a problem.

Let's go through how to catch these and handle them usefully. For this try the following command block:

```
>>> import urllib.error
>>> from urllib.request import urlopen
>>> try:
...     urlopen('http://www.ietf.org/rfc/rfc0.txt')
... except urllib.error.HTTPError as e:
...     print('status', e.code)
```

```
...     print('reason', e.reason)
...     print('url', e.url)
...
status: 404
reason: Not Found
url: http://www.ietf.org/rfc/rfc0.txt
```

Here we've requested RFC 0, which doesn't exist. So the server has returned a 404 status code, and `urllib` has spotted this and raised an `HTTPError`.

You can see that `HTTPError` provide useful attributes regarding the request. In the preceding example, we used the `status`, `reason`, and `url` attributes to get some information about the response.

If something goes wrong lower in the network stack, then the appropriate module will raise an exception. The `urllib` package catches these exceptions and then wraps them as `URLErrors`. For example, we might have specified a host or an IP address that doesn't exist, as shown here:

```
>>> urlopen('http://192.0.2.1/index.html')
...
urllib.error.URLError: <urlopen error [Errno 110] Connection timed
  out>
```

In this instance, we have asked for `index.html` from the `192.0.2.1.` host. The `192.0.2.0/24` IP address range is reserved to be used by documentation only, so you will never encounter a host using the preceding IP address. Hence the TCP connection times out and `socket` raises a timeout exception, which `urllib` catches, re-wraps, and re-raises for us. We can catch these exceptions in the same way as we did in the preceding example.

HTTP headers

Requests, and responses are made up of two main parts, **headers** and a **body**. We briefly saw some HTTP headers when we used our TCP RFC downloader in *Chapter 1, Network Programming and Python*. Headers are the lines of protocol-specific information that appear at the beginning of the raw message that is sent over the TCP connection. The body is the rest of the message. It is separated from the headers by a blank line. The body is optional, its presence depends on the type of request or response. Here's an example of an HTTP request:

```
GET / HTTP/1.1
Accept-Encoding: identity
```

```
Host: www.debian.com
Connection: close
User-Agent: Python-urllib/3.4
```

The first line is called the **request line**. It is comprised of the request **method**, which is GET in this case, the path to the resource, which is / here, and the HTTP version, 1.1. The rest of the lines are request headers. Each line is comprised of a header name followed by a colon and a header value. The request in the preceding output only contains headers, it does not have a body.

Headers are used for several purposes. In a request they can be used for passing extra data, such as cookies and authorization credentials, and for asking the server for preferred formats of resources.

For example, an important header is the Host header. Many web server applications provide the ability to host more than one website on the same server using the same IP address. DNS aliases are set up for the various website domain names, so they all point to the same IP address. Effectively, the web server is given multiple hostnames, one for each website it hosts. IP and TCP (which HTTP runs on), can't be used to tell the server which hostname the client wants to connect to because both of them operate solely on IP addresses. The HTTP protocol allows the client to supply the hostname in the HTTP request by including a Host header.

We'll look at some more request headers in the following section.

Here's an example of a response:

```
HTTP/1.1 200 OK
Date: Sun, 07 Sep 2014 19:58:48 GMT
Content-Type: text/html
Content-Length: 4729
Server: Apache
Content-Language: en

<!DOCTYPE HTML PUBLIC "-//W3C//DTD HTML 4.01//EN"
    "http://www.w3.org/TR/html4/strict.dtd">\n...
```

The first line contains the protocol version, the status code, and the status message. Subsequent lines contain the headers, a blank line, and then the body. In the response, the server can use headers to inform the client about things such as the length of the body, the type of content the response body contains, and the cookie data that the client should store.

Do the following to view a response object's headers:

```
>>> response = urlopen('http://www.debian.org)
>>> response.getheaders()
[('Date', 'Sun, 07 Sep 2014 19:58:48 GMT'), ('Server', 'Apache'),
  ('Content-Location', 'index.en.html'), ('Vary', 'negotiate,accept-
  language,Accept-Encoding')...
```

The `getheaders()` method returns the headers as a list of tuples of the form (`header name`, `header value`). A complete list of HTTP 1.1 headers and their meanings can be found in RFC 7231. Let's look at how to use some headers in requests and responses.

Customizing requests

To make use of the functionality that headers provide, we add headers to a request before sending it. To do this, we can't just use `urlopen()`. We need to follow these steps:

- Create a `Request` object
- Add headers to the request object
- Use `urlopen()` to send the request object

We're going to learn how to customize a request for retrieving a Swedish version of the Debian home page. We will use the `Accept-Language` header, which tells the server our preferred language for the resource it returns. Note that not all servers hold versions of resources in multiple languages, so not all servers will respond to `Accept-Language`Linux home page.

First, we create a `Request` object:

```
>>> from urllib.request import Request
>>> req = Request('http://www.debian.org')
```

Next we add the header:

```
>>> req.add_header('Accept-Language', 'sv')
```

The `add_header()` method takes the name of the header and the contents of the header as arguments. The `Accept-Language` header takes two-letter ISO 639-1 language codes. The code for Swedish is `sv`.

Lastly, we submit the customized request with `urlopen()`:

```
>>> response = urlopen(req)
```

We can check if the response is in Swedish by printing out the first few lines:

```
>>> response.readlines()[:5]
[b'<!DOCTYPE HTML PUBLIC "-//W3C//DTD HTML 4.01//EN"
  "http://www.w3.org/TR/html4/strict.dtd">\n',
  b'<html lang="sv">\n',
  b'<head>\n',
  b'    <meta http-equiv="Content-Type" content="text/html;
  charset=utf-  8">\n',
  b'    <title>Debian -- Det universella operativsystemet </title>\n']
```

Jetta bra! The `Accept-Language` header has informed the server about our preferred language for the response's content.

To view the headers present in a request, do the following:

```
>>> req = Request('http://www.debian.org')
>>> req.add_header('Accept-Language', 'sv')
>>> req.header_items()
[('Accept-language', 'sv')]
```

The `urlopen()` method adds some of its own headers when we run it on a request:

```
>>> response = urlopen(req)
>>> req.header_items()
[('Accept-language', 'sv'), ('User-agent': 'Python-urllib/3.4'),
  ('Host': 'www.debian.org')]
```

A shortcut for adding headers is to add them at the same time that we create the request object, as shown here:

```
>>> headers = {'Accept-Language': 'sv'}
>>> req = Request('http://www.debian.org', headers=headers)
>>> req.header_items()
[('Accept-language', 'sv')]
```

We supply the headers as a `dict` to the `Request` object constructor as the `headers` keyword argument. In this way, we can add multiple headers in one go, by adding more entries to the `dict`.

Let's take a look at some more things that we can do with headers.

Content compression

The `Accept-Encoding` request header and the `Content-Encoding` response header can work together to allow us to temporarily encode the body of a response for transmission over the network. This is typically used for compressing the response and reducing the amount of data that needs to be transferred.

This process follows these steps:

- The client sends a request with acceptable encodings listed in an `Accept-Encoding` header
- The server picks an encoding method that it supports
- The server encodes the body using this encoding method
- The server sends the response, specifying the encoding it has used in a `Content-Encoding` header
- The client decodes the response body using the specified encoding method

Let's discuss how to request a document and get the server to use `gzip` compression for the response body. First, let's construct the request:

```
>>> req = Request('http://www.debian.org')
```

Next, add the `Accept-Encoding` header:

```
>>> req.add_header('Accept-Encoding', 'gzip')
```

And then, submit it with the help of `urlopen()`:

```
>>> response = urlopen(req)
```

We can check if the server is using `gzip` compression by looking at the response's `Content-Encoding` header:

```
>>> response.getheader('Content-Encoding')
'gzip'
```

We can then decompress the body data by using the `gzip` module:

```
>>> import gzip
>>> content = gzip.decompress(response.read())
>>> content.splitlines()[:5]
[b'<!DOCTYPE HTML PUBLIC "-//W3C//DTD HTML 4.01//EN"
  "http://www.w3.org/TR/html4/strict.dtd">',
  b'<html lang="en">',
```

```
b'<head>',
b'    <meta http-equiv="Content-Type" content="text/html;
charset=utf-8">',
b'    <title>Debian -- The Universal Operating System </title>']
```

Encodings are registered with IANA. The current list contains: `gzip`, `compress`, `deflate`, and `identity`. The first three refer to specific compression methods. The last one allows the client to specify that it doesn't want any encoding applied to the content.

Let's see what happens if we ask for no compression by using the `identity` encoding:

```
>>> req = Request('http://www.debian.org')
>>> req.add_header('Accept-Encoding', 'identity')
>>> response = urlopen(req)
>>> print(response.getheader('Content-Encoding'))
None
```

When a server uses the `identity` encoding type, no `Content-Encoding` header is included in the response.

Multiple values

To tell the server that we can accept more than one encoding, add more values to the `Accept-Encoding` header and separate them by commas. Let's try it. We create our `Request` object:

```
>>> req = Request('http://www.debian.org')
```

Then, we add our header, and this time we include more encodings:

```
>>> encodings = 'deflate, gzip, identity'
>>> req.add_header('Accept-Encoding', encodings)
```

Now, we submit the request and then check the response encoding:

```
>>> response = urlopen(req)
>>> response.getheader('Content-Encoding')
'gzip'
```

If needed, relative weightings can be given to specific encodings by adding a q value:

```
>>> encodings = 'gzip, deflate;q=0.8, identity;q=0.0'
```

The q value follows the encoding name, and it is separated by a semicolon. The maximum q value is 1.0, and this is also the default if no q value is given. So, the preceding line should be interpreted as my first preference for encoding is gzip, my second preference is deflate, and my third preference is identity, if nothing else is available.

Content negotiation

Content compression with the Accept-Encoding header and language selection with the Accept-Language header are examples of **content negotiation,** where the client specifies its preferences regarding the format and the content of the requested resource. The following headers can also be used for this:

- Accept: For requesting a preferred file format
- Accept-Charset: For requesting the resource in a preferred character set

There are additional aspects to the content negotiation mechanism, but because it's inconsistently supported and it can become quite involved, we won't be covering it in this chapter. RFC 7231 contain all the details that you need. Take a look at sections such as 3.4, 5.3, 6.4.1, and 6.5.6, if you find that your application requires this.

Content types

HTTP can be used as a transport for any type of file or data. The server can use the Content-Type header in a response to inform the client about the type of data that it has sent in the body. This is the primary means an HTTP client determines how it should handle the body data that the server returns to it.

To view the content type, we inspect the value of the response header, as shown here:

```
>>> response = urlopen('http://www.debian.org')
>>> response.getheader('Content-Type')
'text/html'
```

The values in this header are taken from a list which is maintained by IANA. These values are variously called **content types**, **Internet media types**, or **MIME types** (**MIME** stands for **Multipurpose Internet Mail Extensions**, the specification in which the convention was first established). The full list can be found at http://www.iana.org/assignments/media-types.

There are registered media types for many of the types of data that are transmitted across the Internet, some common ones are:

Media type	Description
text/html	HTML document
text/plain	Plain text document
image/jpeg	JPG image
application/pdf	PDF document
application/json	JSON data
application/xhtml+xml	XHTML document

Another media type of interest is application/octet-stream, which in practice is used for files that don't have an applicable media type. An example of this would be a pickled Python object. It is also used for files whose format is not known by the server. In order to handle responses with this media type correctly, we need to discover the format in some other way. Possible approaches are as follows:

- Examine the filename extension of the downloaded resource, if it has one. The mimetypes module can then be used for determining the media type (go to *Chapter 3, APIs in Action* to see an example of this).

- Download the data and then use a file type analysis tool. TheUse the Python standard library imghdr module can be used for images, and the third-party python-magic package, or the GNU file command, can be used for other types.

- Check the website that we're downloading from to see if the file type has been documented anywhere.

Content type values can contain optional additional parameters that provide further information about the type. This is usually used to supply the character set that the data uses. For example:

```
Content-Type: text/html; charset=UTF-8.
```

In this case, we're being told that the character set of the document is UTF-8. The parameter is included after a semicolon, and it always takes the form of a key/value pair.

Let's discuss an example, downloading the Python home page and using the Content-Type value it returns. First, we submit our request:

```
>>> response = urlopen('http://www.python.org')
```

Then, we check the `Content-Type` value of our response, and extract the character set:

```
>>> format, params = response.getheader('Content-Type').split(';')
>>> params
' charset=utf-8'
>>> charset = params.split('=')[1]
>>> charset
'utf-8'
```

Lastly, we decode our response content by using the supplied character set:

```
>>> content = response.read().decode(charset)
```

Note that quite often, the server either doesn't supply a `charset` in the `Content-Type` header, or it supplies the wrong `charset`. So, this value should be taken as a suggestion. This is one of the reasons that we look at the `Requests` library later in this chapter. It will automatically gather all the hints that it can find about what character set should be used for decoding a response body and make a best guess for us.

User agents

Another request header worth knowing about is the `User-Agent` header. Any client that communicates using HTTP can be referred to as a **user agent**. RFC 7231 suggests that user agents should use the `User-Agent` header to identify themselves in every request. What goes in there is up to the software that makes the request, though it usually comprises a string that identifies the program and version, and possibly the operating system and the hardware that it's running on. For example, the user agent for my current version of Firefox is shown here:

```
Mozilla/5.0 (X11; Linux x86_64; rv:24.0) Gecko/20140722
    Firefox/24.0 Iceweasel/24.7.0
```

Although it has been broken over two lines here, it is a single long string. As you can probably decipher, I'm running Iceweasel (Debian's version of Firefox) version 24 on a 64-bit Linux system. User agent strings aren't intended for identifying individual users. They only identify the product that was used for making the request.

We can view the user agent that `urllib` uses. Perform the following steps:

```
>>> req = Request('http://www.python.org')
>>> urlopen(req)
>>> req.get_header('User-agent')
'Python-urllib/3.4'
```

Here, we have created a request and submitted it using `urlopen`, and `urlopen` added the user agent header to the request. We can examine this header by using the `get_header()` method. This header and its value are included in every request made by `urllib`, so every server we make a request to can see that we are using Python 3.4 and the `urllib` library.

Webmasters can inspect the user agents of requests and then use the information for various things, including the following:

- Classifying visits for their website statistics
- Blocking clients with certain user agent strings
- Sending alternative versions of resources for user agents with known problems, such as bugs when interpreting certain languages like CSS, or not supporting some languages at all, such as JavaScript

The last two can cause problems for us because they can stop or interfere with us accessing the content that we're after. To work around this, we can try and set our user agent so that it mimics a well known browser. This is known as **spoofing**, as shown here:

```
>>> req = Request('http://www.debian.org')
>>> req.add_header('User-Agent', 'Mozilla/5.0 (X11; Linux x86_64;
  rv:24.0) Gecko/20140722 Firefox/24.0 Iceweasel/24.7.0')
>>> response = urlopen(req)
```

The server will respond as if our application is a regular Firefox client. User agent strings for different browsers are available on the web. I'm yet to come across a comprehensive resource for them, but Googling for a browser and version number will usually turn something up. Alternatively you can use Wireshark to capture an HTTP request made by the browser you want to emulate and look at the captured request's user agent header.

Cookies

A cookie is a small piece of data that the server sends in a `Set-Cookie` header as a part of the response. The client stores cookies locally and includes them in any future requests that are sent to the server.

Servers use cookies in various ways. They can add a unique ID to them, which enables them to track a client as it accesses different areas of a site. They can store a login token, which will automatically log the client in, even if the client leaves the site and then accesses it later. They can also be used for storing the client's user preferences or snippets of personalizing information, and so on.

Cookies are necessary because the server has no other way of tracking a client between requests. HTTP is called a **stateless** protocol. It doesn't contain an explicit mechanism for a server to know for sure that two requests have come from the same client. Without cookies to allow the server to add some uniquely identifying information to the requests, things such as shopping carts (which were the original problem that cookies were developed to solve) would become impossible to build, because the server would not be able to determine which basket goes with which request.

We may need to handle cookies in Python because without them, some sites don't behave as expected. When using Python, we may also want to access the parts of a site which require a login, and the login sessions are usually maintained through cookies.

Cookie handling

We're going to discuss how to handle cookies with `urllib`. First, we need to create a place for storing the cookies that the server will send us:

```
>>> from http.cookiejar import CookieJar
>>> cookie_jar = CookieJar()
```

Next, we build something called an `urllib` opener. This will automatically extract the cookies from the responses that we receive and then store them in our cookie jar:

```
>>> from urllib.request import build_opener, HTTPCookieProcessor
>>> opener = build_opener(HTTPCookieProcessor(cookie_jar))
```

Then, we can use our opener to make an HTTP request:

```
>>> opener.open('http://www.github.com')
```

Lastly, we can check that the server has sent us some cookies:

```
>>> len(cookie_jar)
2
```

Whenever we use `opener` to make further requests, the `HTTPCookieProcessor` functionality will check our `cookie_jar` to see if it contains any cookies for that site and then it will automatically add them to our requests. It will also add any further cookies that are received to the cookie jar.

The `http.cookiejar` module also contains a `FileCookieJar` class, that works in the same way as `CookieJar`, but it provides an additional function for easily saving the cookies to a file. This allows persistence of cookies across Python sessions.

Know your cookies

It's worth looking at the properties of cookies in more detail. Let's examine the cookies that GitHub sent us in the preceding section.

To do this, we need to pull the cookies out of the cookie jar. The `CookieJar` module doesn't let us access them directly, but it supports the iterator protocol. So, a quick way of getting them is to create a `list` from it:

```
>>> cookies = list(cookie_jar)
>>> cookies
[Cookie(version=0, name='logged_in', value='no', ...),
 Cookie(version=0, name='_gh_sess', value='eyJzZxNzaW9uX...', ...)
]
```

You can see that we have two `Cookie` objects. Now, let's pull out some information from the first one:

```
>>> cookies[0].name
'logged_in'
>>> cookies[0].value
'no'
```

The cookie's name allows the server to quickly reference it. This cookie is clearly a part of the mechanism that GitHub uses for finding out whether we've logged in yet. Next, let's do the following:

```
>>> cookies[0].domain
'.github.com'
>>> cookies[0].path
'/'
```

The domain and the path are the areas for which this cookie is valid, so our `urllib` opener will include this cookie in any request that it sends to `www.github.com` and its sub-domains, where the path is anywhere below the root.

Now, let's look at the cookie's lifetime:

```
>>> cookies[0].expires
2060882017
```

This is a Unix timestamp; we can convert it to `datetime`:

```
>>> import datetime
>>> datetime.datetime.fromtimestamp(cookies[0].expires)
datetime.datetime(2035, 4, 22, 20, 13, 37)
```

So, our cookie will expire on 22nd of April, 2035. An expiry date is the amount of time that the server would like the client to hold on to the cookie for. Once the expiry date has passed, the client can throw the cookie away and the server will send a new one with the next request. Of course, there's nothing to stop a client from immediately throwing the cookie away, though on some sites this may break functionality that depends on the cookie.

Let's discuss two common cookie flags:

```
>>> print(cookies[0].get_nonstandard_attr('HttpOnly'))
None
```

Cookies that are stored on a client can be accessed in a number of ways:

- By the client as part of an HTTP request and response sequence
- By scripts running in the client, such as JavaScript
- By other processes running in the client, such as Flash

The HttpOnly flag indicates that the client should only allow access to a cookie when the access is part of an HTTP request or response. The other methods should be denied access. This will protect the client against Cross-site scripting attacks (see *Chapter 9, Applications for the Web*, for more information on these). This is an important security feature, and when the server sets it, our application should behaves accordingly.

There is also a secure flag:

```
>>> cookies[0].secure
True
```

If the value is true, the Secure flag indicates that the cookie should only ever be sent over a secure connection, such as HTTPS. Again, we should honor this if the flag has been set such that when our application send requests containing this cookie, it only sends them to HTTPS URLs.

You may have spotted an inconsistency here. Our URL has requested a response over HTTP, yet the server has sent us a cookie, which it's requesting to be sent only over secure connections. Surely the site designers didn't overlook a security loophole like that? Rest assured; they didn't. The response was actually sent over HTTPS. But, how did that happen? Well, the answer lies with redirects.

Redirects

Sometimes servers move their content around. They also make some content obsolete and put up new stuff in a different location. Sometimes they'd like us to use the more secure HTTPS protocol instead of HTTP. In all these cases, they may get traffic that asks for the old URLs, and in all these cases they'd probably prefer to be able to automatically send visitors to the new ones.

The 300 range of HTTP status codes is designed for this purpose. These codes indicate to the client that further action is required on their part to complete the request. The most commonly encountered action is to retry the request at a different URL. This is called a **redirect**.

We'll learn how this works when using `urllib`. Let's make a request:

```
>>> req = Request('http://www.gmail.com')
>>> response = urlopen(req)
```

Simple enough, but now, look at the URL of the response:

```
>>> response.url
'https://accounts.google.com/ServiceLogin?service=mail&passive=true&r
    m=false...'
```

This is not the URL that we requested! If we open this new URL in a browser, then we'll see that it's actually the Google login page (you may need to clear your browser cookies to see this if you already have a cached Google login session). Google redirected us from `http://www.gmail.com` to its login page, and `urllib` automatically followed the redirect. Moreover, we may have been redirected more than once. Look at the `redirect_dict` attribute of our request object:

```
>>> req.redirect_dict
{'https://accounts.google.com/ServiceLogin?service=...': 1,
   'https://mail.google.com/mail/': 1}
```

The `urllib` package adds every URL that we were redirected through to this `dict`. We can see that we have actually been redirected twice, first to `https://mail.google.com`, and second to the login page.

When we send our first request, the server sends a response with a redirect status code, one of 301, 302, 303, or 307. All of these indicate a redirect. This response includes a `Location` header, which contains the new URL. The `urllib` package will submit a new request to that URL, and in the aforementioned case, it will receive yet another redirect, which will lead it to the Google login page.

Since `urllib` follows redirects for us, they generally don't affect us, but it's worth knowing that a response `urllib` returns may be for a URL different from what we had requested. Also, if we hit too many redirects for a single request (more than 10 for `urllib`), then `urllib` will give up and raise an `urllib.error.HTTPError` exception.

URLs

Uniform Resource Locators, or **URLs** are fundamental to the way in which the web operates, and they have been formally described in RFC 3986. A URL represents a resource on a given host. How URLs map to the resources on the remote system is entirely at the discretion of the system admin. URLs can point to files on the server, or the resources may be dynamically generated when a request is received. What the URL maps to though doesn't matter as long as the URLs work when we request them.

URLs are comprised of several sections. Python uses the `urllib.parse` module for working with URLs. Let's use Python to break a URL into its component parts:

```
>>> from urllib.parse import urlparse
>>> result = urlparse('http://www.python.org/dev/peps')
>>> result
ParseResult(scheme='http', netloc='www.python.org', path='/dev/peps',
  params='', query='', fragment='')
```

The `urllib.parse.urlparse()` function interprets our URL and recognizes `http` as the **scheme**, `www.python.org` as the **network location**, and `/dev/peps` as the **path**. We can access these components as attributes of the `ParseResult`:

```
>>> result.netloc
'www.python.org'
>>> result.path
'/dev/peps'
```

For almost all resources on the web, we'll be using the `http` or `https` schemes. In these schemes, to locate a specific resource, we need to know the host that it resides on and the TCP port that we should connect to (together these are the `netloc` component), and we also need to know the path to the resource on the host (the `path` component).

Port numbers can be specified explicitly in a URL by appending them to the host. They are separated from the host by a colon. Let's see what happens when we try this with `urlparse`.

```
>>> urlparse('http://www.python.org:8080/')
ParseResult(scheme='http', netloc='www.python.org:8080', path='/',
  params='', query='', fragment='')
```

The `urlparse` method just interprets it as a part of the netloc. This is fine because this is how handlers such as `urllib.request.urlopen()` expect it to be formatted.

If we don't supply a port (as is usually the case), then the default port 80 is used for `http`, and the default port 443 is used for `https`. This is usually what we want, as these are the standard ports for the HTTP and HTTPS protocols respectively.

Paths and relative URLs

The path in a URL is anything that comes after the host and the port. Paths always start with a forward-slash (/), and when just a slash appears on its own, it's called the **root**. We can see this by performing the following:

```
>>> urlparse('http://www.python.org/')
ParseResult(scheme='http', netloc='www.python.org', path='/',
  params='', query='', fragment='')
```

If no path is supplied in a request, then by default `urllib` will send a request for the root.

When a scheme and a host are included in a URL (as in the previous example), the URL is called an **absolute URL**. Conversely, it's possible to have **relative URLs**, which contain just a path component, as shown here:

```
>>> urlparse('../images/tux.png')
ParseResult(scheme='', netloc='', path='../images/tux.png',
  params='', query='', fragment='')
```

We can see that `ParseResult` only contains a `path`. If we want to use a relative URL to request a resource, then we need to supply the missing scheme, the host, and the base path.

Usually, we encounter relative URLs in a resource that we've already retrieved from a URL. So, we can just use this resource's URL to fill in the missing components. Let's look at an example.

Suppose that we've retrieved the `http://www.debian.org` URL, and within the webpage source code we found the relative URL for the 'About' page. We found that it's a relative URL for `intro/about`.

We can create an absolute URL by using the URL for the original page and the `urllib.parse.urljoin()` function. Let's see how we can do this:

```
>>> from urllib.parse import urljoin
>>> urljoin('http://www.debian.org', 'intro/about')
'http://www.debian.org/intro/about'
```

By supplying `urljoin` with a base URL, and a relative URL, we've created a new absolute URL.

Here, notice how `urljoin` has filled in the slash between the host and the path. The only time that `urljoin` will fill in a slash for us is when the base URL does not have a path, as shown in the preceding example. Let's see what happens if the base URL does have a path.

```
>>> urljoin('http://www.debian.org/intro/', 'about')
'http://www.debian.org/intro/about'
>>> urljoin('http://www.debian.org/intro', 'about')
'http://www.debian.org/about'
```

This will give us varying results. Notice how `urljoin` appends to the path if the base URL ends in a slash, but it replaces the last path element in the base URL if the base URL doesn't end in a slash.

We can force a path to replace all the elements of a base URL by prefixing it with a slash. Do the following:

```
>>> urljoin('http://www.debian.org/intro/about', '/News')
'http://www.debian.org/News'
```

How about navigating to parent directories? Let's try the standard dot syntax, as shown here:

```
>>> urljoin('http://www.debian.org/intro/about/', '../News')
'http://www.debian.org/intro/News'
>>> urljoin('http://www.debian.org/intro/about/', '../../News')
'http://www.debian.org/News'
>>> urljoin('http://www.debian.org/intro/about', '../News')
'http://www.debian.org/News'
```

It work as we'd expect it to. Note the difference between the base URL having and not having a trailing slash.

Lastly, what if the 'relative' URL is actually an absolute URL:

```
>>> urljoin('http://www.debian.org/about', 'http://www.python.org')
'http://www.python.org'
```

The relative URL completely replaces the base URL. This is handy, as it means that we don't need to worry about testing whether a URL is relative or not before using it with `urljoin`.

Query strings

RFC 3986 defines another property of URLs. They can contain additional parameters in the form of key/value pairs that appear after the path. They are separated from the path by a question mark, as shown here:

```
http://docs.python.org/3/search.html?q=urlparse&area=default
```

This string of parameters is called a query string. Multiple parameters are separated by ampersands (&). Let's see how `urlparse` handles it:

```
>>> urlparse('http://docs.python.org/3/search.html?
  q=urlparse&area=default')
ParseResult(scheme='http', netloc='docs.python.org',
  path='/3/search.html', params='', query='q=urlparse&area=default',
  fragment='')
```

So, `urlparse` recognizes the query string as the `query` component.

Query strings are used for supplying parameters to the resource that we wish to retrieve, and this usually customizes the resource in some way. In the aforementioned example, our query string tells the Python docs search page that we want to run a search for the term `urlparse`.

The `urllib.parse` module has a function that helps us turn the `query` component returned by `urlparse` into something more useful:

```
>>> from urllib.parse import parse_qs
>>> result = urlparse
  ('http://docs.python.org/3/search.html?q=urlparse&area=default')
>>> parse_qs(result.query)
{'area': ['default'], 'q': ['urlparse']}
```

The parse_qs() method reads the query string and then converts it into a dictionary. See how the dictionary values are actually in the form of lists? This is because parameters can appear more than once in a query string. Try it with a repeated parameter:

```
>>> result = urlparse
  ('http://docs.python.org/3/search.html?q=urlparse&q=urljoin')
>>> parse_qs(result.query)
{'q': ['urlparse', 'urljoin']}
```

See how both of the values have been added to the list? It's up to the server to decide how it interprets this. If we send this query string, then it may just pick one of the values and use that, while ignoring the repeat. You can only try it, and see what happens.

You can usually figure out what you need to put in a query string for a given page by submitting a query through the web interface using your web browser, and inspecting the URL of the results page. You should be able to spot the text of your search and consequently deduce the corresponding key for the search text. Quite often, many of the other parameters in the query string aren't actually needed for getting a basic result. Try requesting the page using only the search text parameter and see what happens. Then, add the other parameters, if it does not work as expected.

If you submit a form to a page and the resulting page's URL doesn't have a query string, then the page would have used a different method for sending the form data. We'll look at this in the *HTTP methods* section in the following, while discussing the POST method.

URL encoding

URLs are restricted to the ASCII characters and within this set, a number of characters are reserved and need to be escaped in different components of a URL. We escape them by using something called URL encoding. It is often called **percent encoding**, because it uses the percent sign as an escape character. Let's URL-encode a string:

```
>>> from urllib.parse import quote
>>> quote('A duck?')
'A%20duck%3F'
```

The special characters ' ' and ? have been replaced by escape sequences. The numbers in the escape sequences are the characters' ASCII codes in hexadecimal.

The full rules for where the reserved characters need to be escaped are given in RFC 3986, however `urllib` provides us with a couple of methods for helping us construct URLs. This means that we don't need to memorize all of these!

We just need to:

- URL-encode the path
- URL-encode the query string
- Combine them by using the `urllib.parse.urlunparse()` function

Let's see how to use the aforementioned steps in code. First, we encode the path:

```
>>> path = 'pypi'
>>> path_enc = quote(path)
```

Then, we encode the query string:

```
>>> from urllib.parse import urlencode
>>> query_dict = {':action': 'search', 'term': 'Are you quite sure
    this is a cheese shop?'}
>>> query_enc = urlencode(query_dict)
>>> query_enc
'%3Aaction=search&term=Are+you+quite+sure+this+is+a+cheese+shop%3F'
```

Lastly, we compose everything into a URL:

```
>>> from urllib.parse import urlunparse
>>> netloc = 'pypi.python.org'
>>> urlunparse(('http', netloc, path_enc, '', query_enc, ''))
'http://pypi.python.org/pypi?%3Aaction=search&term=Are+you+quite+sure
    +this+is+a+cheese+shop%3F'
```

The `quote()` function has been setup for specifically encoding paths. By default, it ignores slash characters and it doesn't encode them. This isn't obvious in the preceding example, try the following to see how this works:

```
>>> from urllib.parse import quote
>>> path = '/images/users/+Zoot+/'
>>> quote(path)
'/images/users/%2BZoot%2B/'
```

Notice that it ignores the slashes, but it escapes the +. That is perfect for paths.

The `urlencode()` function is similarly intended for encoding query strings directly from dicts. Notice how it correctly percent encodes our values and then joins them with &, so as to construct the query string.

Lastly, the `urlunparse()` method expects a 6-tuple containing the elements matching those of the result of `urlparse()`, hence the two empty strings.

There is a caveat for path encoding. If the elements of a path themselves contain slashes, then we may run into problems. The example is shown in the following commands:

```
>>> username = '+Zoot/Dingo+'
>>> path = 'images/users/{}'.format(username)
>>> quote(path)
'images/user/%2BZoot/Dingo%2B'
```

Notice how the slash in the username doesn't get escaped? This will be incorrectly interpreted as an extra level of directory structure, which is not what we want. In order to get around this, first we need to individually escape any path elements that may contain slashes, and then join them manually:

```
>>> username = '+Zoot/Dingo+'
>>> user_encoded = quote(username, safe='')
>>> path = '/'.join(('', 'images', 'users', username))
'/images/users/%2BZoot%2FDingo%2B'
```

Notice how the username slash is now percent-encoded? We encode the username separately, telling `quote` not to ignore slashes by supplying the `safe=''` argument, which overwrites its default ignore list of `/`. Then, we combine the path elements by using a simple `join()` function.

Here, it's worth mentioning that hostnames sent over the wire must be strictly ASCII, however the `socket` and `http` modules support transparent encoding of Unicode hostnames to an ASCII-compatible encoding, so in practice we don't need to worry about encoding hostnames. There are more details about this process in the `encodings.idna` section of the `codecs` module documentation.

URLs in summary

There are quite a few functions that we've used in the preceding sections. Let's just review what we have used each function for. All of these functions can be found in the `urllib.parse` module. They are as follows:

- Splitting a URL into its components: `urlparse`
- Combining an absolute URL with a relative URL: `urljoin`
- Parsing a query string into a `dict`: `parse_qs`
- URL-encoding a path: `quote`
- Creating a URL-encoded query string from a `dict`: `urlencode`
- Creating a URL from components (reverse of `urlparse`): `urlunparse`

HTTP methods

So far, we've been using requests for asking servers to send web resources to us, but HTTP provides more actions that we can perform. The GET in our request lines is an HTTP **method**, and there are several methods, such as HEAD, POST, OPTION, PUT, DELETE, TRACE, CONNECT, and PATCH.

We'll be looking at several of these in some detail in the next chapter, but there are two methods, we're going to take a quick look at now.

The HEAD method

The HEAD method is the same as the GET method. The only difference is that the server will never include a body in the response, even if there is a valid resource at the requested URL. The HEAD method is used for checking if a resource exists or if it has changed. Note that some servers don't implement this method, but when they do, it can prove to be a huge bandwidth saver.

We use alternative methods with urllib by supplying the method name to a Request object when we create it:

```
>>> req = Request('http://www.google.com', method='HEAD')
>>> response = urlopen(req)
>>> response.status
200
>>> response.read()
b''
```

Here the server has returned a 200 OK response, yet the body is empty, as expected.

The POST method

The POST method is in some senses the opposite of the GET method. We use the POST method for sending data to the server. However, in return the server can still send us a full response. The POST method is used for submitting user input from HTML forms and for uploading files to a server.

When using POST, the data that we wish to send will go in the body of the request. We can put any bytes data in there and declare its type by adding a Content-Type header to our request with an appropriate MIME type.

Let's look at an example for sending some HTML form data to a server by using a POST request, just as browsers do when we submitt a form on a website. The form data always consists of key/value pairs; `urllib` lets us work with regular dictionaries for supplying this (we'll look at where this data comes from in the following section):

```
>>> data_dict = {'P': 'Python'}
```

When posting the HTML form data, the form values must be formatted in the same way as **querystrings** are formatted in a URL, and must be URL-encoded. A `Content-Type` header must also be set to the special MIME type of `application/x-www-form-urlencoded`.

Since this format is identical to querystrings, we can just use the `urlencode()` function on our `dict` for preparing the data:

```
>>> data = urlencode(data_dict).encode('utf-8')
```

Here, we also additionally encode the result to bytes, as it's to be sent as the body of the request. In this case, we use the UTF-8 character set.

Next, we will construct our request:

```
>>> req = Request('http://search.debian.org/cgi-bin/omega',
  data=data)
```

By adding our data as the `data` keyword argument, we are telling `urllib` that we want our data to be sent as the body of the request. This will make the request use the POST method rather than the GET method.

Next, we add the `Content-Type` header:

```
>>> req.add_header('Content-Type', 'application/x-www-form-urlencode;
  charset=UTF-8')
```

Lastly, we submit the request:

```
>>> response = urlopen(req)
```

If we save the response data to a file and open it in a web browser, then we should see some Debian website search results related to Python.

Formal inspection

In the previous section we used the URL `http://search.debian.org/cgibin/omega`, and the dictionary `data_dict = {'P': 'Python'}`. But where did these come from?

We get these by visiting the web page containing the form we would submit to get the results manually. We then inspect the HTML source code of the web page. If we were carrying out the aforementioned search in a web browser, then we would most likely be on the `http://www.debian.org` page, and we would be running a search by typing our search term into the search box at the top right corner and then clicking on **Search**.

Most modern browsers allow you to directly inspect the source for any element on a page. To do this right-click on the element, which in this case is the search box, then select the **Inspect Element** option, as shown in the screenshot here:

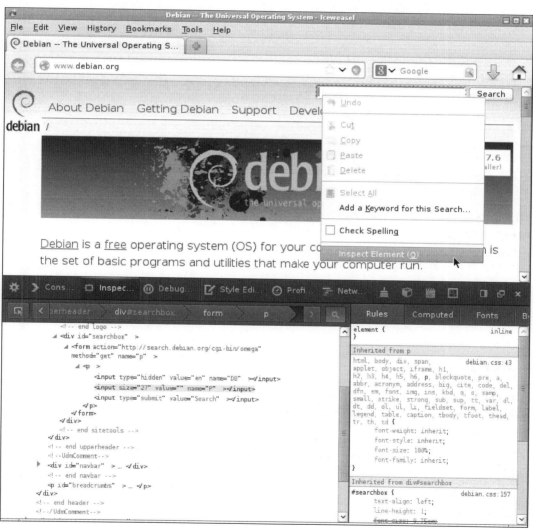

The source code will pop up in a section of the window. In the preceding screenshot, it's at the bottom left corner of the screen. Here, you will see some lines of code that looks like the following example:

```
<form action="http://search.debian.org/cgi-bin/omega"
method="get" name="P">
  <p>
    <input type="hidden" value="en" name="DB"></input>
    <input size="27" value="" name="P"></input>
    <input type="submit" value="Search"></input>
  </p>
</form>
```

You should see the second `<input>` highlighted. This is the tag that corresponds to the search text box. The value of the `name` attribute on the highlighted `<input>` tag is the key that we use in our `data_dict`, which in this case is `P`. The value in our `data_dict` is the term that we want to search for.

To get the URL, we need to look above the highlighted `<input>` for the enclosing `<form>` tag. Here, our URL will be of the value of the `action` attribute, `http://search.debian.org/cgi-bin/omega`. The source code for this web page is included in the source code download for this book, in case Debian changes their website before you read this.

This process can be applied to most HTML pages. To do this, look for the `<input>` corresponding to the input text box, then find the URL from the enclosing `<form>` tag. If you're not familiar with HTML, then this can be a bit of a trial and error process. We'll be looking at some more methods of parsing HTML in the next chapter.

Once we have our input name and URL, we can construct and submit the POST request, as shown in the previous section.

HTTPS

Unless otherwise protected, all HTTP requests and responses are sent in clear text. Anyone with access to the network that the messages travel over can potentially intercept our traffic and read it without hindrance.

Since the web is used for transferring quite a lot of sensitive data, solutions have been created for preventing eavesdroppers from reading the traffic, even if they are able to intercept it. These solutions, for the most part, employ some form of encryption.

The standard method for encrypting HTTP traffic is called HTTP Secure, or **HTTPS**. It uses an encryption mechanism called TLS/SSL, and it is applied to the TCP connection on which the HTTP traffic travels. HTTPS typically uses TCP port 443, as opposed to the default HTTP port 80.

To most users, this process is almost transparent. In principle, we only need to change the http in a URL to an https. Since urllib supports HTTPS, the same is true for our Python clients.

Note that not all servers support HTTPS, so simply changing the URL scheme to https: isn't guaranteed to work for all sites. If this is the case, then the connection attempt may fail in a number of ways, including a socket timeout, a connection reset error, or possibly even an HTTP error, such as a 400 range error or a 500 range error. An increasing number of sites are enabling HTTPS however. Many others are switching to it and using it as their default protocol, so it's worth investigating whether it's available so you can give your application's users extra security.

The Requests library

So that's it for the urllib package. As you can see, access to the standard library is more than adequate for most HTTP tasks. We haven't touched upon all of its capabilities. There are numerous handler classes which we haven't discussed, plus the opener interface is extensible.

However, the API isn't the most elegant, and there have been several attempts made to improve it. One of these is the very popular third-party library called **Requests**. It's available as the requests package on PyPi. It can either be installed through Pip or be downloaded from http://docs.python-requests.org, which hosts the documentation.

The Requests library automates and simplifies many of the tasks that we've been looking at. The quickest way of illustrating this is by trying some examples.

The commands for retrieving a URL with Requests are similar to retrieving a URL with the urllib package, as shown here:

```
>>> import requests
>>> response = requests.get('http://www.debian.org')
```

And we can look at properties of the response object. Try:

```
>>> response.status_code
200
>>> response.reason
'OK'
>>> response.url
'http://www.debian.org/'
>>> response.headers['content-type']
'text/html'
```

Note that the header name in the preceding command is in lowercase. The keys in the `headers` attribute of `Requests` response objects are case insensitive.

There are some convenience attributes that have been added to the response object:

```
>>> response.ok
True
```

The `ok` attribute indicates whether the request was successful. That is, the request contained a status code in the 200 range. Also:

```
>>> response.is_redirect
False
```

The `is_redirect` attribute indicates whether the request was redirected. We can also access the request properties through the response object:

```
>>> response.request.headers
{'User-Agent': 'python-requests/2.3.0 CPython/3.4.1 Linux/3.2.0-4-
   amd64', 'Accept-Encoding': 'gzip, deflate', 'Accept': '*/*'}
```

Notice that `Requests` is automatically handling compression for us. It's including `gzip` and `deflate` in an `Accept-Encoding` header. If we look at the `Content-Encoding` response, then we will see that the response was in fact `gzip` compressed, and `Requests` transparently decompressed it for us:

```
>>> response.headers['content-encoding']
'gzip'
```

We can look at the response content in many more ways. To get the same bytes object as we got from an `HTTPResponse` object, perform the following:

```
>>> response.content
b'<!DOCTYPE HTML PUBLIC "-//W3C//DTD HTML 4.01//EN"
   "http://www.w3.org/TR/html4/strict.dtd">\n<html lang="en">...
```

But `Requests` also performs automatic decoding for us. To get the decoded content, do this:

```
>>> response.text
'<!DOCTYPE HTML PUBLIC "-//W3C//DTD HTML 4.01//EN"
  "http://www.w3.org/TR/html4/strict.dtd">\n<html
  lang="en">\n<head>\n
...
```

Notice that this is now `str` rather than `bytes`. The `Requests` library uses values in the headers for choosing a character set and decoding the content to Unicode for us. If it can't get a character set from the headers, then it uses the `chardet` library (`http://pypi.python.org/pypi/chardet`) to make an estimate from the content itself. We can see what encoding `Requests` has chosen here:

```
>>> response.encoding
'ISO-8859-1'
```

We can even ask it to change the encoding that it has used:

```
>>> response.encoding = 'utf-8'
```

After changing the encoding, subsequent references to the `text` attribute for this response will return the content decoded by using the new encoding setting.

The `Requests` library automatically handles cookies. Give the following a try:

```
>>> response = requests.get('http://www.github.com')
>>> print(response.cookies)
<<class 'requests.cookies.RequestsCookieJar'>
[<Cookie logged_in=no for .github.com/>,
 <Cookie _gh_sess=eyJzZxNz... for ..github.com/>]>
```

The `Requests` library also has a `Session` class, which allows the reuse of cookies, and this is similar to using the `http` module's `CookieJar` and the `urllib` module's `HTTPCookieHandler` objects. Do the following to reuse the cookies in subsequent requests:

```
>>> s = requests.Session()
>>> s.get('http://www.google.com')
>>> response = s.get('http://google.com/preferences')
```

The `Session` object has the same interface as the `requests` module, so we use its `get()` method in the same way as we use the `requests.get()` method. Now, any cookies encountered are stored in the `Session` object, and they will be sent with corresponding requests when we use the `get()` method in the future.

Redirects are also automatically followed, in the same way as when using `urllib`, and any redirected requests are captured in the `history` attribute.

The different HTTP methods are easily accessible, they have their own functions:

```
>>> response = requests.head('http://www.google.com')
>>> response.status_code
200
>>> response.text
''
```

Custom headers are added to to requests in a similar way as they are when using `urllib`:

```
>>> headers = {'User-Agent': 'Mozilla/5.0 Firefox 24'}
>>> response = requests.get('http://www.debian.org', headers=headers)
```

Making requests with query strings is a straightforward process:

```
>>> params = {':action': 'search', 'term': 'Are you quite sure this
  is a cheese shop?'}
>>> response = requests.get('http://pypi.python.org/pypi',
  params=params)
>>> response.url
'https://pypi.python.org/pypi?%3Aaction=search&term=Are+you+quite+sur
  e+this+is+a+cheese+shop%3F'
```

The `Requests` library takes care of all the encoding and formatting for us.

Posting is similarly simplified, although we use the `data` keyword argument here:

```
>>> data = {'P', 'Python'}
>>> response = requests.post('http://search.debian.org/cgi-
  bin/omega', data=data)
```

Handling errors with Requests

Errors in `Requests` are handled slightly differently from how they are handled with `urllib`. Let's work through some error conditions and see how it works. Generate a 404 error by doing the following:

```
>>> response = requests.get('http://www.google.com/notawebpage')
>>> response.status_code
404
```

In this situation, `urllib` would have raised an exception, but notice that `Requests` doesn't. The `Requests` library can check the status code and raise a corresponding exception, but we have to ask it to do so:

```
>>> response.raise_for_status()
...
requests.exceptions.HTTPError: 404 Client Error
```

Now, try it on a successful request:

```
>>> r = requests.get('http://www.google.com')
>>> r.status_code
200
>>> r.raise_for_status()
None
```

It doesn't do anything, which in most situations would let our program exit a `try/except` block and then continue as we would want it to.

What happens if we get an error that is lower in the protocol stack? Try the following:

```
>>> r = requests.get('http://192.0.2.1')
...
requests.exceptions.ConnectionError: HTTPConnectionPool(...
```

We have made a request for a host that doesn't exist and once it has timed out, we get a `ConnectionError` exception.

The `Requests` library simply reduces the workload that is involved in using HTTP in Python as compared to `urllib`. Unless you have a requirement for using `urllib`, I would always recommend using `Requests` for your projects.

Summary

We looked at the principles of the HTTP protocol. We saw how to perform numerous fundamental tasks with the standard library urllib and the third-party Requests packages.

We looked at the structure of HTTP messages, HTTP status codes, the different headers that we may encounter in requests and responses, and how to interpret them and use them for customizing our requests. We looked at how URLs are formed, and how to manipulate and construct them.

We saw how to handle cookies and redirects, how to handle errors that might occur, and how to use secure HTTP connections.

We also covered how to submit data to websites in the manner of submitting a form on a web page, and how to extract the parameters that we need from a page's source code.

Finally, we looked at the third-party Requests package. We saw that as compared to the urllib package, Requests, automates and simplifies many of the tasks that we may routinely need to carry out with HTTP. This makes it a great choice for day-to-day HTTP work.

In the next chapter, we'll be employing what we've learned here to carry out detailed interactions with different web services, querying APIs for data, and uploading our own objects to the web.

3
APIs in Action

When we talk about APIs in relation to Python, we usually refer to the classes and the functions that a module presents to us to interact with. In this chapter, we'll be talking about something different, that is, web APIs.

A web API is a type of API that you interact with through the HTTP protocol. Nowadays, many web services provide a set of HTTP calls, which are designed to be used programmatically by clients, that is, they are meant to be used by machines rather than by humans. Through these interfaces it's possible to automate interaction with the services and to perform tasks such as extracting data, configuring the service in some way, and uploading your own content into the service.

In this chapter, we'll look at:

- Two popular data exchange formats used by web APIs: XML and JSON
- How to interact with two major web APIs: Amazon S3 and Twitter
- How to pull data from HTML pages when an API is not available
- How to make life easier for the webmasters that provide these APIs and websites

There are hundreds of services that offer web APIs. A quite comprehensive and ever-growing list of these services can be found at `http://www.programmableweb.com`.

We're going to start by introducing how XML is used in Python, and then we will explain an XML-based API called the Amazon S3 API.

Getting started with XML

The **Extensible Markup Language** (**XML**) is a way of representing hierarchical data in a standard text format. When working with XML-based web APIs, we'll be creating XML documents and sending them as the bodies of HTTP requests and receiving XML documents as the bodies of responses.

Here's the text representation of an XML document, perhaps this represents the stock at a cheese shop:

```
<?xml version='1.0'?>
<inventory>
    <cheese id="c01">
        <name>Caerphilly</name>
        <stock>0</stock>
    </cheese>
    <cheese id="c02">
        <name>Illchester</name>
        <stock>0</stock>
    </cheese>
</inventory>
```

If you've coded with HTML before, then this may look familiar. XML is a markup based format. It is from the same family of languages as HTML. The data is structured in an hierarchy formed by elements. Each element is represented by two tags, a start tag, for example, `<name>`, and a matching end tag, for example, `</name>`. Between these two tags, we can either put data, such as `Caerphilly`, or add more tags, which represent child elements.

Unlike HTML, XML is designed such that we can define our own tags and create our own data formats. Also, unlike HTML, the XML syntax is always strictly enforced. Whereas in HTML small mistakes, such as tags being closed in the wrong order, closing tags missing altogether, or attribute values missing quotes are tolerated, in XML, these mistakes will result in completely unreadable XML documents. A correctly formatted XML document is called well formed.

The XML APIs

There are two main approaches to working with XML data:

- Reading in a whole document and creating an object-based representation of it, then manipulating it by using an object-oriented API
- Processing the document from start to end, and performing actions as specific tags are encountered

For now, we're going to focus on the object-based approach by using a Python XML API called **ElementTree**. The second so-called pull or event-based approach (also often called **SAX**, as SAX is one of the most popular APIs in this category) is more complicated to set up, and is only needed for processing large XML files. We won't need this to work with Amazon S3.

The basics of ElementTree

We'll be using the Python standard library implementation of the ElementTree API, which is in the xml.etree.ElementTree module.

Let's see how we may create the aforementioned example XML document by using ElementTree. Open a Python interpreter and run the following commands:

```
>>> import xml.etree.ElementTree as ET
>>> root = ET.Element('inventory')
>>> ET.dump(root)
<inventory />
```

We start by creating the root element, that is, the outermost element of the document. We create a root element <inventory> here, and then print its string representation to screen. The <inventory /> representation is an XML shortcut for <inventory></inventory>. It's used to show an empty element, that is, an element with no data and no child tags.

We create the <inventory> element by creating a new ElementTree.Element object. You'll notice that the argument we give to Element() is the name of the tag that is created.

Our <inventory> element is empty at the moment, so let's put something in it. Do this:

```
>>> cheese = ET.Element('cheese')
>>> root.append(cheese)
>>> ET.dump(root)
<inventory><cheese /></inventory>
```

Now, we have an element called <cheese> in our <inventory> element. When an element is directly nested inside another, then the nested element is called a **child** of the outer element, and the outer element is called the **parent**. Similarly, elements that are at the same level are called **siblings**.

Let's add another element, and this time let's give it some content. Add the following commands:

```
>>> name = ET.SubElement(cheese, 'name')
>>> name.text = 'Caerphilly'
>>> ET.dump(root)
<inventory><cheese><name>Caerphilly</name></cheese></inventory>
```

Now, our document is starting to shape up. We do two new things here: first, we use the shortcut class method `ElementTree.SubElement()` to create the new `<name>` element and insert it into the tree as a child of `<cheese>` in a single operation. Second, we give it some content by assigning some text to the element's `text` attribute.

We can remove elements by using the `remove()` method on the parent element, as shown in the following commands:

```
>>> temp = ET.SubElement(root, 'temp')
>>> ET.dump(root)
<inventory><cheese><name>Caerphilly</name></cheese><temp
  /></inventory>
>>> root.remove(temp)
>>> ET.dump(root)
<inventory><cheese><name>Caerphilly</name></cheese></inventory>
```

Pretty printing

It would be useful for us to be able to produce output in a more legible format, such as the example shown at the beginning of this section. The ElementTree API doesn't have a function for doing this, but another XML API, `minidom`, provided by the standard library, does, and it's simple to use. First, import `minidom`:

```
>>> import xml.dom.minidom as minidom
```

Second, use the following command to print some nicely formatted XML:

```
>>> print(minidom.parseString(ET.tostring(root)).toprettyxml())
<?xml version="1.0" ?>
<inventory>
    <cheese>
        <name>Caerphilly</name>
    </cheese>
</inventory>
```

These are not the easiest lines of code at first glance, so let's break them down. The `minidom` library can't directly work with ElementTree elements, so we use ElementTree's `tostring()` function to create a string representation of our XML. We load the string into the `minidom` API by using `minidom.parseString()`, and then we use the `toprettyxml()` method to output our formatted XML.

This can be wrapped into a function so that it becomes more handy. Enter the command block as shown in the following into your Python shell:

```
>>> def xml_pprint(element):
...         s = ET.tostring(element)
...         print(minidom.parseString(s).toprettyxml())
```

Now, just do the following to pretty print:

```
>>> xml_pprint(root)
<?xml version="1.0" ?>
<inventory>
    <cheese>
...
```

Element attributes

In the example shown at the beginning of this section, you may have spotted something in the opening tag of the `<cheese>` element, that is, the `id="c01"` text. This is called an **attribute**. We can use attributes to attach extra information to elements, and there's no limit to the number of attributes an element can have. Attributes are always comprised of an attribute name, which in this case is `id`, and a value, which in this case is `c01`. The values can be any text, but they must be enclosed in quotes.

Now, add the `id` attribute to the `<cheese>` element, as shown here:

```
>>> cheese.attrib['id'] = 'c01'
>>> xml_pprint(cheese)
<?xml version="1.0" ?>
<cheese id="c01">
    <name>Caerphilly</name>
</cheese>
```

The `attrib` attribute of an element is a dict-like object which holds an element's attribute names and values. We can manipulate the XML attributes as we would a regular `dict`.

By now, you should be able to fully recreate the example document shown at the beginning of this section. Go ahead and give it a try.

Converting to text

Once we have an XML tree that we're happy with, usually we would want to convert it into a string to send it over the network. The `ET.dump()` function that we've been using isn't appropriate for this. All the `dump()` function does is print the tag to the screen. It doesn't return a string which we can use. We need to use the `ET.tostring()` function for this, as shown in the following commands:

```
>>> text = ET.tostring(name)
>>> print(text)
b'<name>Caerphilly</name>'
```

Notice that it returns a bytes object. It encods our string for us. The default character set is `us-ascii` but it's better to use UTF-8 for transmitting over HTTP, since it can encode the full range of Unicode characters, and it is widely supported by web applications.

```
>>> text = ET.tostring(name, encoding='utf-8')
```

For now, this is all that we need to know about creating XML documents, so let's see how we can apply it to a web API.

The Amazon S3 API

Amazon S3 is a data storage service. It underpins many of today's high-profile web services. Despite offering enterprise-grade resilience, performance and features, it's pretty easy to start with. It is affordable, and it provides a simple API for automated access. It's one of many cloud services in the growing **Amazon Web Services (AWS)** portfolio.

APIs change every now and then, and they are usually given a version number so that we can track them. We'll be working with the current version of the S3 REST API, "2006-03-01".

You'll notice that in the S3 documentation and elsewhere, the S3 web API is referred to as a **REST API**. **REST** stands for **Representational State Transfer**, and it is a fairly academic conception of how HTTP should be used for APIs, originally presented by Roy Fielding in his PhD dissertation. Although the properties that an API should possess so as to be considered RESTful are quite specific, in practice pretty much any API that is based on HTTP is now slapped with the RESTful label. The S3 API is actually among the most RESTful high-profile APIs, because it appropriately uses a good range of the HTTP methods.

If you want to read more about this topic, Roy Fielding's dissertation is available here `http://ics.uci.edu/~fielding/pubs/dissertation`, and one of the original books that promoted the concept, and is a great read, *RESTful Web Services* by *Leonard Richardson* and *Sam Ruby*, is now available for free download from this page `http://restfulwebapis.org/rws.html`.

Registering with AWS

Before we can access S3, we need to register with AWS. It is the norm for APIs to require registration before allowing access to their features. You can use either an existing Amazon account or create a new one at `http://www.amazonaws.com`. Although S3 is ultimately a paid-for service, if you are using AWS for the first time, then you will get a year's free trial for low-volume use. A year is plenty of time for finishing this chapter! The trial provides 5GB of free S3 storage.

Authentication

Next, we need to discuss authentication, which is an important topic of discussion when using many web APIs. Most web APIs we use will specify a way for supplying authentication credentials that allow requests to be made to them, and typically every HTTP request we make must include authentication information.

APIs require this information for the following reasons:

- To ensure that others can't abuse your application's access permissions
- To apply per-application rate limiting
- To manage delegation of access rights, so that an application can act on the behalf of other users of a service or other services
- Collection of usage statistics

All of the AWS services use an HTTP request signing mechanism for authentication. To sign a request, we hash and sign unique data in an HTTP request using a cryptographic key, then add the signature to the request as a header. By recreating the signature on the server, AWS can ensure that the request has been sent by us, and that it doesn't get altered in transit.

The AWS signature generation process is currently on its 4th version, and an involved discussion would be needed to cover it, so we're going to employ a third-party library, that is, `requests-aws4auth`. This is a companion library for the `Requests` module that automatically handles signature generation for us. It's available at PyPi. So, install it on a command line with the help of `pip`:

```
$ pip install requests-aws4auth
Downloading/unpacking requests-aws4auth

...
```

Setting up an AWS user

To use authentication, we need to acquire some credentials.

We will set this up through the AWS Console. Once you've registered with AWS, log into the Console at `https://console.aws.amazon.com`.

Once you are logged in, you need to perform the steps shown here:

1. Click on your name at the top-right, and then choose **Security Credentials**.

2. Click on **Users**, which is on the list in the left-hand side of the screen, and then click on the **Create New Users** button at the top.

3. Type in the **username**, and make sure that **Generate an access key for each user** has been checked, and then click on the **Create** button in the bottom right-hand corner.

You'll see a new page saying that the user has been created successfully. Click on the **Download credentials** button at the bottom right corner to download a CSV file, which contains the **Access ID** and **Access Secret** for this user. These are important because they will help in authenticating ourselves to the S3 API. Make sure that you store them securely, as they will allow full access to your S3 files.

Then, click on **Close** at the bottom of the screen, and click on the new user in the list that will appear, and then click on the **Attach Policy** button. A list of policy templates will appear. Scroll down this list and select the **AmazonS3FullAccess** policy, as shown in the following screenshot:

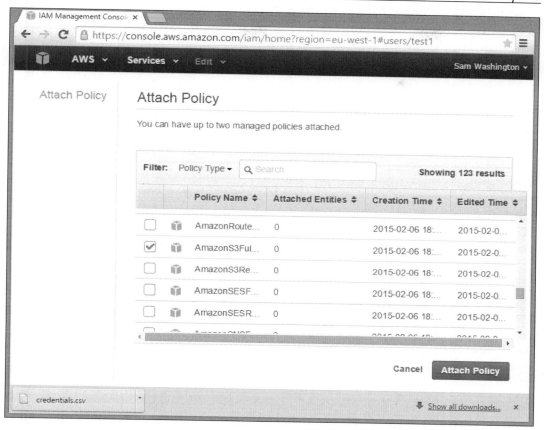

Finally, click on the **Attach Policy** button at the bottom right-hand side when it appears. Now, our user has full access to the S3 service.

Regions

AWS has datacenters around the world, so when we activate a service in AWS we pick the region we want it to live in. There is a list of regions for S3 at `http://docs.aws.amazon.com/general/latest/gr/rande.html#s3_region`.

It's best to choose a region that is closest to the users who will be using the service. For now, you'll be the only user, so just decide on the region that is closest to you for our first S3 tests.

S3 buckets and objects

S3 organizes the data that we store in it using two concepts: buckets and objects. An object is the equivalent of a file, that is, a blob of data with a name, and a bucket is equivalent to a directory. The only difference between buckets and directories is that buckets cannot contain other buckets.

Every bucket has its own URL of the form:

```
http://<bucketname>.s3-<region>.amazonaws.com.
```

In the URL, `<bucketname>` is the name of the bucket and `<region>` is the AWS region where the bucket is present, for example `eu-west-1`. The bucket name and region are set when we create the bucket.

Bucket names are shared globally among all S3 users, and so they must be unique. If you own a domain, then a subdomain of that will make an appropriate bucket name. You could also use your email address by replacing the @ symbol with a hyphen or underscore.

Objects are named when we first upload them. We access objects by adding the object name to the end of the bucket's URL as a path. For example, if we have a bucket called `mybucket.example.com` in the `eu-west-1` region containing the object `cheeseshop.txt`, then we can access it by using the URL `http://mybucket.example.com.s3-eu-west-1.amazonaws.com/cheeseshop.txt`.

Let's create our first bucket through the AWS Console. We can perform most of the operations that the API exposes manually through this web interface, and it's a good way of checking that our API client is performing the desired tasks:

1. Log into the Console at `https://console.aws.amazon.com`.
2. Go to the S3 service. You will see a page, which will prompt you to create a bucket.
3. Click on the **Create Bucket** button.
4. Enter a bucket name, pick a region, and then click on **Create**.
5. You will be taken to the bucket list, and you will be able to see your bucket.

An S3 command-line client

Okay, enough preparation, let's get to coding. For the rest of this section on S3, we will be writing a small command line client that will enable us to interact with the service. We will create buckets, and then upload and download files.

First we'll set up our command line interpreter and initialize the authentication. Create a file called `s3_client.py` and save the following code block in it:

```python
import sys
import requests
import requests_aws4auth as aws4auth
import xml.etree.ElementTree as ET
import xml.dom.minidom as minidom


access_id = '<ACCESS ID>'
access_key = '<ACCESS KEY>'
region = '<REGION>'
endpoint = 's3-{}.amazonaws.com'.format(region)
auth = aws4auth.AWS4Auth(access_id, access_key, region, 's3')
ns = 'http://s3.amazonaws.com/doc/2006-03-01/'


def xml_pprint(xml_string):
    print(minidom.parseString(xml_string).toprettyxml())


def create_bucket(bucket):
    print('Bucket name: {}'.format(bucket))


if __name__ == '__main__':
    cmd, *args = sys.argv[1:]
    globals()[cmd](*args)
```

Downloading the example code

You can download the example code files for all Packt books you have purchased from your account at http://www.packtpub.com. If you purchased this book elsewhere, you can visit http://www.packtpub.com/support and register to have the files e-mailed directly to you.

You'll need to replace <ACCESS ID> and <ACCESS KEY> with the values from the credentials CSV that we downloaded earlier, and <REGION> with the AWS region of your choice.

So, what are we doing here? Well, first we set up our endpoint. An endpoint is a general term for a URL which is used to access an API. Some web APIs have a single endpoint, some have many endpoints, it depends on how the API is designed. The endpoint we generate here is actually only a part of the full endpoint which we'll use when we work with buckets. Our actual endpoint is the endpoint prefixed by a bucket name.

Next, we create our `auth` object. We'll use this in conjunction with `Requests` to add AWS authentication to our API requests.

The `ns` variable is a string, which we'll need for working with XML from the S3 API. We'll discuss this when we use it.

We've included a modified version of our `xml_pprint()` function to help with debugging. And, for now, the `create_bucket()` function is just a placeholder. We'll learn more about this in the next section.

Finally, we have the command interpreter itself - it simply takes the first argument given to the script on the command line and tries to run a function with the same name, passing any remaining command-line arguments to the function. Let's give this a test run. Enter the following in a command prompt:

```
$ python3.4 s3_client.py create_bucket mybucket
Bucket name: mybucket
```

You can see that the script pulls `create_bucket` from the command line arguments and so calls the function `create_bucket()`, passing `myBucket` as an argument.

This framework makes adding functions to expand our client's capabilities a straightforward process. Let's start by making `create_bucket()` do something useful.

Creating a bucket with the API

Whenever we write a client for an API, our main point of reference is the API documentation. The documentation tells us how to construct the HTTP requests for performing operations. The S3 documentation can be found at `http://docs.aws.amazon.com/AmazonS3/latest/API/APIRest.html`. The `http://docs.aws.amazon.com/AmazonS3/latest/API/RESTBucketPUT.html` URL will provide the details of bucket creation.

This documentation tells us that to create a bucket we need to make an HTTP request to our new bucket's endpoint by using the HTTP PUT method. It also tells us that the request body must contain some XML, which specifies the AWS region that we want the bucket to be created in.

So, now we know what we're aiming for, let's discuss our function. First, let's create the XML. Replace the content of `create_bucket()` with the following code block:

```
def create_bucket(bucket):
    XML = ET.Element('CreateBucketConfiguration')
    XML.attrib['xmlns'] = ns
    location = ET.SubElement(XML, 'LocationConstraint')
```

```
location.text = auth.region
data = ET.tostring(XML, encoding='utf-8')
xml_pprint(data)
```

Here we create an XML tree following the format given in the S3 documentation. If we run our client now, then we will see the XML shown here:

```
$ python3.4 s3_client.py create_bucket mybucket.example.com
<?xml version="1.0" ?>
<CreateBucketConfiguration xmlns="http://s3.amazonaws.com/doc/2006-
    03-01/">
    <LocationConstraint>eu-west-1</LocationConstraint>
</CreateBucketConfiguration>
```

This matches the format specified in the documentation. You can see that we've used the ns variable to fill the xmlns attribute. This attribute pops up throughout the S3 XML, having the ns variable pre-defined makes it quicker to work with it.

Now, let's add the code to make the request. Replace the xml_pprint(data) at the end of create_bucket() with the following:

```
url = 'http://{}.{}'.format(bucket, endpoint)
r = requests.put(url, data=data, auth=auth)
if r.ok:
    print('Created bucket {} OK'.format(bucket))
else:
    xml_pprint(r.text)
```

The first line shown here will generate the full URL from our bucket name and endpoint. The second line will make the request to the S3 API. Notice that we have used the requests.put() function to make this request using the HTTP PUT method, rather than by using either the requests.get() method or the requests.post() method. Also, note that we have supplied our auth object to the call. This will allow Requests to handle all the S3 authentication for us!

If all goes well , then we print out a message. In case everything does not go as expected, we print out the response body. S3 returns error messages as XML in the response body. So we use our xml_pprint() function to display it. We'll look at working with these errors in the *Handling errors* section, later on.

Now run the client, and if everything works as expected, then we will get a confirmation message. Make sure that you have picked a bucket that hasn't already been created:

```
$ python3.4 s3_client.py create_bucket mybucket.example.com
Created bucket mybucket.example.com OK
```

When we refresh the S3 Console in our browser, we will see that our bucket has been created.

Uploading a file

Now that we've created a bucket, we can upload some files. Writing a function for uploading a file is similar to creating a bucket. We check the documentation to see how to construct our HTTP request, figure out what information should be collected at the command line, and then write the function.

We need to use an HTTP PUT again. We need the name of the bucket that we want to store the file in and the name that we want the file to be stored under in S3. The body of the request will contain the file data. At the command line, we'll collect the bucket name, the name we want the file to have in the S3 service and the name of the local file to upload.

Add the following function to your s3_client.py file after the create_bucket() function:

```python
def upload_file(bucket, s3_name, local_path):
    data = open(local_path, 'rb').read()
    url = 'http://{}.{}/{}'.format(bucket, endpoint, s3_name)
    r = requests.put(url, data=data, auth=auth)
    if r.ok:
        print('Uploaded {} OK'.format(local_path))
    else:
        xml_pprint(r.text)
```

In creating this function, we follow a pattern similar to that for creating a bucket:

1. Prepare the data that will go in the request body.
2. Construct our URL.
3. Make the request.
4. Check the outcome.

Note that we open the local file in binary mode. The file could contain any type of data, so we don't want text transforms applied. We could pull this data from anywhere, such as a database or another web API. Here, we just use a local file for simplicity.

The URL is the same endpoint that we constructed in `create_bucket()` with the S3 object name appended to the URL path. Later, we can use this URL to retrieve the object.

Now, run the command shown here to upload a file:

```
$ python3.4 s3_client.py mybucket.example.com test.jpg ~/test.jpg
Uploaded ~/test.jpg OK
```

You'll need to replace `mybucket.example.com` with your own bucket name. Once the file gets uploaded, you will see it in the S3 Console.

I have used a JPEG image that was stored in my home directory as the source file. You can use any file, just change the last argument to an appropriate path. However, using a JPEG image will make the following sections easier for you to reproduce.

Retrieving an uploaded file through a web browser

By default, S3 applies restrictive permissions for buckets and objects. The account that creates them has full read-write permissions, but access is completely denied for anyone else. This means that the file that we've just uploaded can only be downloaded if the download request includes authentication for our account. If we try the resulting URL in a browser, then we'll get an access denied error. This isn't very useful if we're trying to use S3 for sharing files with other people.

The solution for this is to use one of S3's mechanisms for changing the permissions. Let's look at the simple task of making our uploaded file public. Change `upload_file()` to the following:

```
def upload_file(bucket, s3_name, local_path, acl='private'):
    data = open(local_path, 'rb').read()
    url = 'http://{}.{}/{}'.format(bucket, endpoint, s3_name)
    headers = {'x-amz-acl': acl}
    r = requests.put(url, data=data, headers=headers, auth=auth)
    if r.ok:
        print('Uploaded {} OK'.format(local_path))
    else:
        xml_pprint(r.text)
```

We have now included a header in our HTTP request, x-amz-acl, which specifies a permission set to be applied to the object. We've also added a new argument to our function signature so that we can specify the permission set on the command line. We have used the so-called **canned ACLs (canned Access Control Lists)**, which have been provided by S3, and are documented at http://docs.aws.amazon.com/AmazonS3/latest/dev/acl-overview.html#canned-acl.

The ACL that we're interested in is called public-read. This will allow anyone to download the file without needing any kind of authentication. We can now re-run our upload, but this time it will apply this ACL to it:

```
$ python3.4 s3_client.py mybucket.example.com test.jpg ~/test.jpg
  public-read
Uploaded test.jpg OK
```

Now, visiting the file's S3 URL in a browser will give us the option to download the file.

Displaying an uploaded file in a web browser

If you have uploaded an image, then you may be wondering why the browser had asked us to save it instead of just displaying it. The reason is that we haven't set the file's Content-Type.

If you remember from the last chapter, the Content-Type header in an HTTP response tells the client, which in this case is our browser, the type of file that is in the body. By default, S3 applies the content type of binary/octet-stream. Because of this Content-Type, the browser can't tell that it's downloading an image, so it just presents it as a file that can be saved. We can fix this by supplying a Content-Type header in the upload request. S3 will store the type that we specify, and it will use it as the Content-Type in the subsequent download responses.

Add the code block shown here to the import at the beginning of s3_client.py:

```
import mimetypes
```

Then change upload_file() to this:

```
def upload_file(bucket, s3_name, local_path, acl='private'):
    data = open(local_path, 'rb').read()
    url = 'http://{}.{}/{}'.format(bucket, endpoint, s3_name)
    headers = {'x-amz-acl': acl}
    mimetype = mimetypes.guess_type(local_path)[0]
    if mimetype:
        headers['Content-Type'] = mimetype
```

```
r = requests.put(url, data=data, headers=headers, auth=auth)
if r.ok:
    print('Uploaded {} OK'.format(local_path))
else:
    xml_pprint(r.text)
```

Here, we have used the `mimetypes` module to guess a suitable `Content-Type` by looking at the file extension of `local_path`. If `mimetypes` can't determine a `Content-Type` from `local_path`, then we don't include the `Content-Type` header, and let S3 apply the default `binary/octet-stream` type.

Unfortunately, in S3 we won't be able to overwrite the metadata for an existing object by using a simple `PUT` request. It's possible to do it by using a `PUT` copy request, but that's beyond the scope of this chapter. For now, it's better to just delete the file from S3 by using the AWS Console before uploading it again. We only need to do this once. Now, our code will automatically add the `Content-Type` for any new file that we upload.

Once you've deleted the file, re-run the client just as shown in the last section, that is, upload the file with the new `Content-Type` and try to download the file in a browser again. If all goes well, then the image will be displayed.

Downloading a file with the API

Downloading a file through the S3 API is similar to uploading it. We simply take the bucket name, the S3 object name and the local filename again but issue a `GET` request instead of a `PUT request`, and then write the data received to disk.

Add the following function to your program, underneath the `upload_file()` function:

```
def download_file(bucket, s3_name, local_path):
    url = 'http://{}.{}/{}'.format(bucket, endpoint, s3_name)
    r = requests.get(url, auth=auth)
    if r.ok:
        open(local_path, 'wb').write(r.content)
        print('Downloaded {} OK'.format(s3_name))
    else:
        xml_pprint(r.text)
```

Now, run the client and download a file, which you have uploaded previously, by using the following command:

```
$ python3.4 s3_client.py download_file mybucket.example.com test.jpg
  ~/test_downloaded.jpg
Downloaded test.jpg OK
```

Parsing XML and handling errors

If you ran into any errors while running the aforementioned code, then you'll notice that a clear error message will not get displayed. S3 embeds error messages in the XML returned in the response body, and until now we've just been dumping the raw XML to the screen. We can improve on this and pull the text out of the XML. First, let's generate an error message so that we can see what the XML looks like. In s3_client.py, replace your access secret with an empty string, as shown here:

```
access_secret = ''
```

Now, try and perform the following operation on the service:

```
$ python3.4 s3_client.py create_bucket failbucket.example.com
<?xml version="1.0" ?>
<Error>
    <Code>SignatureDoesNotMatch</Code>
    <Message>The request signature we calculated does not match the
    signature you provided. Check your key and signing
    method.</Message>
    <AWSAccessKeyId>AKIAJY5II3SZNHZ25SUA</AWSAccessKeyId>
    <StringToSign>AWS4-HMAC-SHA256...</StringToSign>
    <SignatureProvided>e43e2130...</SignatureProvided>
    <StringToSignBytes>41 57 53 34...</StringToSignBytes>
    <CanonicalRequest>PUT...</CanonicalRequest>
    <CanonicalRequestBytes>50 55 54...</CanonicalRequestBytes>
    <RequestId>86F25A39912FC628</RequestId>
    <HostId>kYIZnLclzIW6CmsGA....</HostId>
</Error>
```

The preceding XML is the S3 error information. I've truncated several of the fields so as to show it here. Your code block will be slightly longer than this. In this case, it's telling us that it can't authenticate our request, and this is because we have set a blank access secret.

Parsing XML

Printing all of the XML is too much for an error message. There's a lot of extraneous information which isn't useful to us. It would be better if we could just pull out the useful parts of the error message and display them.

Well, ElementTree gives us some powerful tools for extracting such information from XML. We're going back to XML for a while to explore these tools a little.

First we need to open an interactive Python shell, and then generate the aforementioned error message again by using the following command:

```
>>> import requests
>>> import requests_aws4auth
>>> auth = requests_aws4auth.AWS4Auth('<ID>', '', 'eu-west-1', '')
>>> r = requests.get('http://s3.eu-west-1.amazonaws.com', auth=auth)
```

You'll need to replace `<ID>` with your AWS access ID. Print out `r.text` to make sure that you get an error message, which is similar to the one that we generated earlier.

Now, we can explore our XML. Convert the XML text into an `ElementTree` tree. A handy function for doing this is:

```
>>> import xml.etree.ElementTree as ET
>>> root = ET.fromstring(r.text)
```

We now have an ElementTree instance, with `root` as the root element.

Finding elements

The simplest way of navigating the tree is by using the elements as iterators. Try doing the following:

```
>>> for element in root:
...     print('Tag: ' + element.tag)
Tag: Code
Tag: Message
Tag: AWSAccessKeyId
Tag: StringToSign
Tag: SignatureProvided
...
```

Iterating over `root` returns each of its child elements, and then we print out the tag of an element by using the `tag` attribute.

We can apply a filter to the tags that we iterate over by using the following command:

```
>>> for element in root.findall('Message'):
...     print(element.tag + ': ' + element.text)
Message: The request signature we calculated does not match the
    signature you provided. Check your key and signing method.
```

Here, we have used the findall() method of the root element. This method will provide us with a list of all the direct children of the root element that match the specified tag, which in this case is <Message>.

And this will solve our problem of just extracting the text of the error message. Now, let's update our error handling.

Handling errors

We can go back and add this to our s3_client.py file, but let's include a little more information in the output, and structure the code to allow re-use. Add the following function to the file underneath the download_file() function:

```python
def handle_error(response):
    output = 'Status code: {}\n'.format(response.status_code)
    root = ET.fromstring(response.text)
    code =  root.find('Code').text
    output += 'Error code: {}\n'.format(code)
    message = root.find('Message').text
    output += 'Message: {}\n'.format(message)
    print(output)
```

You'll notice that we have used a new function here, namely, root.find(). This works in the same way as findall() except that it only returns the first matching element, as opposed to a list of all matching elements.

Then, replace each instance of xml_pprint(r.text) in your file with handle_error(r) and then run the client again with the incorrect access secret. Now, you will see a more informative error message:

```
$ python3.4 s3_client.py create_bucket failbucket.example.com
Status code: 403
Error code: SignatureDoesNotMatch
Message: The request signature we calculated does not match the
    signature you provided. Check your key and signing method.
```

Further enhancements

That's as far as we're going to take our client. We've written a command line program that can perform essential operations, such as creating buckets and uploading and downloading objects on the Amazon S3 service. There are still plenty of operations that can be implemented, and these can be found in the S3 documentation; operations such as listing buckets' contents, deleting objects, and copying objects.

We could improve a few other things, especially if we are going to make this into a production application. The command-line parsing mechanism, although compact, is not satisfactory from a security perspective, since anybody with access to the command line can run any built-in python command. It would be better to have a whitelist of functions and to implement a proper command line parser by using one of the standard library modules like `argparse`.

Storing the access ID and the access secret in the source code is also a problem for security. Several serious security incidents have happened because passwords were stored in source code and then uploaded to cloud code repositories. It's much better to load the keys from an external source, such as a file or a database at run time.

The Boto package

We've discussed working directly with the S3 REST API, and this has given us some useful techniques that will allow us to program against similar APIs in the future. In many cases, this will be the only way in which we can interact with a web API.

However, some APIs, including AWS, have ready-to-use packages which expose the functionality of the service without having to deal with the complexities of the HTTP API. These packages generally make the code cleaner and simpler, and they should be preferred for doing production work if they're available.

The AWS package is called **Boto**. We will take a very quick look at the `Boto` package to see how it can provide some of the functionalities that we wrote earlier.

The `boto` package is available in PyPi, so we can install it with `pip`:

```
$ pip install boto
Downloading/unpacking boto
...
```

Now, fire up a Python shell and let's try it out. We need to connect to the service first:

```
>>> import boto
>>> conn = boto.connect_s3('<ACCESS ID>', '<ACCESS SECRET>')
```

You'll need to replace <ACCESS ID> and <ACCESS SECRET> with your access ID and access secret. Now, let's create a bucket:

```
>>> conn.create_bucket('mybucket.example.com')
```

This creates the bucket in the default standard US region. We can supply a different region, as shown here:

```
>>> from boto.s3.connection import Location
>>> conn.create_bucket('mybucket.example.com', location=Location.EU)
```

The region names we need to use for this function are different to the ones we used when creating buckets earlier. To see a list of acceptable region names do this:

```
>>> [x for x in dir(Location) if x.isalnum()]
['APNortheast', 'APSoutheast', 'APSoutheast2', 'CNNorth1', 'DEFAULT',
  'EU', 'SAEast', 'USWest', 'USWest2']
```

Do the following to display a list of the buckets we own:

```
>>> buckets = conn.get_all_buckets()
>>> [b.name for b in buckets]
['mybucket.example.com', 'mybucket2.example.com']
```

We can also list the contents of a bucket. To do so, first, we need to get a reference to it:

```
>>> bucket = conn.get_bucket('mybucket.example.com')
```

And then to list the contents:

```
>>> [k.name for k in bucket.list()]
['cheesehop.txt', 'parrot.txt']
```

Uploading a file is a straightforward process. First, we need to get a reference to the bucket that we want to put it in, and then we need to create a Key object, which will represent our object in the bucket:

```
>>> bucket = conn.get_bucket('mybucket.example.com')
>>> from boto.s3.key import Key
>>> key = Key(bucket)
```

Next, we have to set the Key name and then upload our file data:

```
>>> key.key = 'lumberjack_song.txt'
>>> key.set_contents_from_filename('~/lumberjack_song.txt')
```

The boto package will automatically set the Content-Type when it uploads a file like this, and it uses the same mimetypes module that we used earlier for determining a type.

Downloading also follows a similar pattern. Try the following commands:

```
>>> bucket = conn.get_bucket('mybucket.example.com')
>>> key = bucket.get_key('parrot.txt')
>>> key.get_contents_to_filename('~/parrot.txt')
```

This downloads the `parrot.txt` S3 object in the `mybucket.example.com` bucket and then stores it in the `~/parrot.txt` local file.

Once we have a reference to the key, just use the following to set the ACL:

```
>>> key.set_acl('public-read')
```

I'll leave you to further explore the `boto` package's functionality with the help of the tutorial, which can be found at `https://boto.readthedocs.org/en/latest/s3_tut.html`.

It should be evident that for everyday S3 work in Python, `boto` should be your go to package.

Wrapping up with S3

So, we've discussed some of the uses of the Amazon S3 API, and learned some things about working with XML in Python. These skills should give you a good start in working with any XML based REST API, whether or not it has a pre-built library like `boto`.

However, XML isn't the only data format that is used by web APIs, and the S3 way of working with HTTP isn't the only model used by web APIs. So, we're going to move on and take a look at the other major data format in use today, JSON and another API: Twitter.

JSON

JavaScript Object Notation (JSON) is a standard way of representing simple objects, such as `lists` and `dicts`, in the form of text strings. Although, it was originally developed for JavaScript, JSON is language independent and most languages can work with it. It's lightweight, yet flexible enough to handle a broad range of data. This makes it ideal for exchanging data over HTTP, and a large number of web APIs use this as their primary data format.

Encoding and decoding

We use the `json` module for working with JSON in Python. Let's create a JSON representation of a Python list by using the following commands:

```
>>> import json
>>> l = ['a', 'b', 'c']
>>> json.dumps(l)
'["a", "b", "c"]'
```

We use the `json.dumps()` function for converting an object to a JSON string. In this case, we can see that the JSON string appears to be identical to Python's own representation of a list, but note that this is a string. Confirm this by doing the following:

```
>>> s = json.dumps(['a', 'b', 'c'])
>>> type(s)
<class 'str'>
>>> s[0]
'['
```

Converting JSON to a Python object is also straightforward, as shown here:

```
>>> s = '["a", "b", "c"]'
>>> l = json.loads(s)
>>> l
['a', 'b', 'c']
>>> l[0]
'a'
```

We use the `json.loads()` function, and just pass it a JSON string. As we'll see, this is very powerful when interacting with web APIs. Typically, we will receive a JSON string as the body of an HTTP response, which can simply be decoded using `json.loads()` to provide immediately usable Python objects.

Using dicts with JSON

JSON natively supports a mapping-type object, which is equivalent to a Python `dict`. This means that we can work directly with `dicts` through JSON.

```
>>> json.dumps({'A':'Arthur', 'B':'Brian', 'C':'Colonel'})
'{"A": "Arthur", "C": "Colonel", "B": "Brian"}'
```

Also, it is useful to know how JSON handles nested objects.

```
>>> d = {
...     'Chapman': ['King Arthur', 'Brian'],
...     'Cleese': ['Sir Lancelot', 'The Black Knight'],
...     'Idle': ['Sir Robin', 'Loretta'],
... }
>>> json.dumps(d)
'{"Chapman": ["King Arthur", "Brian"], "Idle": ["Sir
  Robin", "Loretta"], "Cleese": ["Sir Lancelot", "The Black
  Knight"]}'
```

There is just one gotcha though: JSON dictionary keys can only be in the form of strings.

```
>>> json.dumps({1:10, 2:20, 3:30})
'{"1": 10, "2": 20, "3": 30}'
```

Notice, how the keys in the JSON dictionary become string representations of integers? To decode a JSON dictionary that uses numeric keys, we need to manually type-convert them if we want to work with them as numbers. Do the following to accomplish this:

```
>>> j = json.dumps({1:10, 2:20, 3:30})
>>> d_raw = json.loads(j)
>>> d_raw
{'1': 10, '2': 20, '3': 30}
>>> {int(key):val for key,val in d_raw.items()}
{1: 10, 2: 20, 3: 30}
```

We just use a dictionary comprehension to apply int() to the dictionary's keys.

Other object types

JSON cleanly handles only Python lists and dicts, for other object types json may attempt to cast the object type as one or the other, or fail completely. Try a tuple, as shown here:

```
>>> json.dumps(('a', 'b', 'c'))
'["a", "b", "c"]'
```

JSON doesn't have a tuple data type, so the `json` module will cast it to a `list`. If we convert it back:

```
>>> j = json.dumps(('a', 'b', 'c'))
>>> json.loads(j)
['a', 'b', 'c']
```

It will still remain a `list`. The `json` module doesn't support `sets`, so they also need to be recast as `lists`. Try the following commands:

```
>>> s = set(['a', 'b', 'c'])
>>> json.dumps(s)
...
TypeError: {'a', 'c', 'b'} is not JSON serializable
>>> json.dumps(list(s))
'["a", "b", "c"]'
```

This will cause problems similar to the ones caused by tuples. If we convert the JSON back to a Python object, then it will be a `list` and not a `set`.

We almost never encounter web APIs that need these kinds of specialist Python objects, and if we do, then the API should provide some kind of convention for handling it. But we do need to keep track of any conversions that we would need to apply to the outgoing or the incoming objects, if we were storing the data locally in any format other than that of `lists` or `dicts`.

Now that we have an understanding of JSON, let's see how it works in a web API.

The Twitter API

The Twitter API provides access to all the functions that we may want a Twitter client to perform. With the Twitter API, we can create clients that search for recent tweets, find out what's trending, look up user details, follow users' timelines, and even act on the behalf of users by posting tweets and direct messages for them.

We'll be looking at Twitter API version 1.1, the version current at time of writing this chapter.

 Twitter maintains comprehensive documentation for its API, which can be found at `https://dev.twitter.com/overview/documentation`.

A Twitter world clock

To illustrate some of the functionalities of the Twitter API, we're going to write the code for a simple Twitter world clock. Our application will periodically poll its Twitter account for mentions which contain a recognizable city name, and if it finds one, then it will reply to the Tweet with the current local time of that city. In Twitter speak, a mention is any Tweet which includes our account name prefixed by an @, for example, @myaccount.

Authentication for Twitter

Similar to S3, we need to determine how authentication will be managed before we get started. We need to register, and then we need to find out how Twitter expects us to authenticate our requests.

Registering your application for the Twitter API

We need to create a Twitter account, register our application against the account, and then we will receive the authentication credentials for our app. It's also a good idea to set up a second account, which we can use for sending test tweets to the application account. This provides for a cleaner way of checking whether the app is working properly, rather than having the app account send tweets to itself. There's no limit on the number of Twitter accounts that you can create.

To create an account, go to http://www.twitter.com and complete the signup process. Do the following for registering your application once you have a Twitter account:

1. Log into http://apps.twitter.com with your main Twitter account, and then create a new app.
2. Fill out the new app form, note that Twitter application names need to be unique globally.
3. Go to the app's settings and then change the app permissions to have read and write access. You may need to register your mobile number for enabling this. Even if you're unhappy about supplying this, we can create the full app; however the final function that sends a tweet in reply won't be active.

Now we need to get our access credentials, as shown here:

1. Go to the **Keys and Access Tokens** section and then note the **Consumer Key** and the **Access Secret**.
2. Generate an **Access Token**.
3. Note down the **Access Token** and the **Access Secret**.

Authenticating requests

We now have enough information for authenticating requests. Twitter uses an authentication standard called **oAuth,** version 1.0a. It's described in detail at http://oauth.net/core/1.0a/.

The oAuth authentication standard is a little tricky, but fortunately the Requests module has a companion library called requests-oauthlib, which can handle most of the complexity for us. This is available on PyPi, so we can download and install it with pip.

```
$ pip install requests-oauthlib
Downloading/unpacking requests-oauthlib
...
```

Now, we can add authentication to our requests, and then write our application.

A Twitter client

Save the code mentioned here to a file, and save it as twitter_worldclock.py. You'll need to replace <CONSUMER_KEY>, <CONSUMER_SECRET>, <ACCESS_TOKEN>, and <ACCESS_SECRET> with the values that you have taken down from the aforementioned Twitter app configuration:

```python
import requests, requests_oauthlib, sys

consumer_key = '<CONSUMER_KEY>'
consumer_secret = '<CONSUMER_SECRET>'
access_token = '<ACCESS_TOKEN>'
access_secret = '<ACCESS_KEY>'

def init_auth():
    auth_obj = requests_oauthlib.OAuth1(
                    consumer_key, consumer_secret,
                    access_token, access_secret)

    if verify_credentials(auth_obj):
        print('Validated credentials OK')
        return auth_obj
    else:
        print('Credentials validation failed')
        sys.exit(1)

def verify_credentials(auth_obj):
    url = 'https://api.twitter.com/1.1/' \
          'account/verify_credentials.json'
    response = requests.get(url, auth=auth_obj)
    return response.status_code == 200
```

```
if __name__ == '__main__':
    auth_obj = init_auth()
```

Remember that `consumer_secret` and `access_secret` act as the password to your Twitter account, so in a production app they should be loaded from a secure external location instead of being hard-coded into the source code.

In the aforementioned code, we create the `OAuth1` authentication instance, `auth_obj`, in the `init_auth()` function by using our access credentials. We pass this to `Requests` whenever we need to make an HTTP request, and through it `Requests` handles the authentication. You can see an example of this in the `verify_credentials()` function.

In the `verify_credentials()` function, we test whether Twitter recognizes our credentials. The URL that we're using here is an endpoint that Twitter provides purely for testing whether our credentials are valid. It returns an HTTP 200 status code if they are valid or a 401 status code if not.

Now, let's run `twitter_worldclock.py` and if we've registered our application and filled out the tokens and secrets properly, then we should see `Validated credentials OK`. Now that the authentication is working, the basic flow of our program will be, as shown in the following diagram:

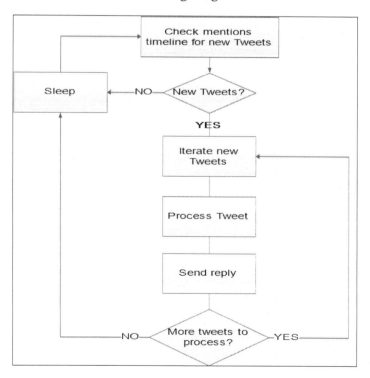

Our program will be running as a daemon, polling Twitter periodically to see whether there are any new tweets for us to process and reply to. When we poll the mentions timeline, we will download any new tweets that were received in a single batch since our last poll, so that we can process all of them without having to poll again.

Polling for Tweets

Let's add a function for checking and retrieving new tweets from our mentions timeline. We'll get this to work before we add the loop. Add the new function underneath `verify_credentials()`, and then add a call this function to the main section, as shown here; also, add `json` to the list of the imports at the beginning of the file:

```
def get_mentions(since_id, auth_obj):
    params = {'count': 200, 'since_id': since_id,
              'include_rts':  0, 'include_entities': 'false'}
    url = 'https://api.twitter.com/1.1/' \
          'statuses/mentions_timeline.json'
    response = requests.get(url, params=params, auth=auth_obj)
    response.raise_for_status()
    return json.loads(response.text)


if __name__ == '__main__':
    auth_obj = init_auth()
    since_id = 1
    for tweet in get_mentions(since_id, auth_obj):
        print(tweet['text'])
```

Using `get_mentions()`, we check for and download any tweets that mention our app account by connecting to the `statuses/mentions_timeline.json` endpoint. We supply a number of parameters, which `Requests` passes on as a query string. These parameters are specified by Twitter and they control how the tweets will be returned to us. They are as follows:

- `'count'`: This specifies the maximum number of tweets that will be returned. Twitter will allow 200 tweets to be received by a single request made to this endpoint.

- `'include_entities'`: This is used for trimming down some extraneous information from the tweets retrieved.

- `'include_rts'`: This tells Twitter not to include any retweets. We don't want the user to receive another time update if someone retweets our reply.

- 'since_id': This tells Twitter to only return the tweets with IDs above this value. Every tweet has a unique 64-bit integer ID, and later tweets have higher value IDs than earlier tweets. By remembering the ID of the last tweet we process and then passing it as this parameter, Twitter will filter out the tweets that we've already seen.

Before running the aforementioned, we want to generate some mentions for our account so that we have something to download. Log into your Twitter test account and then create a couple of tweets that contain @username, where you replace username with your app account's username. After this, when you go into the **Mentions** section of the **Notifications** tab of your app account, you will see these tweets.

Now, if we run the aforementioned code, then we will get the text of our mentions printed to screen.

Processing the Tweets

The next step is to parse our mentions and then generate the times that we want to include in our replies. Parsing is a straightforward process. In this, we just check the 'text' value of the tweets, but it takes a little more work to generate the times. In fact, for this, we'll need a database of cities and their time zones. This is available in the pytz package, which can be found at PyPi. For doing this, install the following package:

```
$ pip install pytz
Downloading/unpacking pytz
...
```

And then, we can write our tweet processing function. Add this function underneath get_mentions(), and then add datetime and pytz to the list of the imports at the beginning of the file:

```
def process_tweet(tweet):
    username = tweet['user']['screen_name']
    text = tweet['text']
    words = [x for x in text.split() if
                        x[0] not in ['@', '#']]
    place = ' '.join(words)
    check = place.replace(' ', '_').lower()
    found = False
    for tz in pytz.common_timezones:
        tz_low = tz.lower()
        if check in tz_low.split('/'):
```

```
                    found = True
                    break
        if found:
            timezone = pytz.timezone(tz)
            time = datetime.datetime.now(timezone).strftime('%H:%M')
            reply = '@{} The time in {} is currently
            {}'.format(username, place, time)
        else:
            reply = "@{} Sorry, I didn't recognize " \
                            "'{}' as a city".format(username, place)
        print(reply)

    if __name__ == '__main__':
        auth_obj = init_auth()
        since_id = 1
        for tweet in get_mentions(since_id, auth_obj):
            process_tweet(tweet)
```

The bulk of process_tweet() is used for formatting the tweet's text and processing the time zone data. First we will remove any @username mentions and #hashtags from the tweet. Then, we prepare the remaining tweet text to be compared with the time zone names database. The time zone names database is held in pytz.common_timezones, but the names also contain regions, which are separated from the names with slashes (/). Also, in these names underscores are used in place of spaces.

We scan through the database checking against the formatted tweet text. If a match is found, then we construct a reply, which contains the local time of the matched time zone. For this, we use the datetime module along with a time zone object generated by pytz. If we don't find a match in the time zone database, then we compose a reply to let the user know the same. Then, we print our reply to screen to check if it's working as expected.

Again, before running this, we may want to create a few tweets that contain just a city name and mention our world clock app account, so that the function has something to process. Some cities that appear in the time zone database are Dublin, New York, and Tokyo.

Give it a try! When you run it, you will get some tweet reply texts on the screen, which contain the cities and the current local times for those cities.

Rate limits

If we run the aforementioned several times, then we'll find that it will stop working after a while. Either the credentials will temporarily fail to validate, or the HTTP request in get_mentions() will fail.

This is because Twitter applies rate limits to its API, which means that our application is only allowed to make a certain number of requests to an endpoint in a given amount of time. The limits are listed in the Twitter documentation and they vary according to the authentication route (as discussed later) and endpoint. We are using `statuses/mentions_timeline.json`, so our limit is 15 requests for every 15 minutes. If we exceed this, then Twitter will respond with a `429 Too many requests` status code. This will force us to wait till the next 15 minute window starts before it lets us get any useful data back.

Rate limits are a common feature of web APIs, so it's useful to have ways of testing efficiently when using them. One approach to testing with data from rate-limited APIs is to download some data once and then store it locally. After this, load it from the file instead of pulling it from the API. Download some test data by using the Python interpreter, as shown here:

```
>>> from twitter_worldclock import *
>>> auth_obj = init_auth()
Credentials validated OK
>>> mentions = get_mentions(1, auth_obj)
>>> json.dump(mentions, open('test_mentions.json', 'w'))
```

You'll need to be in the same folder as `twitter_worldclock.py` when you run this. This creates a file called `test_mentions.json`, which contains our JSONized mentions. Here, the `json.dump()` function writes the supplied data into a file rather than returning it as a string.

Instead of calling the API, we can use this data by modifying our program's main section to look like the following:

```
if __name__ == '__main__':
    mentions = json.load(open('test_mentions.json'))
    for tweet in mentions:
        process_tweet(tweet)
```

Sending a reply

The final function that we need to perform is sending a tweet in response to a mention. For this, we use the `statuses/update.json` endpoint. If you've not registered your mobile number with your app account, then this won't work. So, just leave your program as it is. If you have registered your mobile number, then add this function under `process_tweets()`:

```
def post_reply(reply_to_id, text, auth_obj):
    params = {
```

```
    'status': text,
    'in_reply_to_status_id': reply_to_id}
url = 'https://api.twitter.com/1.1./statuses/update.json'
response = requests.post(url, params=params, auth=auth_obj)
response.raise_for_status()
```

And add this below the `print()` call at the end of `process_tweet()`, at the same indentation level:

```
post_reply(tweet['id'], reply, auth_obj)
```

Now, if you run this and then check your test account's Twitter notifications, you will see some replies.

The `post_reply()` function just calls the endpoint by using the following parameters to inform Twitter on what to post:

- `status`: This is the text of our reply tweet.
- `in_reply_to_status_id`: This is the ID of the tweet that we're replying to. We supply this so that Twitter can link the tweets as a conversation.

When testing this, we might get some `403` status code responses. This is okay, it's just that Twitter refuses to let us post two tweets with identical text in a row, which we may find happens with this set up, depending on what test tweets we send.

Final touches

The building blocks are in place, and we can add our main loop to make the program a daemon. Add the `time` module to the imports at the top, and then change the main section to what is shown here:

```
if __name__ == '__main__':
    auth_obj = init_auth()
    since_id = 1
    error_count = 0
    while error_count < 15:
        try:
            for tweet in get_mentions(since_id, auth_obj):
                process_tweet(tweet)
                since_id = max(since_id, tweet['id'])
            error_count = 0
        except requests.exceptions.HTTPError as e:
            print('Error: {}'.format(str(e)))
            error_count += 1
        time.sleep(60)
```

This will call `get_mentions()` every 60 seconds and then process any new tweets that have been downloaded. If we hit any HTTP errors, then it will retry the process 15 times before exiting the program.

Now if we run our program, then it will run continuously, replying to tweets that mention the world clock app account. Give it a try, run the program, and then send some tweets from your test account. After a minute, you will see some replies to your notifications.

Taking it further

Now that we've written a basic functional Twitter API client, there are certainly some things that we could improve upon. Although we don't have space in this chapter to explore enhancements in detail, it's worth mentioning a few to inform future projects you may want to undertake.

Polling and the Twitter streaming APIs

You may have already spotted a problem that our client will only pull a maximum of 200 tweets per poll. In each poll, Twitter provides the most recent tweets first. This means that if we get more than 200 tweets in 60 seconds, then we will permanently lose the tweets that come in first. In fact, there is no complete solution for this using the `statuses/mentions_timeline.json` endpoint.

Twitter's solution for this problem is to provide an alternative type of API, which is called a **streaming API**. When connecting to these APIs, the HTTP response connection is actually left open and the incoming tweets are continuously streamed through it. The `Requests` package provides neat functionality for handling this. The `Requests` response objects have an `iter_lines()` method, which runs indefinitely. It is capable of outputting a line of data whenever the server sends one, which can then be processed by us. If you do find that you need this, then there's an example that will help you in getting started in the Requests documentation, and it can be found at `http://docs.python-requests.org/en/latest/user/advanced/#streaming-requests`.

Alternative oAuth flows

Our setup for having our app operate against our main account and having a second account for sending the test tweets is a little clunky, especially so if you use your app account for regular tweeting. Wouldn't it be better to have a separate account dedicated to handling the world clock tweets?

Well, yes it would. The ideal set up is to have a main account on which you register the app, and which you can also use it as a regular Twitter account, and have the app process tweets for a second dedicated world clock account.

oAuth makes this possible, but there are some extra steps that are needed to get it to work. We would need the world clock account to authorize our app to act on its behalf. You'll notice that the oAuth credentials mentioned earlier are comprised of two main elements, **consumer** and **access**. The consumer element identifies our application, and the access element proves that the account the access credentials came from authorized our app to act on its behalf. In our app we shortcut the full account authorization process by having the app act on behalf of the account through which it was registered, that is, our app account. When we do this, Twitter lets us acquire the access credentials directly from the dev.twitter.com interface. To use a different user account, we would have needed to have inserted a step where the user is taken to Twitter, which would be opened in a web browser, where the user would have to log in and then explicitly authorize our application.

This process is demonstrated in the requests-oauthlib documentation, which can be found at https://requests-oauthlib. readthedocs.org/en/latest/oauth1_workflow.html.

HTML and screen scraping

Although more and more services are offering their data through APIs, when a service doesn't do this then the only way of getting the data programmatically is to download its web pages and then parse the HTML source code. This technique is called **screen scraping**.

Though it sounds simple enough in principle, screen scraping should be approached as a last resort. Unlike XML, where the syntax is strictly enforced and data structures are usually reasonably stable and sometimes even documented, the world of web page source code is a messy one. It is a fluid place, where the code can change unexpectedly and in a way that can completely break your script and force you to rework the parsing logic from scratch.

Still, it is sometimes the only way to get essential data, so we're going to take a brief look at developing an approach toward scraping. We will discuss ways to reduce the impact when the HTML code does change.

You should always check a site's terms and conditions before scraping. Some websites explicitly disallow automated parsing and retrieval. Breaching the terms may result in your IP address being barred. However, in most cases, as long as you don't republish the data and don't make excessively frequent requests, you should be okay.

HTML parsers

We'll be parsing HTML just as we parsed XML. We again have a choice between pull-style APIs and object-oriented APIs. We are going to use ElementTree for the same reasons as mentioned before.

There are several HTML parsing libraries that are available. They're differentiated by their speed, the interfaces that they offer for navigating within HTML documents, and their ability at handling badly constructed HTML. The Python standard library doesn't include an object-oriented HTML parser. The universally recommended third-party package for this is lxml, which is primarily an XML parser. However, it does include a very good HTML parser. It's quick, it offers several ways of navigating documents, and it is tolerant of broken HTML.

The lxml library can be installed on Debian and Ubuntu through the python-lxml package. If you need an up-to-date version or if you're not able to install the system packages, then lxml can be installed through pip. Note that you'll need a build environment for this. Debian usually comes with an environment that has already been set up but if it's missing, then the following will install one for both Debian and Ubuntu:

```
$ sudo apt-get install build-essential
```

Then you should be able to install lxml, like this:

```
$ sudo STATIC_DEPS=true pip install lxml
```

If you hit compilation problems on a 64-bit system, then you can also try:

```
$ CFLAGS="$CFLAGS -fPIC" STATIC_DEPS=true pip install lxml
```

On Windows, installer packages are available from the lxml website at http://lxml.de/installation.html. Check the page for links to third-party installers in case an installer for your version of Python isn't available.

The next best library, in case lxml doesn't work for you, is BeautifulSoup. BeautifulSoup is pure Python, so it can be installed with pip, and it should run anywhere. Although it has its own API, it's a well-respected and capable library, and it can, in fact, use lxml as a backend library.

Show me the data

Before we start parsing HTML, we need something to parse! Let's grab the version and codename of the latest stable Debian release from the Debian website. Information about the current stable release can be found at `https://www.debian.org/releases/stable/`.

The information that we want is displayed in the page title and in the first sentence:

So, we should extract the "*jessie*" codename and the 8.0 version number.

Parsing HTML with lxml

Let's open a Python shell and get to parsing. First, we'll download the page with `Requests`.

```
>>> import requests
>>> response = requests.get('https://www.debian.org/releases/stable')
```

Next, we parse the source into an `ElementTree` tree. This is the same as it is for parsing XML with the standard library's `ElementTree`, except here we will use the `lxml` specialist `HTMLParser`.

```
>>> from lxml.etree import HTML
>>> root = HTML(response.content)
```

The `HTML()` function is a shortcut that reads the HTML that is passed to it, and then it produces an XML tree. Notice that we're passing `response.content` and not `response.text`. The `lxml` library produces better results when it uses the raw response rather than the decoded Unicode text.

The `lxml` library's `ElementTree` implementation has been designed to be 100 percent compatible with the standard library's, so we can start exploring the document in the same way as we did with XML:

```
>>> [e.tag for e in root]
['head', 'body']
>>> root.find('head').find('title').text
'Debian -- Debian \u201cjessie\u201d Release Information'
```

In the preceding code, we have printed out the text content of the document's `<title>` element, which is the text that appears in the tab in the preceding screenshot. We can already see it contains the codename that we want.

Zeroing in

Screen scraping is the art of finding a way to unambiguously address the elements in the HTML that contain the information that we want, and extract the information from only those elements.

However, we also want the selection criteria to be as simple as possible. The less we rely on the contents of the document, the lesser the chance of it being broken if the page's HTML changes.

Let's inspect the HTML source of the page, and see what we're dealing with. For this, either use `View Source` in a web browser, or save the HTML to a file and open it in a text editor. The page's source code is also included in the source code download for this book. Search for the text `Debian 8.0`, so that we are taken straight to the information we want. For me, it looks like the following block of code:

```
<body>
...
<div id="content">
<h1>Debian &ldquo;jessie&rdquo; Release Information</h1>
<p><b>Debian 8.0</b> was
released October 18th, 2014.
The release included many major
changes, described in
...
```

I've skipped the HTML between the `<body>` and the `<div>` to show that the `<div>` is a direct child of the `<body>` element. From the above, we can see that we want the contents of the `<p>` tag child of the `<div>` element.

If we navigated to this element by using the `ElementTree` functions, which we have used before, then we'd end up with something like the following:

```
>>> root.find('body').findall('div')[1].find('p').text
Debian 8.0 was.
```

. . .

But this isn't the best approach, as it depends quite heavily on the HTML structure. A change, such as a `<div>` tag being inserted before the one that we needed, would break it. Also, in more complex documents, this can lead to horrendous chains of method calls, which are hard to maintain. Our use of the `<title>` tag in the previous section to get the codename is an example of a good technique, because there is always only one `<head>` and one `<title>` tag in a document. A better approach to finding our `<div>` would be to make use of the `id="content"` attribute it contains. It's a common web page design pattern to break a page into a few top-level `<divs>` for the major page sections like the header, the footer and the content, and to give the `<divs>` id attributes which identify them as such.

Hence, if we could search for `<div>`s with an `id` attribute of `"content"`, then we'd have a clean way of selecting the right `<div>`. There is only one `<div>` in the document that is a match, and it's unlikely that another`<div>` like that will be added to the document. This approach doesn't depend on the document structure, and so it won't be affected by any changes that are made to the structure. We'll still need to rely on the fact that the `<p>` tag in the `<div>` is the first `<p>` tag that appears, but given that there is no other way to identify it, this is the best we can do.

So, how do we run such a search for our content `<div>`?

Searching with XPath

In order to avoid exhaustive iteration and the checking of every element, we need to use **XPath**, which is more powerful than what we've used so far. It is a query language that was developed specifically for XML, and it's supported by `lxml`. Plus, the standard library implementation provides limited support for it.

We're going to take a quick look at XPath, and in the process we will find the answer to the question posed earlier.

To get started, use the Python shell from the last section, and do the following:

```
>>> root.xpath('body')
[<Element body at 0x39e0908>]
```

This is the simplest form of XPath expression: it searches for children of the current element that have tag names that match the specified tag name. The current element is the one we call xpath() on, in this case root. The root element is the top-level <html> element in the HTML document, and so the returned element is the <body> element.

XPath expressions can contain multiple levels of elements. The searches start from the node the xpath() call is made on and work down the tree as they match successive elements in the expression. We can use this to find just the <div> child elements of <body>:

```
>>> root.xpath('body/div')
```

```
[<Element div at 0x39e06c8>, <Element div at 0x39e05c8>, <Element div at 0x39e0608>]
```

The body/div expression means match <div> children of <body> children of the current element. Elements with the same tag can appear more than once at the same level in an XML document, so an XPath expression can match multiple elements, hence the xpath() function always returns a list.

The preceding queries are relative to the element that we call xpath() on, but we can force a search from the root of the tree by adding a slash to the start of the expression. We can also perform a search over all the descendants of an element, with the help of a double-slash. To do this, try the following:

```
>>> root.xpath('//h1')
```

```
[<Element h1 at 0x2ac3b08>]
```

Here, we've directly found our <h1> element by only specifying a single tag, even though it's several levels below root. This double-slash at the beginning of the expression will always search from the root, but we can prefix this with a dot if we want it to start searching from the context element.

```
>>> root.find('head').xpath('.//h1')
```

```
[]
```

This will not find anything because there are no <h1> descendents of <head>.

XPath conditions

So, we can be quite specific by supplying paths, but the real power of XPath lies in applying additional conditions to the elements in the path. In particular, our aforementioned problem, which is, testing element attributes.

```
>>> root.xpath('//div[@id="content"]')
```

```
[<Element div at 0x39e05c8>]
```

The square brackets after div, [@id="content"], form a condition that we place on the <div> elements that we're matching. The @ sign before id means that id refers to an attribute, so the condition means: only elements with an id attribute equal to "content". This is how we can find our content <div>.

Before we employ this to extract our information, let's just touch on a couple of useful things that we can do with conditions. We can specify just a tag name, as shown here:

```
>>> root.xpath('//div[h1]')
[<Element div at 0x39e05c8>]
```

This returns all <div> elements which have an <h1> child element. Also try:

```
>>> root.xpath('body/div[2]'):
[<Element div at 0x39e05c8>]
```

Putting a number as a condition will return the element at that position in the matched list. In this case this is the second <div> child element of <body>. Note that these indexes start at 1, unlike Python indexing which starts at 0.

There's a lot more that XPath can do, the full specification is a **World Wide Web Consortium (W3C)** standard. The latest version can be found at http://www.w3.org/TR/xpath-3/.

Pulling it together

Now that we've added XPath to our superpowers, let's finish up by writing a script to get our Debian version information. Create a new file, get_debian_version.py, and save the following to it:

```python
import re
import requests
from lxml.etree import HTML

response = requests.get('http://www.debian.org/releases/stable/')
root = HTML(response.content)
title_text = root.find('head').find('title').text
release = re.search('\u201c(.*)\u201d', title_text).group(1)
p_text = root.xpath('//div[@id="content"]/p[1]')[0].text
version = p_text.split()[1]

print('Codename: {}\nVersion: {}'.format(release, version))
```

Here, we have downloaded and parsed the web page by pulling out the text that we want with the help of XPath. We have used a regular expression to pull out *jessie*, and a `split` to extract the version 8.0. Finally we print it out.

So, run it like it is shown here:

```
$ python3.4 get_debian_version.py
Codename: jessie
Version: 8.0
```

Magnificent. Well, darned nifty, at least. There are some third-party packages available which can speed up scraping and form submission, two popular ones are Mechanize and Scrapy. Check them out at `http://mechanize.sourceforge.net`, and `http://scrapy.org`.

With great power...

As an HTTP client developer, you may have different priorities to the webmasters that run websites. A webmaster will typically provide a site for human users; possibly offering a service designed for generating revenue, and it is most likely that all this will need to be done with the help of very limited resources. They will be interested in analyzing how humans use their site, and may have areas of the site they would prefer that automated clients didn't explore.

HTTP clients that automatically parse and download pages on websites are called various things, such as *bots*, *web crawlers*, and *spiders*. Bots have many legitimate uses. All the search engine providers make extensive use of bots for crawling the web and building their huge page indexes. Bots can be used to check for dead links, and to archive sites for repositories, such as the Wayback Machine. But, there are also many uses that might be considered as illegitimate. Automatically traversing an information service to extract the data on its pages and then repackaging that data for presentation elsewhere without permission of the site owners, downloading large batches of media files in one go when the spirit of the service is online viewing and so on could be considered as illegitimate. Some sites have terms of service which explicitly bar automated downloads. Although some actions such as copying and republishing copyrighted material are clearly illegitimate, some other actions are subject to interpretation. This gray area is a subject of ongoing debate, and it is unlikely that it will ever be resolved to everyone's satisfaction.

However, even when they do serve a legitimate purpose, in general, bots do make webmasters lives somewhat more difficult. They pollute the webserver logs, which webmasters use for calculating statistics on how their site is being used by their human audience. Bots also consume bandwidth and other server resources.

Using the methods that we are looking at in this chapter, it is quite straightforward to write a bot that performs many of the aforementioned functions. Webmasters provide us with services that we will be using, so in return, we should respect the aforementioned areas and design our bots in such a way that they impact them as little as possible.

Choosing a User Agent

There are a few things that we can do to help our webmasters out. We should always pick an appropriate user agent for our client. The principle way in which webmasters filter out bot traffic from their logfiles is by performing user agent analysis.

There are lists of the user agents of known bots, for example, one such list can be found at `http://www.useragentstring.com/pages/Crawlerlist`.

Webmasters can use these in their filters. Many webmasters also simply filter out any user agents that contain the words *bot*, *spider*, or *crawler*. So, if we are writing an automated bot rather than a browser, then it will make the webmasters' lives a little easier if we use a user agent that contains one of these words. Many bots used by the search engine providers follow this convention, some examples are listed here:

- `Mozilla/5.0 compatible; bingbot/2.0; http://www.bing.com/bingbot.htm`
- `Baiduspider: http://www.baidu.com/search/spider.htm`
- `Mozilla/5.0 compatible; Googlebot/2.1; http://www.google.com/bot.html`

There are also some guidelines in section 5.5.3 of the HTTP RFC 7231.

The Robots.txt file

There is an unofficial but standard mechanism to tell bots if there are any parts of a website that they should not crawl. This mechanism is called `robots.txt`, and it takes the form of a text file called, unsurprisingly, `robots.txt`. This file always lives in the root of a website so that bots can always find it. It has rules that describe the accessible parts of the website. The file format is described at `http://www.robotstxt.org`.

The Python standard library provides the `urllib.robotparser` module for parsing and working with `robots.txt` files. You can create a parser object, feed it a `robots.txt` file and then you can simply query it to see whether a given URL is permitted for a given user agent. A good example can be found in the documentation in the standard library. If you check every URL that your client might want to access before you access it, and honor the webmasters wishes, then you'll be helping them out.

Finally, since we may be making quite a lot of requests as we test out our fledgling clients, it's a good idea to make local copies of the web pages or the files that you want your client to parse and test it against them. In this way, we'll be saving bandwidth for ourselves and for the websites.

Summary

We've covered a lot of ground in this chapter, but you should now be able to start making real use of the web APIs that you encounter.

We looked at XML, how to construct documents, parse them and extract data from them by using the `ElementTree` API. We looked at both the Python `ElementTree` implementation and `lxml`. We also looked at how the XPath query language can be used efficiently for extracting information from documents.

We looked at the Amazon S3 service and wrote a client that lets us perform basic operations, such as creating buckets, and uploading and downloading files through the S3 REST API. We learned about setting access permissions and setting content types, such that the files work properly in web browsers.

We looked at the JSON data format, how to convert Python objects into the JSON data format and how to convert them back to Python objects.

We then explored the Twitter API and wrote an on-demand world clock service, through which we learned how to read and process tweets for an account, and how to send a tweet as a reply.

We saw how to extract or scrape information from the HTML source of web pages. We saw how to work with HTML when using `ElementTree` and the `lxml` HTML parser. We also learned how to use XPath to help make this process more efficient.

And finally, we looked at how we can give back to the webmasters that provide us with all the data. We discussed a few ways in which we can code our clients to make the webmasters lives a little easier and respect how they would like us to use their sites.

So, that's it for HTTP for now. We'll re-visit HTTP in *Chapter 9, Applications for the Web*, where we'll be looking at using Python for constructing the server-side of web applications. In the next chapter, we'll discuss the other great workhorse of the Internet: e-mail.

4
Engaging with E-mails

E-mail is one of the most popular ways of digital communication. Python has a rich number of built-in libraries for dealing with e-mails. In this chapter, we will learn how to use Python to compose, send, and retrieve e-mails. The following topics will be covered in this chapter:

- Sending e-mails with SMTP through the `smtplib` library
- Securing e-mails transport with TLS
- Retrieving e-mails by using POP3 with `poplib`
- Retrieving e-mails by using IMAP with `imapclient`
- Manipulating e-mails on the server with IMAP
- Sending e-mails with the help of the `logging` module

E-mail terminologies

Before we start composing our first e-mail with the help of Python, let us revisit some of the elementary concepts of e-mail. Often, an end-user uses a piece of software or a graphical user interface (GUI) for composing, sending, and receiving e-mails. This piece of software is known as an e-mail client, for example, Mozilla Thunderbird, Microsoft Outlook, and so on are e-mail clients. The same tasks can be done by a web interface, that is, a webmail client interface. Some common examples of these are: Gmail, Yahoo mail, Hotmail and so on.

The mail that you send from your client interface does not reach the receiver's computer directly. Your mail travels through a number of specialized e-mail servers. These servers run a piece of software called the **Mail Transfer Agent (MTA)**, and its primary job is to route the e-mail to the appropriate destinations by analyzing the mail header, among other things.

Lots of other things also happen en-route, and then the mail reaches the recipient's local e-mail gateway. Then, the recipient can retrieve the e-mail by using his or her e-mail client.

A few protocols are involved in the aforementioned process. The most common of those have been listed here:

- **Simple Mail Transfer Protocol (SMTP)**: The SMTP protocol is used by the MTA for delivering your e-mail to the recipient's e-mail server. The SMTP protocol can only be used for sending e-mails from one host to another.

- **Post Office Protocol 3 (POP3)**: The POP3 protocol provides a simple and standardized way for the users to gain access to the mailboxes and then download the messages to their computers. When using the POP3 protocol, your e-mail messages will be downloaded from the Internet service provider's (ISP) mail server to the local computer. You can also leave the copies of your e-mails on the ISP server.

- **Internet Message Access Protocol (IMAP)**: The IMAP protocol also provides a simple and standardized way for accessing your e-mail from the ISP's local server. IMAP is a client/server protocol in which the e-mails are received and held for you by your ISP. As this requires only a small data transfer, this scheme works well even over a slow connection, such as the mobile phone network. Only if you send a request to read a specific e-mail, that email message will be downloaded from the ISP. You can also do some other interesting things, such as creating and manipulating folders or mailboxes on the server, deleting messages, and so on.

Python has three modules, `smtplib`, `poplib`, and `imaplib`, which support SMTP, POP3, and the IMAP protocols respectively. Each module has options for transmitting the information securely by using the **Transport Layer Security (TLS)** protocol. Each protocol also uses some form of authentication for ensuring the confidentiality of the data.

Sending e-mails with SMTP

We can send an e-mail from a Python script by using `smtplib` and `e-mail` packages. The `smtplib` module provides an SMTP objects which is used for sending mail by using either an SMTP or an **Extended SMTP (ESMTP)** protocol. The `e-mail` module helps us in constructing the e-mail messages with the help of the various header information and attachments. This module conforms to the **Internet Message Format (IMF)** described at `http://tools.ietf.org/html/rfc2822.html`.

Composing an e-mail message

Let us construct the e-mail message by using classes from the email module. The email.mime module provides classes for creating the e-mail and MIME objects from scratch. **MIME** is an acronym for **Multi-purpose Internet Mail Extensions**. This is an extension of the original Internet e-mail protocol. This is widely used for exchanging different kinds of data files, such as audio, video, images, applications, and so on.

Many classes have been derived from the MIME base class. We will use an SMTP client script using email.mime.multipart.MIMEMultipart() class as an example. It accepts passing the e-mail header information through a keyword dictionary. Let's have a look at how we can specify an e-mail header by using the MIMEMultipart() object. Multi-part mime refers to sending both the HTML and the TEXT part of an e-mail message in a single e-mail. When an e-mail client receives a multipart message, it accepts the HTML version if it can render HTML, otherwise it presents the plain text version, as shown in the following code block:

```
from email.mime.multipart import MIMEMultipart()
msg = MIMEMultipart()
msg['To'] = recipient
msg['From'] = sender
msg['Subject'] = 'Email subject..'
```

Now, attach a plain text message to this multi-part message object. We can wrap a plain-text message by using the MIMEText() object. The constructor of this class takes the additional arguments. For example, we can pass text and plain as its arguments. The data of this message can be set by using the set_payload() method, as shown here:

```
part = MIMEText('text', 'plain')
message = 'Email message ….'
part.set_payload(message)
```

Now, we will attach the plain text message to the Multi-part message, as shown here:

```
msg.attach(part)
```

The message is ready to be routed to the destination mail server by using one or more SMTP MTA servers. But, obviously, the script only talks to a specific MTA and that MTA handles the routing of the message.

Sending an e-mail message

The `smtplib` module supplies us with an SMTP class, which can be initialized by an SMTP server socket. Upon successful initialization, this will give us an SMTP session object. The SMTP client will establish a proper SMTP session with the server. This can be done by using the `ehlo()` method for an SMTP `session` object. The actual message sending will be done by applying the `sendmail()` method to the SMTP session. So, a typical SMTP session will look like the following:

```
session = smtplib.SMTP(SMTP_SERVER, SMTP_PORT)
session.ehlo()
session.sendmail(sender, recipient, msg.as_string())
session.quit()
```

In our example SMTP client script, we have made use of Google's free Gmail service. If you have a Gmail account, then you can send an e-mail from a Python script to that account by using SMTP. Your e-mail may get blocked initially, as Gmail may detect that it had been sent from a less secure e-mail client. You can change your Gmail account settings and enable your account to send/receive e-mails from less secure e-mail clients. You can learn more about sending e-mail from an app on the Google website, which can be found at `https://support.google.com/a/answer/176600?hl=en`.

If you don't have a Gmail account, then you can use a local SMTP server setup in a typical Linux box and run this script. The following code shows how to send an e-mail through a public SMTP server:

```python
#!/usr/bin/env python3
# Listing 1 - First email client
import smtplib

from email.mime.image import MIMEImage
from email.mime.multipart import MIMEMultipart
from email.mime.text import MIMEText

SMTP_SERVER = 'aspmx.l.google.com'
SMTP_PORT = 25

def send_email(sender, recipient):
    """ Send email message """
    msg = MIMEMultipart()
```

```
msg['To'] = recipient
msg['From'] = sender
subject = input('Enter your email subject: ')
msg['Subject'] = subject
message = input('Enter your email message. Press Enter when
finished. ')
part = MIMEText('text', "plain")
part.set_payload(message)
msg.attach(part)
# create smtp session
session = smtplib.SMTP(SMTP_SERVER, SMTP_PORT)
session.ehlo()
#session.set_debuglevel(1)
# send mail
session.sendmail(sender, recipient, msg.as_string())
print("You email is sent to {0}.".format(recipient))
session.quit()

if __name__ == '__main__':
    sender = input("Enter sender email address: ")
    recipient = input("Enter recipient email address: ")
    send_email(sender, recipient)
```

If you run this script, then you can see that the output is similar to what is mentioned here. For the sake of anonymity, real e-mail addresses have not been shown in the following example:

```
$ python3 smtp_mail_sender.py
Enter sender email address: <SENDER>@gmail.com
Enter recipeint email address: <RECEIVER>@gmail.com
Enter your email subject: Test mail
Enter your email message. Press Enter when finished. This message can be
ignored
You email is sent to <RECEIVER>@gmail.com.
```

This script will send a very simple e-mail message by using Python's standard library module, smtplib. For composing the message, MIMEMultipart and MIMEText classes have been imported from the email.mime submodule. This submodule has various types of classes for composing e-mail messages with different types of attachments, for example, MIMEApplication(), MIMEAudio(), MIMEImage(), and so on.

In this example, the send_mail() function has been called by two arguments: sender and receiver. Both of these arguments are e-mail addresses. An e-mail message is constructed by the MIMEMultipart() message class. The essential headers, such as To, From, and Subject have been added to this class namespace. The body of the message is composed with the instance of the MIMEText() class. This is done by the class set_payload() method. Then, this payload is attached to the main message by the attach() method.

In order to communicate with the SMTP server, a session with the server will be created by instantiating the smtplib module's SMTP() class. The server name and the port arguments will be passed to the constructor. According to the SMTP protocol, an extended hello message through ehlo() method will be sent by the client to the server. The message will be sent by the sendmail() method.

Notice that if the set_debuglevel() method is called on an SMTP session object, then it will produce additional debug messages. The line is commented out in the preceding example. Un-commenting that line will produce a debug message such as:

```
$ python3 smtp_mail_sender.py
Enter sender email address: <SENDER>@gmail.com
Enter recipeint email address: <RECEIVER>@gmail.com
Enter your email subject: Test email
Enter your email message. Press Enter when finished. This is a test email
send: 'mail FROM:<SENDER@gmail.com> size=339\r\n'
reply: b'250 2.1.0 OK hg2si4622244wib.38 - gsmtp\r\n'
reply: retcode (250); Msg: b'2.1.0 OK hg2si4622244wib.38 - gsmtp'
send: 'rcpt TO:<RECEIVER@gmail.com>\r\n'
reply: b'250 2.1.5 OK hg2si4622244wib.38 - gsmtp\r\n'
reply: retcode (250); Msg: b'2.1.5 OK hg2si4622244wib.38 - gsmtp'
send: 'data\r\n'
reply: b'354  Go ahead hg2si4622244wib.38 - gsmtp\r\n'
reply: retcode (354); Msg: b'Go ahead hg2si4622244wib.38 - gsmtp'
data: (354, b'Go ahead hg2si4622244wib.38 - gsmtp')
send: 'Content-Type: multipart/mixed;
  boundary="===============1431208306=="\r\nMIME-Version: 1.0\r\nTo:
  RECEIVER@gmail.com\r\nFrom: SENDER@gmail.com\r\nSubject: Test
  email\r\n\r\n--===============1431208306==\r\nContent-Type:
  text/plain; charset="us-ascii"\r\nMIME-Version: 1.0\r\nContent-
  Transfer-Encoding: 7bit\r\n\r\nThis is a test email\r\n--
  ===============1431208306==--\r\n.\r\n'
```

```
reply: b'250 2.0.0 OK 1414233177 hg2si4622244wib.38 - gsmtp\r\n'
reply: retcode (250); Msg: b'2.0.0 OK 1414233177 hg2si4622244wib.38 -
   gsmtp'
data: (250, b'2.0.0 OK 1414233177 hg2si4622244wib.38 - gsmtp')
You email is sent to RECEIVER@gmail.com.
send: 'quit\r\n'
reply: b'221 2.0.0 closing connection hg2si4622244wib.38 - gsmtp\r\n'
reply: retcode (221); Msg: b'2.0.0 closing connection
   hg2si4622244wib.38 - gsmtp'
```

This is interesting because the message has been sent through a public SMTP server in a step-by-step fashion.

Sending e-mails securely with TLS

TLS protocol is a successor of **SSL** or **Secure Socket Layer**. This ensures that the communication between the client and the server is secure. This is done by sending the message in an encrypted format so that unauthorized people cannot see the message. It is not difficult to use TLS with `smtplib`. After you create an SMTP session object, you need to call the `starttls()` method. Before sending an e-mail, you need to login to the server by using the SMTP server credentials.

Here is an example for the second e-mail client:

```python
#!/usr/bin/env python3
# Listing 2
import getpass
import smtplib

from email.mime.image import MIMEImage
from email.mime.multipart import MIMEMultipart
from email.mime.text import MIMEText

SMTP_SERVER = 'smtp.gmail.com'
SMTP_PORT = 587 # ssl port 465, tls port 587

def send_email(sender, recipient):
    """ Send email message """
    msg = MIMEMultipart()
    msg['To'] = recipient
    msg['From'] = sender
```

```
msg['Subject'] = input('Enter your email subject: ')
message = input('Enter your email message. Press Enter when
finished. ')
part = MIMEText('text', "plain")
part.set_payload(message)
msg.attach(part)
# create smtp session
session = smtplib.SMTP(SMTP_SERVER, SMTP_PORT)
session.set_debuglevel(1)
session.ehlo()
session.starttls()
session.ehlo
password = getpass.getpass(prompt="Enter you email password:
")
# login to server
session.login(sender, password)
# send mail
session.sendmail(sender, recipient, msg.as_string())
print("You email is sent to {0}.".format(recipient))
session.quit()

if __name__ == '__main__':
    sender = input("Enter sender email address: ")
    recipient = input("Enter recipeint email address: ")
    send_email(sender, recipient)
```

The preceding code is similar to our first example, except for the authentication to
the server. In this case, the SMTP user is authenticated against the server. If we run
the script after turning on the SMTP debugging, then we would be seeing an output
similar to the following:

```
$ python3 smtp_mail_sender_tls.py
Enter sender email address: SENDER@gmail.com
Enter recipeint email address: RECEPIENT@gmail.com
Enter your email subject: Test email
Enter your email message. Press Enter when finished. This is a test
  email that can be ignored.
```

After the user input, communication with the server will begin. It will start by the
ehlo() method. In response to this command, the SMTP server will send a few
response lines with the return code 250. This response will include the features
supported by the server.

The summary of these responses will indicate that the server is ready to proceed with the client, as shown in the following:

```
send: 'ehlo debian6box.localdomain.loc\r\n'
reply: b'250-mx.google.com at your service, [77.233.155.107]\r\n'
reply: b'250-SIZE 35882577\r\n'
reply: b'250-8BITMIME\r\n'
reply: b'250-STARTTLS\r\n'
reply: b'250-ENHANCEDSTATUSCODES\r\n'
reply: b'250-PIPELINING\r\n'
reply: b'250-CHUNKING\r\n'
reply: b'250 SMTPUTF8\r\n'
reply: retcode (250); Msg: b'mx.google.com at your service,
   [77.233.155.107]\nSIZE
   35882577\n8BITMIME\nSTARTTLS\nENHANCEDSTATUSCODES\nPIPELINING\
   nCHUNKING\nSMTPUTF8'
```

After the initial command, the client will use the `starttls()` method to upgrade the connection to TLS, as shown here:

```
send: 'STARTTLS\r\n'
reply: b'220 2.0.0 Ready to start TLS\r\n'
reply: retcode (220); Msg: b'2.0.0 Ready to start TLS'
Enter you email password:
send: 'ehlo debian6box.localdomain.loc\r\n'
reply: b'250-mx.google.com at your service, [77.233.155.107]\r\n'
reply: b'250-SIZE 35882577\r\n'
reply: b'250-8BITMIME\r\n'
reply: b'250-AUTH LOGIN PLAIN XOAUTH XOAUTH2 PLAIN-CLIENTTOKEN
   OAUTHBEARER\r\n'
reply: b'250-ENHANCEDSTATUSCODES\r\n'
reply: b'250-PIPELINING\r\n'
reply: b'250-CHUNKING\r\n'
reply: b'250 SMTPUTF8\r\n'
reply: retcode (250); Msg: b'mx.google.com at your service,
   [77.233.155.107]\nSIZE 35882577\n8BITMIME\nAUTH LOGIN PLAIN XOAUTH
   XOAUTH2 PLAIN-CLIENTTOKEN
   OAUTHBEARER\nENHANCEDSTATUSCODES\nPIPELINING\nCHUNKING\nSMTPUTF8'
```

In the authentication phase, the authentication data is sent by the client-side script with the help of the login() method. Note that the authentication token is a base-64 encoded string and the username and password are separated by a null byte. There other supported authentication protocols exists for the sophisticated clients. The following is the example of authentication token:

```
send: 'AUTH PLAIN A...dvXXDDCCD.......sscdsvsdvsfd...12344555\r\n'
reply: b'235 2.7.0 Accepted\r\n'
reply: retcode (235); Msg: b'2.7.0 Accepted'
```

After the client is authenticated, it can send e-mail messages by using the sendmail() method. Three arguments are passed to this method, sender, recipient, and the message. The sample output is shown here:

```
send: 'mail FROM:<SENDER@gmail.com> size=360\r\n'
reply: b'250 2.1.0 OK xw9sm8487512wjc.24 - gsmtp\r\n'
reply: retcode (250); Msg: b'2.1.0 OK xw9sm8487512wjc.24 - gsmtp'
send: 'rcpt TO:<RECEPIENT@gmail.com>\r\n'
reply: b'250 2.1.5 OK xw9sm8487512wjc.24 - gsmtp\r\n'
reply: retcode (250); Msg: b'2.1.5 OK xw9sm8487512wjc.24 - gsmtp'
send: 'data\r\n'
reply: b'354  Go ahead xw9sm8487512wjc.24 - gsmtp\r\n'
reply: retcode (354); Msg: b'Go ahead xw9sm8487512wjc.24 - gsmtp'
data: (354, b'Go ahead xw9sm8487512wjc.24 - gsmtp')
send: 'Content-Type: multipart/mixed;
  boundary="===============1501937935=="\r\nMIME-Version: 1.0\r\n
To: <Output omitted>-===============1501937935==--\r\n.\r\n'
reply: b'250 2.0.0 OK 1414235750 xw9sm8487512wjc.24 - gsmtp\r\n'
reply: retcode (250); Msg: b'2.0.0 OK 1414235750 xw9sm8487512wjc.24 -
  gsmtp'
data: (250, b'2.0.0 OK 1414235750 xw9sm8487512wjc.24 - gsmtp')
You email is sent to RECEPIENT@gmail.com.
send: 'quit\r\n'
reply: b'221 2.0.0 closing connection xw9sm8487512wjc.24 - gsmtp\r\n'
reply: retcode (221); Msg: b'2.0.0 closing connection
  xw9sm8487512wjc.24 - gsmtp'
```

Retrieving e-mails by using POP3 with poplib

The stored e-mail messages can be downloaded and read by the local computer. The POP3 protocol can be used to download the messages from the e-mail server. Python has a module called `poplib`, and it can be used for this purpose. This module provides two high-level classes, `POP()` and `POP3_SSL()`, which implement the POP3 and POP3S protocols respectively for communicating with a POP3/POP3S server. It accepts three arguments, host, port, and timeout. If port is omitted, then the default port (110) can be used. The optional timeout parameter determines the length (in seconds) of the connection timeout at the server.

The secure version of `POP3()` is its subclass `POP3_SSL()`. It takes additional parameters, such as keyfile and certfile, which are used for supplying the SSL certificate files, namely the private key and certificate chain file.

Writing for a POP3 client is also very straightforward. To do this, instantiate a mailbox object by initializing the `POP3()` or `POP3_SSL()` class. Then, invoke the `user()` and `pass_()` methods to login to the server by using the following command:

```
mailbox = poplib.POP3_SSL(<POP3_SERVER>, <SERVER_PORT>)
mailbox.user('username')
    mailbox.pass_('password')
```

Now, you can call the various methods for manipulating your accounts and messages. A few interesting methods have been listed here:

- `stat()`: This method returns the mailbox status according to tuples of two integers, that is, the message count and the size of the mailbox.

- `list()`: This method sends a request for getting a message list, which has been demonstrated in the example shown later in this section.

- `retr()`: This method gives an argument message a number that indicates the message that has to be retrieved. It also marks the message as read.

- `dele()`: This method provides an argument for the message that has to be deleted. On many POP3 servers, the deletion is not performed until QUIT. You can reset the delete flag by using the `rset()` method.

- `quit()`: This method takes you off the connection by committing a few changes and disconnecting you from the server.

Let us see how we can read out the e-mail messages by accessing the Google's secure POP3 e-mail server. By default, the POP3 server listens on port 995 securely. The following is an example of fetching an e-mail by using POP3:

```python
#!/usr/bin/env python3
import getpass
import poplib

GOOGLE_POP3_SERVER = 'pop.googlemail.com'
POP3_SERVER_PORT = '995'

def fetch_email(username, password):
    mailbox = poplib.POP3_SSL(GOOGLE_POP3_SERVER,
    POP3_SERVER_PORT)
    mailbox.user(username)
    mailbox.pass_(password)
    num_messages = len(mailbox.list()[1])
    print("Total emails: {0}".format(num_messages))
    print("Getting last message")
    for msg in mailbox.retr(num_messages)[1]:
        print(msg)
    mailbox.quit()

if __name__ == '__main__':
    username = input("Enter your email user ID: ")
    password = getpass.getpass(prompt="Enter your email password:
    ")
    fetch_email(username, password)
```

As you can see in the preceding code, the `fetch_email()` function has created a mailbox object by calling `POP3_SSL()` along with the server socket. The username and the password are set on this object by calling the `user()` and `pass_()` method. Upon successful authentication, we can invoke the POP3 commands by using methods, such as the `list()` method, which is called to list the e-mails. In this example, the total number of messages has been displayed on the screen. Then, the `retr()` method has been used for retrieving the content of a single message.

A sample output has been shown here:

```
$ python3 fetch_email_pop3.py
Enter your email user ID: <PERSON1>@gmail.com
Enter your email password:
Total emails: 330
```

```
Getting last message
b'Received: by 10.150.139.7 with HTTP; Tue, 7 Oct 2008 13:20:42 -0700
   (PDT)'
b'Message-ID: <fc9dd8650810...@mail.gmail.com>'
b'Date: Tue, 7 Oct 2008 21:20:42 +0100'
b'From: "Mr Person1" <PERSON1@gmail.com>'
b'To: "Mr Person2" <PERSON2@gmail.com>'
b'Subject: Re: Some subject'
b'In-Reply-To: <1bec119d...@mail.gmail.com>'
b'MIME-Version: 1.0'
b'Content-Type: multipart/alternative; '
b'\tboundary="----=_Part_63057_22732713.1223410842697"'
b'References: <fc9dd8650809270....@mail.gmail.com>'
b'\t <1bec119d0810060337p557bc....@mail.gmail.com>'
b'Delivered-To: PERSON1@gmail.com'
b''
b'------=_Part_63057_22732713.1223410842697'
b'Content-Type: text/plain; charset=ISO-8859-1'
b'Content-Transfer-Encoding: quoted-printable'
b'Content-Disposition: inline'
b''
b'Dear Person2,'
```

Retrieving e-mails by using IMAP with imaplib

As we mentioned previously, accessing e-mail over the IMAP protocol doesn't necessarily download the message to the local computer or mobile phone. So, this can be very efficient, even when used over any low bandwidth Internet connection.

Python provides a client-side library called imaplib, which can be used for accessing e-mails over the IMAP protocol. This provides the IMAP4() class, which implements the IMAP protocol. It takes two arguments, that is, host and port for implementing this protocol. By default, 143 has been used as the port number.

The derived class, that is, IMAP4_SSL(), provides a secure version of the IMAP4 protocol. It connects over an SSL encrypted socket. So, you will need an SSL friendly socket module. The default port is 993. Similar to POP3_SSL(), you can supply the path to a private key and a certificate file path.

A typical example of what an IMAP client looks like can be seen here:

```
mailbox = imaplib.IMAP4_SSL(<IMAP_SERVER>, <SERVER_PORT>)
    mailbox.login('username', 'password')
    mailbox.select('Inbox')
```

The aforementioned code will try to initiate an IMAP4 encrypted client session. After the `login()` method is successful, you can apply the various methods on the created object. In the aforementioned code snippet, the `select()` method has been used. This will select a user's mailbox. The default mailbox is called `Inbox`. A full list of methods supported by this mailbox object is available on the Python Standard library documentation page, which can be found at `https://docs.python.org/3/library/imaplib.html`.

Here, we would like to demonstrate how you can search the mailbox by using the `search()` method. It accepts a character set and search criterion parameter. The character set parameter can be `None`, where a request for no specific character will be sent to the server. However, at least one criterion needs to be specified. For performing advance search for sorting the messages, you can use the `sort()` method.

Similar to POP3, we will use a secure IMAP connection for connecting to the server by using the `IMAP4_SSL()` class. Here's a lightweight example of a Python IMAP client:

```python
#!/usr/bin/env python3
import getpass
import imaplib
import pprint

GOOGLE_IMAP_SERVER = 'imap.googlemail.com'
IMAP_SERVER_PORT = '993'

def check_email(username, password):
    mailbox = imaplib.IMAP4_SSL(GOOGLE_IMAP_SERVER,
    IMAP_SERVER_PORT)
    mailbox.login(username, password)
    mailbox.select('Inbox')
```

```
        tmp, data = mailbox.search(None, 'ALL')
        for num in data[0].split():
            tmp, data = mailbox.fetch(num, '(RFC822)')
            print('Message: {0}\n'.format(num))
            pprint.pprint(data[0][1])
            break
        mailbox.close()
        mailbox.logout()


    if __name__ == '__main__':
        username = input("Enter your email username: ")
        password = getpass.getpass(prompt="Enter you account password:
        ")
        check_email(username, password)
```

In this example, an instance of `IMPA4_SSL()`, that is, the mailbox object, has been created. In this, we have taken the server address and port as arguments. Upon successfully logging in with the `login()` method, you can use the `select()` method for choosing the mail box folder that you want to access. In this example, the `Inbox` folder has been selected. In order to read the messages, we need to request for the data from the Inbox. One way to do that is to use the `search()` method. Upon the successful reception of some mail metadata, we can use the `fetch()` method for retrieving the e-mail message envelope part and data. In this example, the RFC 822 type of standard text message has been sought with the help of the `fetch()` method. We can use the Python pretty print or the print module for showing the output on the screen. Finally, apply the `close()` and the `logout()` methods to the mailbox object.

The preceding code will display an output similar to the following:

```
$ python3 fetch_email_imap.py
Enter your email username: RECIPIENT@gmail.comn
Enter you Google password:
Message b'1'
b'X-Gmail-Received:
    3ec65fa310559efe27307d4e37fdc95406deeb5a\r\nDelivered-To:
    RECIPIENT@gmail.com\r\nReceived: by 10.54.40.10 with SMTP id
    n10cs1955wrn;\r\n
    [Message omitted]
```

Sending e-mail attachments

In the previous section, we have seen how plain text messages can be sent by using the SMTP protocol. In this section, let us explore how to send attachments through e-mail messages. We can use our second example, in which we have sent an e-mail by using TLS, for this. While composing the e-mail message, in addition to adding a plain text message, include the additional attachment field.

In this example, we can use the MIMEImage type for the email.mime.image sub-module. A GIF type of image will be attached to the e-mail message. It is assumed that a GIF image can be found anywhere in the file system path. This file path is generally taken on the basis of the user input.

The following example shows how to send an attachment along with your e-mail message:

```python
#!/usr/bin/env python3

import os
import getpass
import re
import sys
import smtplib

from email.mime.image import MIMEImage
from email.mime.multipart import MIMEMultipart
from email.mime.text import MIMEText

SMTP_SERVER = 'aspmx.l.google.com'
SMTP_PORT = 25

def send_email(sender, recipient):
    """ Sends email message """
    msg = MIMEMultipart()
    msg['To'] = recipient
    msg['From'] = sender
    subject = input('Enter your email subject: ')
    msg['Subject'] = subject
    message = input('Enter your email message. Press Enter when
    finished. ')
```

```
        part = MIMEText('text', "plain")
        part.set_payload(message)
        msg.attach(part)
        # attach an image in the current directory
        filename = input('Enter the file name of a GIF image: ')
        path = os.path.join(os.getcwd(), filename)
        if os.path.exists(path):
            img = MIMEImage(open(path, 'rb').read(), _subtype="gif")
            img.add_header('Content-Disposition', 'attachment',
            filename=filename)
            msg.attach(img)
        # create smtp session
        session = smtplib.SMTP(SMTP_SERVER, SMTP_PORT)
        session.ehlo()
        session.starttls()
        session.ehlo
        # send mail
        session.sendmail(sender, recipient, msg.as_string())
        print("You email is sent to {0}.".format(recipient))
        session.quit()

    if __name__ == '__main__':
        sender = input("Enter sender email address: ")
        recipient = input("Enter recipeint email address: ")
        send_email(sender, recipient)
```

If you run the preceding script, then it will ask the usual, that is, the e-mail sender, the recipient, the user credentials, and the location of the image file.

```
$ python3 smtp_mail_sender_mime.py
Enter sender email address: SENDER@gmail.com
Enter recipeint email address: RECIPIENT@gmail.com
Enter your email subject: Test email with attachment
Enter your email message. Press Enter when finished. This is a test email
with atachment.
Enter the file name of a GIF image: image.gif
You email is sent to RECIPIENT@gmail.com.
```

Sending e-mails via the logging module

In any modern programming language, the logging facilities are provided with common features. Similarly, Python's logging module is very rich in features and flexibilities. We can use the different types of log handlers with the logging module, such as the console or the file logging handler. One way in which you can maximize your logging benefits is by e-mailing the log messages to the user just as the log is being produced. Python's logging module provides a type of handler called `BufferingHandler`, which is capable of buffering the log data.

An example of extending `BufferingHandler` has been displayed later. A child class called `BufferingSMTPHandler` is defined by `BufferingHandler`. In this example, an instance of the logger object is created by using the logging module. Then, an instance of `BufferingSMTPHandler` is tied to this logger object. The logging level is set to DEBUG so that it can log any message. A sample list of four words has been used for creating the four log entries. Each log entry should resemble the following:

```
<Timestamp> INFO   First line of log
```

```
This accumulated log message will be emailed to a local user as set
  on top of the script.
```

Now, let us take a look at the full code. The following is an example of sending an e-mail with the help of the logging module:

```
import logging.handlers
import getpass

MAILHOST = 'localhost'
FROM = 'you@yourdomain'
TO = ['%s@localhost' %getpass.getuser()]
SUBJECT = 'Test Logging email from Python logging module
  (buffering)'

class BufferingSMTPHandler(logging.handlers.BufferingHandler):
    def __init__(self, mailhost, fromaddr, toaddrs, subject,
    capacity):
        logging.handlers.BufferingHandler.__init__(self, capacity)
        self.mailhost = mailhost
        self.mailport = None
        self.fromaddr = fromaddr
        self.toaddrs = toaddrs
        self.subject = subject
```

```
        self.setFormatter(logging.Formatter("%(asctime)s
        %(levelname)-5s %(message)s"))

    def flush(self):
        if len(self.buffer) > 0:
            try:
                import smtplib
                port = self.mailport
                if not port:
                    port = smtplib.SMTP_PORT
                smtp = smtplib.SMTP(self.mailhost, port)
                msg = "From: %s\r\nTo: %s\r\nSubject:
                %s\r\n\r\n" % (self.fromaddr,
                    ",".join(self.toaddrs), self.subject)
                for record in self.buffer:
                    s = self.format(record)
                    print(s)
                    msg = msg + s + "\r\n"
                smtp.sendmail(self.fromaddr, self.toaddrs, msg)
                smtp.quit()
            except:
                self.handleError(None) # no particular record
            self.buffer = []

def test():
    logger = logging.getLogger("")
    logger.setLevel(logging.DEBUG)
    logger.addHandler(BufferingSMTPHandler(MAILHOST, FROM, TO,
    SUBJECT, 10))
    for data in ['First', 'Second', 'Third', 'Fourth']:
        logger.info("%s line of log", data)
    logging.shutdown()

if __name__ == "__main__":
    test()
```

As you can see, our BufferingSMTPHandler method only overrides one method, that is, flush(). On the constructor, __init__(), the basic variable is setup as well as the logging format by using the setFormatter() method. In the flush() method, we have created an instance of an SMTP() object. The SMTP message header has been created by using the data available. The log message has been appended to the e-mail message, and the sendmail() method has been called to send the e-mail message. The code in the flush() method is wrapped inside a try-except block.

The output of the script discussed will be similar to the following:

```
$ python3 logger_mail_send.py
2014-10-25 13:15:07,124 INFO  First line of log
2014-10-25 13:15:07,127 INFO  Second line of log
2014-10-25 13:15:07,127 INFO  Third line of log
2014-10-25 13:15:07,129 INFO  Fourth line of log
```

Now, when you check the e-mail message with the e-mail command (native to Linux/UNIX machines), you can expect that the e-mail would have been received by the local user, as shown in the following:

```
$ mail
Mail version 8.1.2 01/15/2001.  Type ? for help.
"/var/mail/faruq": 1 message 1 new
>N  1 you@yourdomain    Sat Oct 25 13:15   20/786    Test Logging
   email from Python logging module (buffering)
```

You can view the content of the message by typing the message ID on the command prompt with &, as shown in the following output:

```
& 1
Message 1:
From you@yourdomain Sat Oct 25 13:15:08 2014
Envelope-to: faruq@localhost
Delivery-date: Sat, 25 Oct 2014 13:15:08 +0100
Date: Sat, 25 Oct 2014 13:15:07 +0100
From: you@yourdomain
To: faruq@localhost
Subject: Test Logging email from Python logging module (buffering)

2014-10-25 13:15:07,124 INFO  First line of log
2014-10-25 13:15:07,127 INFO  Second line of log
2014-10-25 13:15:07,127 INFO  Third line of log
2014-10-25 13:15:07,129 INFO  Fourth line of log
```

Finally, you can quit the mail program by typing the shortcut q on the command prompt, as shown here:

```
& q
Saved 1 message in /home/faruq/mbox
```

Summary

This chapter demonstrates how Python can interact with the three major e-mail handling protocols: SMTP, POP3, and IMAP. In each of these cases, how to work the client code has been explained. Finally, an example for using SMTP in the Python's logging module has been shown.

In the next chapter, you will learn how to use Python to work with remote systems to perform various tasks, such as administrative tasks by using SSH, file transfer through FTP, Samba, and so forth. Some remote monitoring protocols, such as SNMP, and the authentication protocols, such as LDAP, will also be discussed briefly. So, enjoy writing more Python codes in the next chapter.

5
Interacting with Remote Systems

If your computer is connected to the Internet or a **local area network (LAN)**, then it's time to talk to the other computers on the network. In a typical home, office, or campus LAN, you will find that many different types of computers are connected to the network. Some computers act as the servers for specific services, such as a file server, a print server, a user authentication management server, and so on. In this chapter, we will explore how the computers in a network can interact with each other and how they can access a few services through the Python scripts. The following task list will give you an overview of the topics that will be covered in this chapter:

- Accessing SSH terminals with `paramiko`
- Transferring files through SFTP
- Transferring files with the help of FTP
- Reading the SNMP packets
- Reading the LDAP packets
- Sharing the files with the help of SAMBA

This chapter requires quite a few third-party packages, such as `paramiko`, `pysnmp`, and so on. You can use your operating system's package management tool for installing them. Here's a quick how-to on installing the `paramiko` module in Ubuntu 14, python3, and the other modules that are required for understanding the topics covered in this chapter:

```
sudo apt-get install python3
sudo apt-get install python3-setuptools
sudo easy_install3 paramiko
sudo easy_install3 python3-ldap
sudo easy_install3 pysnmp
sudo easy_install3 pysmb
```

Secure shell – access using Python

SSH has become a very popular network protocol for performing secure data communication between two computers. It provides an excellent cryptographic support, so that unrelated third-parties cannot see the content of the data during the transmission process. Details of the SSH protocol can be found in these RFC documents: RFC4251-RFC4254, available at `http://www.rfc-editor.org/rfc/rfc4251.txt`.

Python's `paramiko` library provides a very good support for the SSH-based network communication. You can use Python scripts to benefit from the advantages of SSH-based remote administration, such as the remote command-line login, command execution, and the other secure network services between two networked computers. You may also be interested in using the `pysftp` module, which is based on `paramiko`. More details regarding this package can be found at PyPI: `https://pypi.python.org/pypi/pysftp/`.

The SSH is a client/server protocol. Both of the parties use the SSH key pairs to encrypt the communication. Each key pair has one private and one public key. The public key can be published to anyone who may be interested in that. The private key is always kept private and secure from everyone except the owner of the key.

The SSH public and private keys can be generated and digitally signed by an external or an internal certificate authority. But that brings a lot of overhead to a small organization. So, alternatively, the keys can be generated randomly by utility tools, such as `ssh-keygen`. The public key needs to be available to all participating parties. When the SSH client connects to the server for the first time, it registers the public key of the server on a special file called `~/.ssh/known_hosts` file. So, the subsequent connection to the server ensures that the client is talking to the same server as it spoke to before. On the server side, if you would like to restrict access to certain clients who have certain IP addresses, then the public keys of the permitted hosts can be stored to another special file called `ssh_known_hosts` file. Of course, if you re-build the machines, such as the server machine, then the old public key of the server won't match with that of the one stored in the `~/.ssh/known_hosts` file. So, the SSH client will raise an exception and prevent you from connecting to it. You can delete the old key from that file and then try to re-connect, as if for the first time.

We can use the `paramiko` module to create an SSH client and then connect it to the SSH server. This module will supply the `SSHClient()` class.

```
ssh_client = paramiko.SSHClient()
```

By default, the instance of this client class will reject the unknown host keys. So, you can set up a policy for accepting the unknown host keys. The built-in `AutoAddPolicy()` class will add the host keys as and when they are discovered. Now, you need to run the `set_missing_host_key_policy()` method along with the following argument on the `ssh_client` object.

```
ssh_client.set_missing_host_key_policy(paramiko.AutoAddPolicy())
```

If, you want to restrict connecting only to certain hosts, then you can define your own policy and replace it with the `AutoAddPolicy()` class.

You may also be interested in adding the system host keys by using the `load_system_host_keys()` method.

```
ssh_client.load_system_host_keys()
```

So far, we have discussed how to encrypt the connection. However, SSH needs your authentication credentials. This means that the client needs to prove to the server that a specific user is talking, not someone else. This can be done in a few ways. The simplest way is by using the username and the password combination. Another popular way is by using the key-based authentication method. This means that the user's public key can be copied to the server. There's a specific tool for doing that. This comes with the later versions of the SSH. Here's an example of how to use `ssh-copy-id`.

`ssh-copy-id -i ~/.ssh/id_rsa.pub faruq@debian6box.localdomain.loc`

This command will copy the SSH public key of the faruq user to a machine, `debian6box.localdomain.loc`:

Here, we can simply call the `connect()` method along with the target hostname and the SSH login credentials. To run any command on the target host, we need to invoke the `exec_command()` method by passing the command as its argument.

```
ssh_client.connect(hostname, port, username, password)
stdin, stdout, stderr = ssh_client.exec_command(cmd)
```

The following code listing shows how to do SSH login to a target host and then run a simple `ls` command:

```
#!/usr/bin/env python3

import getpass
import paramiko
```

```
HOSTNAME = 'localhost'
PORT = 22

def run_ssh_cmd(username, password, cmd, hostname=HOSTNAME,
    port=PORT):
    ssh_client = paramiko.SSHClient()
    ssh_client.set_missing_host_key_policy(\
        paramiko.AutoAddPolicy())
    ssh_client.load_system_host_keys()
    ssh_client.connect(hostname, port, username, password)
    stdin, stdout, stderr = ssh_client.exec_command(cmd)
    print(stdout.read())

if __name__ == '__main__':
    username = input("Enter username: ")
    password = getpass.getpass(prompt="Enter password: ")
    cmd = 'ls -l /dev'
    run_ssh_cmd(username, password, cmd)
```

Before running it, we need to ensure that the SSH server daemon is running on the target host (which in this case is the localhost). As shown in the following screenshot, we can use the netstat command for doing that. This command will show all the running services that are listening to a particular port:

The preceding script will make an SSH connection to the localhost and the run the `ls -l /dev/` command. The output of this script will be similar to the following screenshot:

```
faruq@debian6box: ~/projects/learnpynet/ch5
File  Edit  View  Terminal  Help
faruq@debian6box:ch5$
faruq@debian6box:ch5$ python 5_1_ssh_with_paramiko.py
Enter username: faruq
Enter password:
Command: ls -l /dev
stdout:
total 0
drwxr-xr-x  2 root root         300 Jan  8 04:50 block
drwxr-xr-x  2 root root          80 Jan  8 04:50 bsg
drwxr-xr-x  3 root root          60 Jan  8 04:50 bus
lrwxrwxrwx  1 root root           3 Jan  8 04:50 cdrom -> sr0
drwxr-xr-x  2 root root        2720 Jan 14 18:38 char
crw-------  1 root root       5,   1 Jan  8 04:51 console
lrwxrwxrwx  1 root root          11 Jan  8 04:50 core -> /proc/kcore
crw-------  1 root root      10,  62 Jan  8 04:50 cpu_dma_latency
drwxr-xr-x  6 root root         120 Jan  8 04:50 disk
```

Inspecting the SSH packets

It would be very interesting to see the network packet exchange between the client and the server. We can use either the native `tcpdump` command or the third-party Wireshark tool to capture network packets. With `tcpdump`, you can specify the target network interface (`-i lo`) and the port number (port 22) options. In the following packet capture session, five packet exchanges have been shown during an SSH client/server communication session:

```
root@debian6box:~# tcpdump -i lo port 22

tcpdump: verbose output suppressed, use -v or -vv for full protocol
  decode

listening on lo, link-type EN10MB (Ethernet), capture size 65535
  bytes

12:18:19.761292 IP localhost.50768 > localhost.ssh: Flags [S], seq
  3958510356, win 32792, options [mss 16396,sackOK,TS val 57162360
  ecr 0,nop,wscale 6], length 0

12:18:19.761335 IP localhost.ssh > localhost.50768: Flags [S.], seq
  1834733028, ack 3958510357, win 32768, options [mss 16396,sackOK,TS
  val 57162360 ecr 57162360,nop,wscale 6], length 0

12:18:19.761376 IP localhost.50768 > localhost.ssh: Flags [.], ack 1,
  win 513, options [nop,nop,TS val 57162360 ecr 57162360], length 0
```

```
12:18:19.769430 IP localhost.50768 > localhost.ssh: Flags [P.], seq
  1:25, ack 1, win 513, options [nop,nop,TS val 57162362 ecr
  57162360], length 24
```

```
12:18:19.769467 IP localhost.ssh > localhost.50768: Flags [.], ack
  25, win 512, options [nop,nop,TS val 57162362 ecr 57162362], length
  0
```

Although, it's very quick and easy to run `tcpdump`, the command does not interpret it in the same way as the other GUI tools, such as Wireshark, interpret it. The preceding session can be captured in Wireshark, as shown in the following screenshot:

Protocol	Info
TCP	50768 > 22 [SYN] Seq=0 Win=32792 Len=0 MSS=16396 TSV=57162360 TSER=0 WS=6
TCP	22 > 50768 [SYN, ACK] Seq=0 Ack=1 Win=32768 Len=0 MSS=16396 TSV=57162360 TSER=57162360 WS
TCP	50768 > 22 [ACK] Seq=1 Ack=1 Win=32832 Len=0 TSV=57162360 TSER=57162360
SSH	Client Protocol: SSH-2.0-paramiko_1.7.6\r
TCP	22 > 50768 [ACK] Seq=1 Ack=25 Win=32768 Len=0 TSV=57162362 TSER=57162362
SSHv2	Server Protocol: SSH-2.0-OpenSSH_5.5p1 Debian-6+squeeze5\r
TCP	50768 > 22 [ACK] Seq=25 Ack=42 Win=32832 Len=0 TSV=57162369 TSER=57162369
SSHv2	Client: Key Exchange Init
SSHv2	Server: Key Exchange Init
TCP	50768 > 22 [ACK] Seq=441 Ack=826 Win=34368 Len=0 TSV=57162382 TSER=57162372
SSHv2	Client: Diffie-Hellman Key Exchange Init
TCP	22 > 50768 [ACK] Seq=826 Ack=585 Win=34944 Len=0 TSV=57162421 TSER=57162411
SSHv2	Server: New Keys
TCP	50768 > 22 [ACK] Seq=585 Ack=1546 Win=35968 Len=0 TSV=57162447 TSER=57162447
SSHv2	Client: New Keys
TCP	22 > 50768 [ACK] Seq=1546 Ack=601 Win=34944 Len=0 TSV=57162522 TSER=57162522
TCP	[TCP segment of a reassembled PDU]
TCP	22 > 50768 [ACK] Seq=1546 Ack=653 Win=34944 Len=0 TSV=57162527 TSER=57162527
TCP	[TCP segment of a reassembled PDU]
TCP	50768 > 22 [ACK] Seq=653 Ack=1598 Win=35968 Len=0 TSV=57162527 TSER=57162527
TCP	50768 > 22 [PSH, ACK] Seq=653 Ack=1598 Win=35968 Len=644 TSV=57162550 TSER=57162527[Malfc
TCP	22 > 50768 [PSH, ACK] Seq=1598 Ack=1297 Win=36224 Len=68 TSV=57162553 TSER=57162550[Malfc
TCP	50768 > 22 [ACK] Seq=1297 Ack=1666 Win=35968 Len=0 TSV=57162553 TSER=57162553

This clearly shows how the first three packets complete the TCP handshake process. Then, the subsequent SSH packets negotiate the connection between the client and the server. It's interesting to see how the client and the server negotiate the encryption protocols. In this example, the client port is `50768` and the server port is `22`. The client first initiates the SSH packet exchange and then indicates that it would like to talk over the `SSHv2` protocol. Then, the server agrees on that and continues the packet exchange.

Transferring files through SFTP

SSH can be used effectively for securely transferring files between two computer nodes. The protocol used in this case is the **secure file transfer protocol (SFTP)**. The Python `paramiko` module will supply the classes required for creating the SFTP session. This session can then perform a regular SSH login.

```
ssh_transport = paramiko.Transport(hostname, port)
ssh_transport.connect(username='username', password='password')
```

The SFTP session can be created from the SSH transport. The paramiko's working in the SFTP session will support the normal FTP commands such as `get()`.

```
sftp_session = paramiko.SFTPClient.from_transport(ssh_transport)
sftp_session.get(source_file, target_file)
```

As you can see, the SFTP `get` command requires the source file's path and the target file's path. In the following example, the script will download a `test.txt` file, which is located on the user's home directory, through SFTP:

```python
#!/usr/bin/env python3

import getpass
import paramiko

HOSTNAME = 'localhost'
PORT = 22
FILE_PATH = '/tmp/test.txt'

def sftp_download(username, password, hostname=HOSTNAME,
    port=PORT):
    ssh_transport = paramiko.Transport(hostname, port)
    ssh_transport.connect(username=username, password=password)
    sftp_session =
    paramiko.SFTPClient.from_transport(ssh_transport)
    file_path = input("Enter filepath: ") or FILE_PATH
    target_file = file_path.split('/')[-1]
    sftp_session.get(file_path, target_file)
    print("Downloaded file from: %s" %file_path)
    sftp_session.close()

if __name__ == '__main__':
    hostname = input("Enter the target hostname: ")
    port = input("Enter the target port: ")
    username = input("Enter yur username: ")
    password = getpass.getpass(prompt="Enter your password: ")
    sftp_download(username, password, hostname, int(port))
```

In this example, a file has been downloaded with the help of SFTP. Notice, how paramiko has created the SFTP session by using the SFTPClient.from_ transport(ssh_transport) class.

The script can be run as shown in the following screenshot. Here, we will first create a temporary file called /tmp/test.txt, then complete the SSH login, and then download that file by using SFTP. Lastly, we will check the content of the file.

```
root@localhost: ~/learnpynet/ch5
File  Edit  View  Search  Terminal  Help
[root@localhost ch5]# echo 'This is a test file' > /tmp/test.txt
[root@localhost ch5]# python 5_2_sftp_file_transfer.py
Enter the target hostname: localhost
Enter the target port: 22
Enter yur username: faruq
Enter your password:
Enter filepath: /tmp/test.txt
Downloaded file from: /tmp/test.txt
[root@localhost ch5]# cat /tmp/test.txt
This is a test file
[root@localhost ch5]#
```

Transferring files with FTP

Unlike SFTP, FTP uses the plain-text file transfer method. This means any username or password transferred through the wire can be detected by an unrelated third-party. Even though FTP is a very popular file transfer protocol, people frequently use this for transferring a file from their PCs to the remote servers.

In Python, ftplib is a built-in module used for transferring the files to and from the remote machines. You can create an anonymous FTP client connection with the FTP() class.

```
ftp_client = ftplib.FTP(path, username, email)
```

Then you can invoke the normal FTP commands, such as CWD. In order to download a binary file, you need to create a file-handler such as the following:

```
file_handler = open(DOWNLOAD_FILE_NAME, 'wb')
```

In order to retrieve the binary file from the remote host, the syntax shown here can be used along with the RETR command:

```
ftp_client.retrbinary('RETR remote_file_name', file_handler.write)
```

In the following code snippet, an example of a full FTP file download can be seen:

```python
#!/usr/bin/env python
import ftplib


FTP_SERVER_URL = 'ftp.kernel.org'
DOWNLOAD_DIR_PATH = '/pub/software/network/tftp'
DOWNLOAD_FILE_NAME = 'tftp-hpa-0.11.tar.gz'


def ftp_file_download(path, username, email):
    # open ftp connection
    ftp_client = ftplib.FTP(path, username, email)
    # list the files in the download directory
    ftp_client.cwd(DOWNLOAD_DIR_PATH)
    print("File list at %s:" %path)
    files = ftp_client.dir()
    print(files)
    # downlaod a file
    file_handler = open(DOWNLOAD_FILE_NAME, 'wb')
    #ftp_cmd = 'RETR %s ' %DOWNLOAD_FILE_NAME
    ftp_client.retrbinary('RETR tftp-hpa-0.11.tar.gz',
    file_handler.write)
    file_handler.close()
    ftp_client.quit()


if __name__ == '__main__':
    ftp_file_download(path=FTP_SERVER_URL,   username='anonymous',
        email='nobody@nourl.com')
```

The preceding code illustrates how an anonymous FTP can be downloaded from `ftp.kernel.org`, which is the official website that hosts the Linux kernel. The `FTP()` class takes three arguments, such as the initial filesystem path on the remote server, the username, and the email address of the `ftp` user. For anonymous downloads, no username and password is required. So, the script can be downloaded from the `tftp-hpa-0.11.tar.gz` file, which can be found on the `/pub/software/network/tftp` path.

Inspecting FTP packets

If we capture the FTP session in Wireshark on port 21 of the public network interface, then we can see how the communication happens in plain-text. This will show you why SFTP should be preferred. In the following figure, we can see that, after successfully establishing connection with a client the server sends the banner message: 220 Welcome to kernel.org. Following this, the client will anonymously send a request for login. In response, the server will ask for a password. The client can send the user's e-mail address for authentication.

Source	Destination	Protocol	Info
10.0.2.15	199.204.44.	TCP	36688 > 21 [SYN] Seq=0 Win=5840 Len=0 MSS=1460 TSV=57325322 TSER=0 WS=6
199.204.44.	10.0.2.15	TCP	21 > 36688 [SYN, ACK] Seq=0 Ack=1 Win=65535 Len=0 MSS=1460
10.0.2.15	199.204.44.	TCP	36688 > 21 [ACK] Seq=1 Ack=1 Win=5840 Len=0
199.204.44.	10.0.2.15	FTP	Response: 220 Welcome to kernel.org
10.0.2.15	199.204.44.	TCP	36688 > 21 [ACK] Seq=1 Ack=28 Win=5840 Len=0
10.0.2.15	199.204.44.	FTP	Request: USER anonymous
199.204.44.	10.0.2.15	TCP	21 > 36688 [ACK] Seq=28 Ack=17 Win=65535 Len=0
199.204.44.	10.0.2.15	FTP	Response: 331 Please specify the password.
10.0.2.15	199.204.44.	FTP	Request: PASS nobody@nourl.com
199.204.44.	10.0.2.15	TCP	21 > 36688 [ACK] Seq=62 Ack=40 Win=65535 Len=0
199.204.44.	10.0.2.15	FTP	Response: 230 Login successful.
10.0.2.15	199.204.44.	FTP	Request: CWD /pub/software/network/tftp
199.204.44.	10.0.2.15	TCP	21 > 36688 [ACK] Seq=85 Ack=72 Win=65535 Len=0
199.204.44.	10.0.2.15	FTP	Response: 250 Directory successfully changed.
10.0.2.15	199.204.44.	FTP	Request: TYPE A
199.204.44.	10.0.2.15	TCP	21 > 36688 [ACK] Seq=122 Ack=80 Win=65535 Len=0
199.204.44.	10.0.2.15	FTP	Response: 200 Switching to ASCII mode.
10.0.2.15	199.204.44.	FTP	Request: PASV
199.204.44.	10.0.2.15	TCP	21 > 36688 [ACK] Seq=152 Ack=86 Win=65535 Len=0
199.204.44.	10.0.2.15	FTP	Response: 227 Entering Passive Mode (199,204,44,194,118,250)
10.0.2.15	199.204.44.	TCP	36688 > 21 [ACK] Seq=86 Ack=204 Win=5840 Len=0
10.0.2.15	199.204.44.	FTP	Request: LIST
199.204.44.	10.0.2.15	TCP	21 > 36688 [ACK] Seq=204 Ack=92 Win=65535 Len=0
199.204.44.	10.0.2.15	FTP	Response: 150 Here comes the directory listing.
10.0.2.15	199.204.44.	TCP	36688 > 21 [ACK] Seq=92 Ack=243 Win=5840 Len=0
199.204.44.	10.0.2.15	FTP	Response: 226 Directory send OK.
10.0.2.15	199.204.44.	TCP	36688 > 21 [ACK] Seq=92 Ack=267 Win=5840 Len=0
10.0.2.15	199.204.44.	FTP	Request: TYPE I

To your surprise, you can see that the password has been sent in clear-text. In the following screenshot, the contents of the password packet have been displayed. It shows the supplied fake e-mail address, nobody@nourl.com.

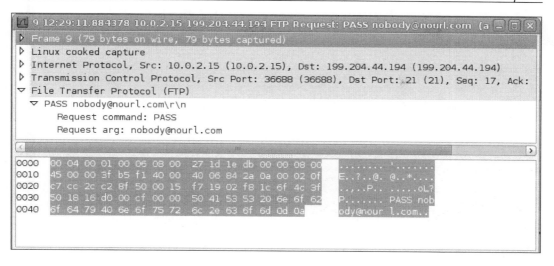

Fetching Simple Network Management Protocol data

SNMP is a ubiquitous network protocol that is used by the network routers, such as switches, servers, and so on, for communicating the device's configuration, performance data, and the commands that are meant for the control devices. Although SNMP starts with the word *simple,* it's not a simple protocol. Internally, each device's information is stored in a sort of a database of information called the **management information base (MIB)**. The SNMP protocol offers varying levels of security depending on the protocol version number. In SNMP v1 and v2c, the data is protected by a pass phrase known as the community string. In SNMP v3, a username and a password are required for storing the data. And, the data can be encrypted with the help of SSL. In our example, we will use the v1 and v2c versions of the SNMP protocol.

SNMP is a client/server-based network protocol. The server daemon provides the requested information to the clients. In your machine, if SNMP has been installed and configured properly, then you can use the `snmpwalk` utility command to query the basic system information by using the following syntax:

```
# snmpwalk -v2c -c public localhost
iso.3.6.1.2.1.1.1.0 = STRING: "Linux debian6box 2.6.32-5-686 #1 SMP
  Tue May 13 16:33:32 UTC 2014 i686"
iso.3.6.1.2.1.1.2.0 = OID: iso.3.6.1.4.1.8072.3.2.10
iso.3.6.1.2.1.1.3.0 = Timeticks: (88855240) 10 days, 6:49:12.40
iso.3.6.1.2.1.1.4.0 = STRING: "Me <me@example.org>"
iso.3.6.1.2.1.1.5.0 = STRING: "debian6box"
iso.3.6.1.2.1.1.6.0 = STRING: "Sitting on the Dock of the Bay"
```

The output of the preceding command will show the MIB number and its values. For example, the MIB number `iso.3.6.1.2.1.1.1.0` shows that it's a string type value, such as `Linux debian6box 2.6.32-5-686 #1 SMP Tue May 13 16:33:32 UTC 2014 i686`.

In Python, you can use a third-party library called `pysnmp` for interfacing with the `snmp` daemon. You can install the `pysnmp` module by using pip.

```
$ pip install pysnmp
```

This module provides a useful wrapper for the `snmp` commands. Let's learn how to create an `snmpwalk` command. To begin, import a command generator.

```
from pysnmp.entity.rfc3413.oneliner import cmdgen
cmd_generator = cmdgen.CommandGenerator()
```

Then define the necessary default values for the connection assuming that the `snmpd` daemon has been running on port `161` of the local machine and the community string has been set to public.

```
SNMP_HOST = 'localhost'
SNMP_PORT = 161
SNMP_COMMUNITY = 'public'
```

Now invoke the `getCmd()` method with the help of the necessary data.

```
error_notify, error_status, error_index, var_binds =
cmd_generator.getCmd(
    cmdgen.CommunityData(SNMP_COMMUNITY),
    cmdgen.UdpTransportTarget((SNMP_HOST, SNMP_PORT)),
    cmdgen.MibVariable('SNMPv2-MIB', 'sysDescr', 0),
    lookupNames=True, lookupValues=True
)
```

You can see that `cmdgen` takes the following parameters:

- `CommunityData()`: Set the community string as public.
- `UdpTransportTarget()`: This is the host target, where the `snmp` agent is running. This is specified in a pair of the hostname and the UDP port.
- `MibVariable`: This is a tuple of values that includes the MIB version number and the MIB target string (which in this case is `sysDescr`; this refers to the description of the system).

The output of this command consists of a four-value tuple. Out of those, three are related to the errors returned by the command generator, and the fourth one is related to the actual variables that bind the returned data.

The following example shows how the preceding method can be used for fetching the SNMP host description string from a running SNMP daemon:

```
from pysnmp.entity.rfc3413.oneliner import cmdgen

SNMP_HOST = 'localhost'
SNMP_PORT = 161
SNMP_COMMUNITY = 'public'

if __name__ == '__manin__':
    cmd_generator = cmdgen.CommandGenerator()

    error_notify, error_status, error_index, var_binds =
    cmd_generator.getCmd(
        cmdgen.CommunityData(SNMP_COMMUNITY),
        cmdgen.UdpTransportTarget((SNMP_HOST, SNMP_PORT)),
        cmdgen.MibVariable('SNMPv2-MIB', 'sysDescr', 0),
        lookupNames=True, lookupValues=True
    )

    # Check for errors and print out results
    if error_notify:
        print(error_notify)
    elif error_status:
        print(error_status)
    else:
        for name, val in var_binds:
            print('%s = %s' % (name.prettyPrint(),
            val.prettyPrint()))
```

After running the preceding example, an output similar to the following will appear:

```
$ python 5_4_snmp_read.py
SNMPv2-MIB::sysDescr."0" = Linux debian6box 2.6.32-5-686 #1 SMP Tue
   May 13 16:33:32 UTC 2014 i686
```

Inspecting SNMP packets

We can inspect the SNMP packet by capturing the packets on port 161 of your network interface. If the server is running locally, then listening on the loopbook interface is sufficient. The snmp-get request format and the snmp-get response packet formats, which are produced by Wireshak, is shown in the following screenshot:

In response to the SNMP get request from the client, an SNMP get response will be generated by the server. This can be seen in the following screenshot:

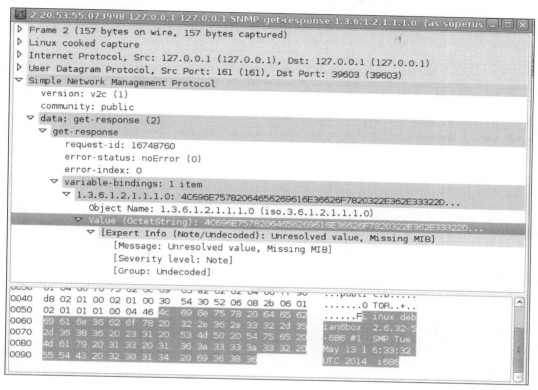

Reading Light-weight Directory Access Protocol data

LDAP has been used for a long time for accessing and managing distributed directory information. This is an application level protocol that works over the IP network. Directory service is heavily used in organizations for managing the information about the users, the computer systems, the networks, the applications, and so on. The LDAP protocol contains plenty of technical jargon. It is a client/server-based protocol. So, the LDAP client will make a request to a properly configured LDAP server. After initializing the LDAP connection, the connection will need to be authenticated by using a few parameters. A simple BIND operation will establish an LDAP session. In a simple case, you can set up a simple anonymous BIND that would not need no password or any other credentials.

If you a run a simple LDAP query with the help of `ldapsearch`, then you will see results such as:

```
# ldapsearch  -x -b "dc=localdomain,dc=loc" -h 10.0.2.15 -p 389


# extended LDIF
#
# LDAPv3
# base <dc=localdomain,dc=loc> with scope subtree
# filter: (objectclass=*)
# requesting: ALL
#


# localdomain.loc
dn: dc=localdomain,dc=loc
objectClass: top
objectClass: dcObject
objectClass: organization
o: localdomain.loc
dc: localdomain


# admin, localdomain.loc
dn: cn=admin,dc=localdomain,dc=loc
objectClass: simpleSecurityObject
objectClass: organizationalRole
cn: admin
description: LDAP administrator
# groups, localdomain.loc
dn: ou=groups,dc=localdomain,dc=loc
ou: groups
objectClass: organizationalUnit
objectClass: top
```

```
# users, localdomain.loc
dn: ou=users,dc=localdomain,dc=loc
ou: users
objectClass: organizationalUnit
objectClass: top

# admin, groups, localdomain.loc
dn: cn=admin,ou=groups,dc=localdomain,dc=loc
cn: admin
gidNumber: 501
objectClass: posixGroup

# Faruque Sarker, users, localdomain.loc
dn: cn=Faruque Sarker,ou=users,dc=localdomain,dc=loc
givenName: Faruque
sn: Sarker
cn: Faruque Sarker
uid: fsarker
uidNumber: 1001
gidNumber: 501
homeDirectory: /home/users/fsarker
loginShell: /bin/sh
objectClass: inetOrgPerson
objectClass: posixAccount

# search result
search: 2
result: 0 Success

# numResponses: 7
# numEntries: 6
```

The preceding communication can be captured with the help of Wireshark. You need to capture the packets on port 389. As shown in the following screenshot, the LDAP client-server communication will be established after a `bindRequest` has been successfully sent. It's not secure to communicate anonymously with the LDAP server. For the sake of simplicity, in the following example the search has been done without binding with any of the credentials.

Protocol	Info
TCP	43101 > 389 [SYN] Seq=0 Win=32792 Len=0 MSS=16396 TSV=58228296 TSER=0 WS=6
TCP	389 > 43101 [SYN, ACK] Seq=0 Ack=1 Win=32768 Len=0 MSS=16396 TSV=58228296 TSER=58228296 WS=6
TCP	43101 > 389 [ACK] Seq=1 Ack=1 Win=32832 Len=0 TSV=58228296 TSER=58228296
LDAP	bindRequest(1) "dc=localdomain,dc=loc" simple
TCP	389 > 43101 [ACK] Seq=1 Ack=36 Win=32768 Len=0 TSV=58228297 TSER=58228297
LDAP	bindResponse(1) unwillingToPerform (unauthenticated bind (DN with no password) disallowed)
TCP	43101 > 389 [ACK] Seq=36 Ack=68 Win=32832 Len=0 TSV=58228297 TSER=58228297
LDAP	searchRequest(2) "ou=users,dc=localdomain,dc=loc" wholeSubtree
LDAP	searchResEntry(2) "cn=Faruque Sarker,ou=users,dc=localdomain,dc=loc"
LDAP	searchResDone(2) success [1 result]
TCP	43101 > 389 [ACK] Seq=119 Ack=157 Win=32832 Len=0 TSV=58228298 TSER=58228297
LDAP	unbindRequest(3)
TCP	389 > 43101 [FIN, ACK] Seq=157 Ack=126 Win=32768 Len=0 TSV=58228300 TSER=58228300
TCP	43101 > 389 [FIN, ACK] Seq=126 Ack=158 Win=32832 Len=0 TSV=58228301 TSER=58228300
TCP	389 > 43101 [ACK] Seq=158 Ack=127 Win=32768 Len=0 TSV=58228301 TSER=58228301

The Python's third-party `python-ldap` package provides the necessary functionality for interacting with an LDAP server. You can install this package with the help of `pip`.

```
$ pip install python-ldap
```

To begin with, you will have to initialize the LDAP connection:

```
import ldap
    ldap_client = ldap.initialize("ldap://10.0.2.15:389/")
```

Then the following code will show how a simple BIND operation can be performed:

```
    ldap_client.simple_bind("dc=localdomain,dc=loc")
```

Then you can perform an ldap search. It requires you to specify the necessary parameters, such as base DN, filter, and attributes. Here is an example of the syntax that is required for searching for the users on an LDAP server:

```
    ldap_client.search_s( base_dn, ldap.SCOPE_SUBTREE, filter, attrs )
```

Here is a complete example for finding user information by using the LDAP protocol:

```
    import ldap

    # Open a connection
    ldap_client = ldap.initialize("ldap://10.0.2.15:389/")
```

```
# Bind/authenticate with a user with apropriate rights to add
  objects

ldap_client.simple_bind("dc=localdomain,dc=loc")

base_dn = 'ou=users,dc=localdomain,dc=loc'
filter = '(objectclass=person)'
attrs = ['sn']

result = ldap_client.search_s( base_dn, ldap.SCOPE_SUBTREE,
    filter, attrs )
print(result)
```

The preceding code will search the LDAP directory subtree with the
ou=users,dc=localdomain,dc=loc base DN and the [sn] attributes.
The search is limited to the person objects.

Inspecting LDAP packets

If we analyze the communication between the LDAP client and the server, then we
can see the format of the LDAP search request and response. The parameters that we
have used in our code have a direct relationship with the searchRequest section of
an LDAP packet. As shown in the following screenshot produced by Wireshark, it
contains data, such as baseObject, scope and Filter.

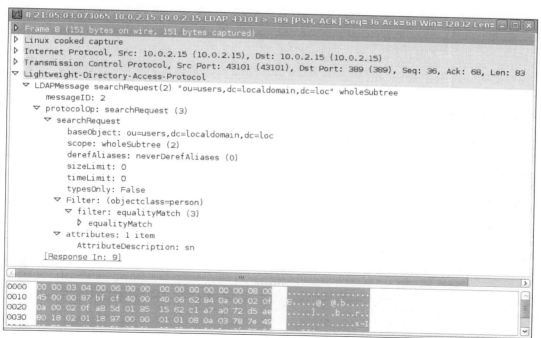

The LDAP search request generates a server response, which has been shown here:

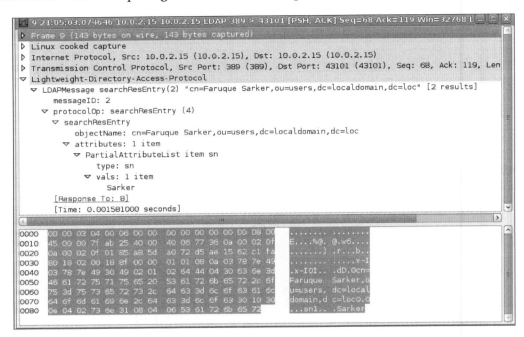

When the LDAP server returns the search response, we can see the format of the response. As shown in the preceding screenshot, it contains the result of the search and the associated attributes.

Here is an example of searching a user from an LDAP server:

```python
#!/usr/bin/env python
import ldap
import ldap.modlist as modlist

LDAP_URI = "ldap://10.0.2.15:389/"
BIND_TO = "dc=localdomain,dc=loc"
BASE_DN = 'ou=users,dc=localdomain,dc=loc'
SEARCH_FILTER = '(objectclass=person)'
SEARCH_FILTER = ['sn']

if __name__ == '__main__':
    # Open a connection
    l = ldap.initialize(LDAP_URI)
    # bind to the server
    l.simple_bind(BIND_TO)
    result = l.search_s( BASE_DN, ldap.SCOPE_SUBTREE,
    SEARCH_FILTER,  SEARCH_FILTER )
    print(result)
```

In a properly configured LDAP machine, the preceding script will return a result that will be similar to the following:

```
$ python 5_5_ldap_read_record.py
[('cn=Faruque Sarker,ou=users,dc=localdomain,dc=loc', {'sn':
   ['Sarker']})]
```

Sharing files with SAMBA

In a LAN environment, you will often need to share the files between different types of machines, such as Windows and Linux machines. The protocol used for sharing the files and the printers among these machines is either the **Server Message Block (SMB)** protocol or its enhanced version called the **Common Internet File System (CIFS)** protocol. CIFS runs over TCP/IP and it is used by the SMB clients and servers. In Linux, you will find a package called Samba, which implements the SMB protocol.

If you are running a Linux virtual machine within a Windows box with the help of software, such as VirtualBox, then we can test file sharing among the Windows and the Linux machines. Let us create a folder at `C:\share` on the Windows machine as you can see in the following screenshot:

Now, right-click on the folder and then go to the **Sharing** tab. There are two buttons: **Share** and **Advanced sharing**. You can click on the latter and it will open the advanced sharing dialog box. Now you can adjust the share permissions. If this share is active, then you will be able to see this share from your Linux virtual machine. If you run the following command on your Linux box, then you will see the previously defined file-share:

```
$smbclient -L 10.0.2.2 -U WINDOWS_USERNAME%PASSWPRD  -W WORKGROUP
Domain=[FARUQUESARKER] OS=[Windows 8 9200] Server=[Windows 8 6.2]

        Sharename       Type        Comment
        ---------       ----        -------
        ADMIN$          Disk        Remote Admin
        C$              Disk        Default share
        IPC$            IPC         Remote IPC
        Share           Disk
```

The following screenshot shows how you can share a folder under Windows 7 as discussed previously:

The preceding file share can be accessed from your Python script by using a third-party module called pysmb. You can use the pip command-line tool for installing pysmb:

```
$ pip install pysmb
```

This module provides an SMBConnection class, where you can pass the necessary parameters for accessing an SMB/CIFS share. For example, the following code will help you to access a file-share:

```
from smb.SMBConnection import SMBConnection
smb_connection = SMBConnection(username, password,
    client_machine_name, server_name, use_ntlm_v2 = True,
    domain='WORKGROUP', is_direct_tcp=True)
```

If the preceding works, then the following assertion will be true:

```
assert smb_connection.connect(server_ip, 445)
```

You can list the shared files by using the listShares() method:

```
shares =   smb_connection.listShares()
for share in shares:
    print share.name
```

If you can use the tmpfile module copying a file from your windows share. For example, if you create a file in the C:\Share\test.rtf path, then the additional code shown here will copy that file by using the SMB protocol:

```
import tempfile
files = smb_connection.listPath(share.name, '/')

for file in files:
    print file.filename

file_obj = tempfile.NamedTemporaryFile()
file_attributes, filesize = smb_connection.retrieveFile('Share',
    '/test.rtf', file_obj)
file_obj.close()
```

If we put the entire code into a single source file, then it will look like the following listing:

```
#!/usr/bin/env python
import tempfile
from smb.SMBConnection import SMBConnection

SAMBA_USER_ID = 'FaruqueSarker'
PASSWORD = 'PASSWORD'
CLIENT_MACHINE_NAME = 'debian6box'
SAMBA_SERVER_NAME = 'FARUQUESARKER'
SERVER_IP = '10.0.2.2'
```

```
SERVER_PORT = 445
SERVER_SHARE_NAME = 'Share'
SHARED_FILE_PATH = '/test.rtf'


if __name__ == '__main__':

    smb_connection = SMBConnection(SAMBA_USER_ID, PASSWORD,
    CLIENT_MACHINE_NAME, SAMBA_SERVER_NAME, use_ntlm_v2 = True,
    domain='WORKGROUP', is_direct_tcp=True)
    assert smb_connection.smb_connectionect(SERVER_IP, SERVER_PORT
    = 445)
    shares =  smb_connection.listShares()

    for share in shares:
        print share.name

    files = smb_connection.listPath(share.name, '/')
    for file in files:
        print file.filename

    file_obj = tempfile.NamedTemporaryFile()
    file_attributes, filesize =
    smb_connection.retrieveFile(SERVER_SHARE_NAME,
    SHARED_FILE_PATH, file_obj)

    # Retrieved file contents are inside file_obj
    file_obj.close()
```

Inspecting SAMBA packets

If we capture the SMABA packets on port 445, then we can see how the Windows Server communicates with the Linux SAMBA client over the CIFS protocol.
In the following two screenshots, a detailed communication between the client and the server, has been presented. The connection setup has been shown in the following screenshot:

Source	Destination	Protocol	Info
10.0.2.15	10.0.2.2	TCP	37676 > 445 [SYN] Seq=0 Win=5840 Len=0 MSS=1460 TSV=58421434 TSER=0 WS=6
10.0.2.2	10.0.2.15	TCP	445 > 37676 [SYN, ACK] Seq=0 Ack=1 Win=65535 Len=0 MSS=1460
10.0.2.15	10.0.2.2	TCP	37676 > 445 [ACK] Seq=1 Ack=1 Win=5840 Len=0
10.0.2.15	10.0.2.2	SMB	Negotiate Protocol Request
10.0.2.2	10.0.2.15	TCP	445 > 37676 [ACK] Seq=1 Ack=63 Win=65535 Len=0
10.0.2.2	10.0.2.15	SMB2	NegotiateProtocol Response
10.0.2.15	10.0.2.2	TCP	37676 > 445 [ACK] Seq=63 Ack=453 Win=6432 Len=0
10.0.2.15	10.0.2.2	SMB2	SessionSetup Request, NTLMSSP_NEGOTIATE
10.0.2.2	10.0.2.15	TCP	445 > 37676 [ACK] Seq=453 Ack=229 Win=65535 Len=0
10.0.2.2	10.0.2.15	SMB2	SessionSetup Response, Error: STATUS_MORE_PROCESSING_REQUIRED, NTLMSSP_CHALLENGE
10.0.2.15	10.0.2.2	SMB2	SessionSetup Request, NTLMSSP_AUTH, User: WORKGROUP\FaruqueSarker
10.0.2.2	10.0.2.15	TCP	445 > 37676 [ACK] Seq=778 Ack=683 Win=65535 Len=0
10.0.2.2	10.0.2.15	SMB2	SessionSetup Response
10.0.2.15	10.0.2.2	SMB2	TreeConnect Request Tree: \\FARUQUESARKER\IPC$
10.0.2.2	10.0.2.15	TCP	445 > 37676 [ACK] Seq=863 Ack=799 Win=65535 Len=0
10.0.2.2	10.0.2.15	SMB2	TreeConnect Response
10.0.2.15	10.0.2.2	SMB2	Create Request File: srvsvc
10.0.2.2	10.0.2.15	TCP	445 > 37676 [ACK] Seq=947 Ack=935 Win=65535 Len=0
10.0.2.2	10.0.2.15	SMB2	Create Response File: srvsvc
10.0.2.15	10.0.2.2	DCERPC	Bind: call_id: 2, 2 context items, 1st SRVSVC V3.0
10.0.2.2	10.0.2.15	TCP	445 > 37676 [ACK] Seq=1103 Ack=1167 Win=65535 Len=0
10.0.2.2	10.0.2.15	SMB2	Write Response
10.0.2.15	10.0.2.2	SMB2	Read Request Len:1024 Off:0 File: srvsvc
10.0.2.2	10.0.2.15	TCP	445 > 37676 [ACK] Seq=1187 Ack=1284 Win=65535 Len=0
10.0.2.2	10.0.2.15	DCERPC	Bind_ack: call_id: 2 Unknown result (3), reason: Local limit exceeded
10.0.2.15	10.0.2.2	SRVSVC	NetShareEnumAll request
10.0.2.2	10.0.2.15	TCP	445 > 37676 [ACK] Seq=1363 Ack=1512 Win=65535 Len=0
10.0.2.2	10.0.2.15	SRVSVC	NetShareEnumAll response

The following screenshot shows how a file copy session is performed:

Source	Destination	Protocol	Info
10.0.2.15	10.0.2.2	SMB2	Close Request File: srvsvc
10.0.2.2	10.0.2.15	TCP	445 > 37676 [ACK] Seq=1891 Ack=1604 Win=65535 Len=0
10.0.2.2	10.0.2.15	SMB2	Close Response
10.0.2.15	10.0.2.2	SMB2	TreeConnect Request Tree: \\FARUQUESARKER\Share
10.0.2.2	10.0.2.15	TCP	445 > 37676 [ACK] Seq=2019 Ack=1722 Win=65535 Len=0
10.0.2.2	10.0.2.15	SMB2	TreeConnect Response
10.0.2.15	10.0.2.2	SMB2	Create Request File: (
10.0.2.2	10.0.2.15	TCP	445 > 37676 [ACK] Seq=2103 Ack=1934 Win=65535 Len=0
10.0.2.2	10.0.2.15	SMB2	Create Response File:
10.0.2.15	10.0.2.2	SMB2	Find Request File: SMB2_FIND_BOTH_DIRECTORY_INFO Pattern: *
10.0.2.2	10.0.2.15	TCP	445 > 37676 [ACK] Seq=2347 Ack=2036 Win=65535 Len=0
10.0.2.2	10.0.2.15	SMB2	Find Response SMB2_FIND_BOTH_DIRECTORY_INFO Pattern: *
10.0.2.15	10.0.2.2	SMB2	Find Request File: SMB2_FIND_BOTH_DIRECTORY_INFO Pattern: *
10.0.2.2	10.0.2.15	TCP	445 > 37676 [ACK] Seq=2845 Ack=2138 Win=65535 Len=0
10.0.2.2	10.0.2.15	SMB2	Find Response, Error: STATUS_NO_MORE_FILES SMB2_FIND_BOTH_DIRECTORY_INFO Pattern: *
10.0.2.15	10.0.2.2	SMB2	Close Request File:
10.0.2.2	10.0.2.15	TCP	445 > 37676 [ACK] Seq=2922 Ack=2230 Win=65535 Len=0
10.0.2.2	10.0.2.15	SMB2	Close Response
10.0.2.15	10.0.2.2	SMB2	Create Request File: test.rtf
10.0.2.2	10.0.2.15	TCP	445 > 37676 [ACK] Seq=3050 Ack=2458 Win=65535 Len=0
10.0.2.2	10.0.2.15	SMB2	Create Response File: test.rtf
10.0.2.15	10.0.2.2	SMB2	GetInfo Request FILE_INFO/SMB2_FILE_STREAM_INFO File: test.rtf
10.0.2.2	10.0.2.15	TCP	445 > 37676 [ACK] Seq=3294 Ack=2566 Win=65535 Len=0
10.0.2.2	10.0.2.15	SMB2	GetInfo Response
10.0.2.15	10.0.2.2	SMB2	Read Request Len:187 Off:0 File: test.rtf
10.0.2.2	10.0.2.15	TCP	445 > 37676 [ACK] Seq=3408 Ack=2683 Win=65535 Len=0
10.0.2.2	10.0.2.15	SMB2	Read Response
10.0.2.15	10.0.2.2	SMB2	Close Request File: test.rtf

A typical SAMBA packet format has been shown in the following screenshot. The important field of this packet is the NT_STATUS field. Typically, if the connection is successful, then it will show STATUS_SUCESS. Otherwise, it will print a different code. This is shown in the following screenshot:

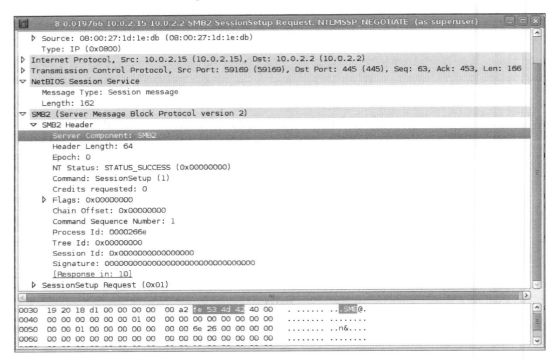

Summary

In this chapter, we have come across several network protocols and Python libraries, which are used for interacting with remote systems. SSH and SFTP are used for securely connecting and transferring files to the remote hosts. FTP is still used as a simple file transfer mechanism. However, it's not secure due to user credentials being transferred over the wire as plain-text. We also examined Python libraries for dealing with SNMP, LDAP, and SAMBA packets.

In the next chapter, one of the most common networking protocols — that is, DNS and IP — will be discussed. We will explore TCP/IP networking using Python scripts.

6
IP and DNS

Every computer that is connected to a network needs an IP address. In *Chapter 1, Network Programming and Python*, an introduction to TCP/IP networking was presented. The IP address labels a machine's network interface with a numeric identifier, which also identifies the location of the machine, albeit with limited reliability. **Domain Name System (DNS)** is a core network service that maps the names to the IP addresses and vice-verse. In this chapter, we will mainly focus on manipulating the IP and DNS protocols with the help of Python. In addition to this, we will briefly discuss the **Network Time Protocol (NTP)**, which helps in synchronizing the time with a centralized time server. The following topics will be discussed here:

- Retrieving the network configuration of a local machine
- Manipulating the IP addresses
- The GeoIP look-ups
- Working with DNS
- Working with NTP

Retrieving the network configuration of a local machine

Before doing anything else, let's ask in the Python language, *What's my name?*. In networking terms, this is equivalent to finding out the machine's name or the host's name. On the shell command-line, this can be discovered by using the `hostname` command. In Python, you can do this by using the socket module.

```
>>> import socket
>>> socket.gethostname()
'debian6box.localdomain.loc'
```

Now, we would like to see the local machine IP. This can be seen by using the `ifconfig` command in Linux and by using the `ipconfig` command in the Windows OS. But, we'd like to do this in Python by using the following built-in function:

```
>>> socket.gethostbyname('debian6box.localdomain.loc')
'10.0.2.15'
```

As you can see, this is the IP of the first network interface. It can also show us the IP of the loopback interface (127.0.0.1) if your DNS or hostfile has not been configured properly. In Linux/UNIX, the following line can be added to your `/etc/hosts` file for obtaining the correct IP address:

```
10.0.2.15          debian6box.localdomain.loc          debian6box
```

This process is known as a host-file based name resolution. You can send a query to a DNS server and ask for the IP address of a specific host. If the name has been registered properly, then you will get a response from the server. But, before making a query to the remote server, let us first discover some more information about the network interface and the gateway machine of your network.

In every LAN, a host is configured to act as a gateway, which talks to the *outside* world. In order to find the network address and the netmask, we can use the Python third-party library netifaces (version > 0.10.0). This will pull all the relevant information. For example, you can call `netifaces.gateways()` for finding the gateways that are configured to the outside world. Similarly, you can enumerate the network interfaces by calling `netifaces.interfaces()`. If you would like to know all the IP addresses of a particular interface *eth0*, then you can call `netifaces.ifaddresses('eth0')`. The following code listing shows the way in which you can list all the gateways and IP addresses of a local machine:

```python
#!/usr/bin/env python
import socket
import netifaces

if __name__ == '__main__':
    # Find host info
    host_name = socket.gethostname()
    ip_address = socket.gethostbyname(host_name)
    print("Host name: {0}".format(host_name))

    # Get interfaces list
    ifaces = netifaces.interfaces()
    for iface in ifaces:
```

```
        ipaddrs = netifaces.ifaddresses(iface)
        if netifaces.AF_INET in ipaddrs:
            ipaddr_desc = ipaddrs[netifaces.AF_INET]
            ipaddr_desc = ipaddr_desc[0]
            print("Network interface: {0}".format(iface))
            print("\tIP address: {0}".format(ipaddr_desc['addr']))
            print("\tNetmask: {0}".format(ipaddr_desc['netmask']))
    # Find the gateway
    gateways = netifaces.gateways()
    print("Default gateway:
    {0}".format(gateways['default'][netifaces.AF_INET][0]))
```

If you run this code, then this will print a summary of the local network configuration, which will be similar to the following:

```
$ python 6_1_local_network_config.py
Host name: debian6box
Network interface: lo
  IP address: 127.0.0.1
  Netmask: 255.0.0.0
Network interface: eth0
  IP address: 10.0.2.15
  Netmask: 255.255.255.0
Default gateway: 10.0.2.2
```

Manipulating IP addresses

Often you will need to manipulate IP addresses and perform some sort of operations on them. Python3 has a built-in `ipaddress` module to help you in carrying out this task. It has convenient functions for defining the IP addresses and the IP networks and for finding lots of useful information. For example, if you would like to know how many IP addresses exist in a given subnet, for instance, `10.0.1.0/255.255.255.0` or `10.0.2.0/24`, then you can find them with the help of the code snippet shown here. This module will provide several classes and factory functions; for example, the IP address and the IP network has separate classes. Each class has a variant for both IP version 4 (IPv4) and IP version 6 (IPv6). Some of the features have been demonstrated in the following section:

IP network objects

Let us import the `ipaddress` module and define a `net4` network.

```
>>> import ipaddress as ip
>>> net4 = ip.ip_network('10.0.1.0/24')
```

Now, we can find some useful information, such as `netmask`, the network/broadcast address, and so on, of `net4`:

```
>>> net4.netmask
IP4Address(255.255.255.0)
```

The `netmask` properties of `net4` will be displayed as an `IP4Address` object. If you are looking for its string representation, then you can call the `str()` method, as shown here:

```
>>> str(net4.netmask)
'255.255.255.0'
```

Similarly, you can find the network and the broadcast addresses of `net4`, by doing the following:

```
>>> str(net4.network_address)
10.0.1.0
>>> str(net4.broadcast_address)
10.0.1.255
```

How many addresses does `net4` hold in total? This can be found by using the command shown here:

```
>>> net4.num_addresses
256
```

So, if we subtract the network and the broadcast addresses, then the total available IP addresses will be 254. We can call the `hosts()` method on the `net4` object. It will produce a Python generator, which will supply all the hosts as `IPv4Adress` objects.

```
>>> all_hosts = list(net4.hosts())
>>> len(all_hosts)
254
```

You can access the individual IP addresses by following the standard Python list access notation. For example, the first IP address would be the following:

```
>>> all_hosts[0]
IPv4Address('10.0.1.1')
```

You can access the last IP address by using the list notation for accessing the last item of a list, as shown here:

```
>>> all_hosts[-1]
IPv4Address('10.0.1.1')
```

We can also find the subnet information from the IPv4Network objects, as follows:

```
>>> subnets = list( net4.subnets())
>>> subnets
[ IPv4Network('10.0.1.0/25'), IPv4Network('10.0.1.128/25')  ]
```

Any IPv4Network object can tell about its parent supernet, which is the opposite of the subnet.

```
>>> net4.supernet()
IPv4Network('10.0.1.0/23')
```

Network interface objects

In the ipaddress module, a convenient class is used for representing an interface's IP configuration in detail. The IPv4 Interface class takes an arbitrary address and behaves like a network address object. Let us define and discuss our network interface eth0, as shown in following screenshot:

```
root@localhost: ~/learnpynet
File  Edit  View  Search  Terminal  Help
[root@localhost learnpynet]# python
Python 3.3.2 (default, Aug 14 2014, 14:25:52)
[GCC 4.8.2 20140120 (Red Hat 4.8.2-16)] on linux
Type "help", "copyright", "credits" or "license" for more information.
>>> import ipaddress as ip
>>> eth0 = ip.IPv4Interface('192.168.0.1/24')
>>> eth0.ip
IPv4Address('192.168.0.1')
>>> eth0.with_prefixlen
'192.168.0.1/24'
>>> eth0.with_netmask
'192.168.0.1/255.255.255.0'
>>> eth0.network
IPv4Network('192.168.0.0/24')
>>> str(eth0.network)
'192.168.0.0/24'
>>> str(eth0.ip)
'192.168.0.1'
>>> eth0.is_private
True
>>> eth0.is_reserved
False
>>> eth0.is_multicast
False
```

As you can see in the preceding screenshot, a network interface eth0 with the IPv4Address class has been defined. It has some interesting properties, such as IP, network address, and so on. In the same way as with the network objects, you can check if the address is private, reserved, or multicast. These address ranges have been defined in various RFC documents. The ipaddress module's help page will show you the links to those RFC documents. You can search this information in other places as well.

The IP address objects

The IP address classes have many more interesting properties. You can perform some arithmetic and logical operations on those objects. For example, if an IP address is greater than another IP address, then you can add numbers to the IP address objects, and this will give you a corresponding IP address. Let's see a demonstration of this in the following screenshot:

```
root@localhost:~/learnpynet

File   Edit   View   Search   Terminal   Help
>>> import ipaddress as ip
>>> eth0 = ip.ip_address('192.168.1.1')
>>> lo = ip.ip_address('127.0.0.1')
>>> eth0.is_private
True
>>> lo.is_private
False
>>> lo.is_reserved
False
>>> eth1 = ip.ip_address('192.168.2.1')
>>> eth1 = eth1 + 1
>>> eth1
IPv4Address('192.168.2.2')
>>> eth0 == eth1
False
>>> lo.is_loopback
True
>>> str(lo)
'127.0.0.1'
>>> net = ip.ip_network('192.168.1.0/24')
>>> eth0 in net
True
>>> eth1 in net
False
>>> eth1 = eth0 + 1
>>> eth1 in net
True
>>>
```

Demonstration of the ipaddress module

Here, the eth0 interface has been defined with a private IP address, which is 192.168.1.1, and eth1 has been defined with another private IP address, which is 192.168.2.1. Similarly the loopback interface lo is defined with IP address 127.0.0.1. As you can see, you can add numbers to the IP address and it will give you the next IP address with the same sequence.

You can check if an IP is a part of a specific network. Here, a network net has been defined by the network address, which is 192.168.1.0/24, and the membership of eth0 and eth1 has been tested against that. A few other interesting properties, such as is_loopback, is_private, and so on, have also been tested here.

Planning IP addresses for your local area network

If you are wondering how to pick-up a suitable IP subnet, then you can experiment with the ipaddress module. The following code snippet will show an example of how to choose a specific subnet, based on the number of necessary host IP addresses for a small private network:

```python
#!/usr/bin/env python
import ipaddress as ip

CLASS_C_ADDR = '192.168.0.0'

if __name__ == '__main__':
    not_configed = True
    while not_configed:
        prefix = input("Enter the prefixlen (24-30): ")
        prefix = int(prefix)
        if prefix not in range(23, 31):
            raise Exception("Prefixlen must be between 24 and 30")
        net_addr = CLASS_C_ADDR + '/' + str(prefix)
        print("Using network address:%s " %net_addr)
        try:
            network = ip.ip_network(net_addr)
        except:
            raise Exception("Failed to create network object")
        print("This prefix will give %s IP addresses"
            %(network.num_addresses))
        print("The network configuration will be")
        print("\t network address: %s"
            %str(network.network_address))
        print("\t netmask: %s" %str(network.netmask))
```

```
print("\t broadcast address: %s"
%str(network.broadcast_address))
first_ip, last_ip = list(network.hosts())[0],
list(network.hosts())[-1]
print("\t host IP addresses: from %s to %s" %(first_ip,
last_ip))
ok = input("Is this configuration OK [y/n]? ")
ok = ok.lower()
if ok.strip() == 'y':
    not_configed = False
```

If you run this script, then it will show an output similar to the following:

```
# python 6_2_net_ip_planner.py
Enter the prefixlen (24-30): 28
Using network address:192.168.0.0/28
This prefix will give 16 IP addresses
The network configuration will be
   network address: 192.168.0.0
   netmask: 255.255.255.240
   broadcast address: 192.168.0.15
   host IP addresses: from 192.168.0.1 to 192.168.0.14
Is this configuration OK [y/n]? n
Enter the prefixlen (24-30): 26
Using network address:192.168.0.0/26
This prefix will give 64 IP addresses
The network configuration will be
   network address: 192.168.0.0
   netmask: 255.255.255.192
   broadcast address: 192.168.0.63
   host IP addresses: from 192.168.0.1 to 192.168.0.62
Is this configuration OK [y/n]? y
```

GeoIP look-ups

At times, it will be necessary for many applications to look-up the location of the IP addresses. For example, many website owners can be interested in tracking the location of their visitors and in classifying their IPs according to criteria, such as country, city, and so on. There is a third-party library called **python-geoip,** which has a robust interface for giving you the answer to your IP location query. This library is provided by MaxMind, which also provides the option for shipping a recent version of the Geolite2 database as the `python-geoip-geolite2` package. This includes the GeoLite2 data created by MaxMind, which is available at www. maxmind.com under the creative commons Attribution-ShareAlike 3.0 Unported License. You can also buy a commercial license from their website.

Let's see an example of how to use this Geo-lookup library.:

```
import socket
from geoip import geolite2
import argparse


if __name__ == '__main__':
    # Setup commandline arguments
    parser = argparse.ArgumentParser(description='Get IP Geolocation
info')
    parser.add_argument('--hostname', action="store", dest="hostname",
required=True)

    # Parse arguments
    given_args = parser.parse_args()
    hostname =  given_args.hostname
    ip_address = socket.gethostbyname(hostname)
    print("IP address: {0}".format(ip_address))

    match = geolite2.lookup(ip_address)
    if match is not None:
        print('Country: ',match.country)
        print('Continent: ',match.continent)
        print('Time zone: ', match.timezone)
```

This script will show an output similar to the following:

```
$ python 6_3_geoip_lookup.py --hostname=amazon.co.uk
IP address: 178.236.6.251
Country:  IE
Continent:  EU
Time zone:  Europe/Dublin
```

You can find more information about this package from the developer's website, which is at `http://pythonhosted.org/python-geoip/`.

DNS look-ups

The IP address can be translated into human readable strings called domain names. DNS is a big topic in the world of networking. In this section, we will create a DNS client in Python, and see how this client will talk to the server by using Wirshark.

A few DNS cleint libraries are available from PyPI. We will focus on the `dnspython` library, which is available at `http://www.dnspython.org/`. You can install this library by using either the `easy_install` command or the `pip` command:

```
$ pip install dnspython
```

Making a simple query regarding the IP address of a host is very simple. You can use the `dns.resolver` submodule, as follows:

```
import dns.resolver
answers = dns.resolver.query('python.org', 'A')
for rdata in answers:
    print('IP', rdata.to_text())
```

If you want to make a reverse look-up, then you need to use the `dns.reversename` submodule, as shown here:

```
import dns.reversename
name = dns.reversename.from_address("127.0.0.1")
print name
print dns.reversename.to_address(name)
```

Now, let's create an interactive DNS client script that will do a complete look-up of the possible records, as shown here:

```python
import dns.resolver


if __name__ == '__main__':
    loookup_continue = True
    while loookup_continue:
        name = input('Enter the DNS name to resolve: ')
        record_type = input('Enter the query type
        [A/MX/CNAME]: ')
        answers = dns.resolver.query(name, record_type)
        if record_type == 'A':
            print('Got answer IP address: %s' %[x.to_text() for x
            in answers])
        elif record_type == 'CNAME':
            print('Got answer Aliases: %s' %[x.to_text() for x in
            answers])
        elif record_type == 'MX':
            for rdata in answers:
                print('Got answers for Mail server records:')
                print('Mailserver', rdata.exchange.to_text(), 'has
                preference', rdata.preference)
            print('Record type: %s is not implemented'
            %record_type)
        lookup_more = input("Do you want to lookup more
        records? [y/n]: " )
        if lookup_more.lower() == 'n':
            loookup_continue = False
```

If you run this script with some input, then you will have an output similar to the following:

```
$ python 6_4_dns_client.py
Enter the DNS name to resolve: google.com
Enter the query type [A/MX/CNAME]: MX
Got answers for Mail server records:
Mailserver alt4.aspmx.l.google.com. has preference 50
Got answers for Mail server records:
Mailserver alt2.aspmx.l.google.com. has preference 30
Got answers for Mail server records:
```

```
Mailserver alt3.aspmx.1.google.com. has preference 40

Got answers for Mail server records:

Mailserver aspmx.1.google.com. has preference 10

Got answers for Mail server records:

Mailserver alt1.aspmx.1.google.com. has preference 20

Do you want to lookup more records? [y/n]: y

Enter the DNS name to resolve: www.python.org

Enter the query type [A/MX/CNAME]: A

Got answer IP address: ['185.31.18.223']

Do you want to lookup more records? [y/n]: y

Enter the DNS name to resolve: pypi.python.org

Enter the query type [A/MX/CNAME]: CNAME

Got answer Aliases: ['python.map.fastly.net.']

Do you want to lookup more records? [y/n]: n
```

Inspecting DNS client/server communication

In previous chapters, perhaps you noticed how we captured network packets between the client and the server by using Wireshark. Here is an example of the session capturing, while a Python package was being installed from PyPI:

Source	Destination	Protocol	Info
10.0.2.15	192.168.1.1	DNS	Standard query A pypi.python.org
10.0.2.15	192.168.1.1	DNS	Standard query AAAA pypi.python.org
192.168.1.1	10.0.2.15	DNS	Standard query response CNAME python.map.fastly.net
192.168.1.1	10.0.2.15	DNS	Standard query response CNAME python.map.fastly.net A 185.31.19.223
10.0.2.15	192.168.1.1	DNS	Standard query A pypi.python.org
10.0.2.15	192.168.1.1	DNS	Standard query AAAA pypi.python.org
192.168.1.1	10.0.2.15	DNS	Standard query response CNAME python.map.fastly.net A 185.31.19.223
192.168.1.1	10.0.2.15	DNS	Standard query response CNAME python.map.fastly.net
10.0.2.15	192.168.1.1	DNS	Standard query A pypi.python.org
192.168.1.1	10.0.2.15	DNS	Standard query response CNAME python.map.fastly.net A 185.31.19.223
10.0.2.15	192.168.1.1	DNS	Standard query AAAA pypi.python.org
192.168.1.1	10.0.2.15	DNS	Standard query response CNAME python.map.fastly.net
10.0.2.15	192.168.1.1	DNS	Standard query A pypi.python.org
10.0.2.15	192.168.1.1	DNS	Standard query AAAA pypi.python.org
192.168.1.1	10.0.2.15	DNS	Standard query response CNAME python.map.fastly.net A 185.31.19.223
192.168.1.1	10.0.2.15	DNS	Standard query response CNAME python.map.fastly.net
10.0.2.15	192.168.1.1	DNS	Standard query A pypi.python.org
10.0.2.15	192.168.1.1	DNS	Standard query AAAA pypi.python.org
192.168.1.1	10.0.2.15	DNS	Standard query response CNAME python.map.fastly.net A 185.31.19.223
192.168.1.1	10.0.2.15	DNS	Standard query response CNAME python.map.fastly.net
10.0.2.15	192.168.1.1	DNS	Standard query A pypi.python.org
10.0.2.15	192.168.1.1	DNS	Standard query AAAA pypi.python.org
192.168.1.1	10.0.2.15	DNS	Standard query response CNAME python.map.fastly.net A 185.31.19.223
192.168.1.1	10.0.2.15	DNS	Standard query response CNAME python.map.fastly.net

FDNS client/server communication

In Wireshark you can specify `port 53` by navigating to **Capture | Options | Capture filter**. This will capture all the DNS packets that were sent to/from your machine.

As you can see in the following screenshot, the client and the server have several request/response cycles the DNS records. It was started with a standard request for the host's address (A) and it was followed by a suitable response.

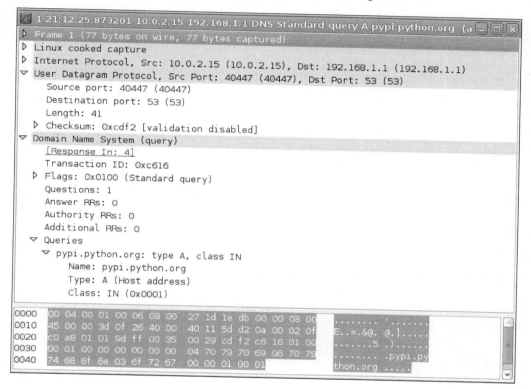

If you look deep inside a packet, then you can see the request format of the response from the server, as shown in the following screenshot:

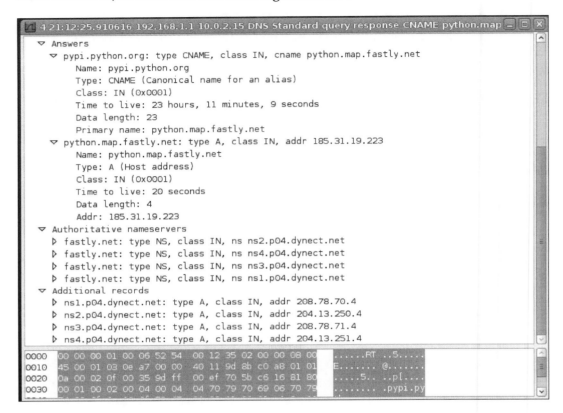

NTP clients

The final topic that will be covered in this chapter is NTP. Synchronizing time with a centralized time server is a key step in any corporate network. We would like to compare the log files between various servers and see if the timestamp on each server is accurate; the log events may not then co-relate. Many authentication protocols, such as Kerberos, strictly rely on the accuracy of the time stamp reported by the client to the servers. Here, a third-party Python `ntplib` library will be introduced, and then the communication between the NTP client and the server will be investigated.

To create an NTP client, you need to call the ntplib's NTPCLient class.

```
import ntplib
from time import ctime
c = ntplib.NTPClient()
response = c.request('pool.ntp.org')
print ctime(response.tx_time)
```

Here, we have selected pool.ntp.org, which is a load-balanced webserver. So, a pool of the NTP servers will be ready to respond to the client's request. Let's find more information regarding this from the response that was returned by an NTP server.

```
import ntplib
from time import ctime

HOST_NAME = 'pool.ntp.org'

if __name__ == '__main__':
    params = {}
    client = ntplib.NTPClient()
    response = client.request(HOST_NAME)
    print('Received time: %s' %ctime(response.tx_time))
    print('ref_clock: ',ntplib.ref_id_to_text(response.ref_id,
    response.stratum))
    print('stratum: ',response.stratum)
    print('last_update: ', response.ref_time)
    print('offset: %f' %response.offset)
    print('precision: ', response.precision)
    print('root_delay: %.6f' %response.root_delay)
    print('root_dispersion: %.6f' %response.root_dispersion)
```

The detailed response will look like the following:

```
$ python 6_5_ntp_client.py
Received time: Sat Feb 28 17:08:29 2015
ref_clock:  213.136.0.252
stratum:  2
last_update:  1425142998.2
offset:  -4.777519
precision:  -23
root_delay: 0.019608
root_dispersion: 0.036987
```

The preceding information was supplied by the NTP server to the client. This information can be used to determine the accuracy of the supplied time server. For example, the stratum value 2 indicates that the NTP server will query another NTP server with the stratum value 1, which may have a directly attached time source. For more information about the NTP protocol, you may either read the RFC 958 document at `https://tools.ietf.org/html/rfc958` or visit `http://www.ntp.org/`.

Inspecting the NTP client/server communication

You may be able to learn more about NTP by looking at captured packets. For this purpose, the preceding NTP client/server communication has been captured as shown in the following two screenshots:

The first screenshot shows the NTP client request. If you look inside the flag fields, then you will see the client's version number.

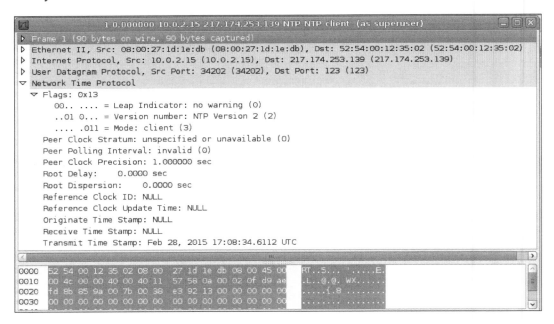

Similarly, the NTP server response has been shown in the following screenshot:

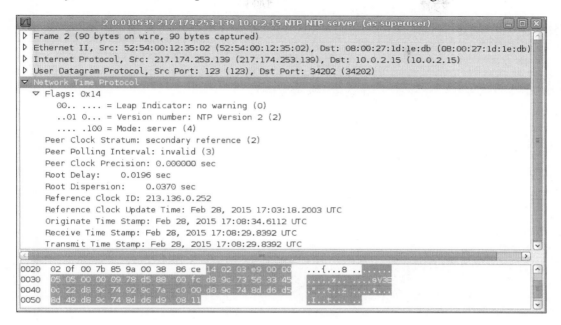

Summary

In this chapter, the standard Python libraries for IP address manipulation were discussed. Two third-party libraries `dnspython` and `ntplib` have been presented to interact with the DNS and the NTP servers respectively. As you have seen through the aforementioned examples, these libraries provide you with the necessary interface for talking to those services.

In the following chapter, we will introduce socket programming in Python. This is another interesting and popular topic for networking programmers. There, you will find both low and high-level Python libraries for programming with BSD sockets.

7

Programming with Sockets

After you have interacted with various clients/servers in Python, you will be keen to create your own custom clients and servers for any protocol of your choice. Python provides a good coverage on the low-level networking interface. It all starts with BSD socket interface. As you can assume, Python has a `socket` module that gives you the necessary functionality to work with the socket Interface. If you have ever done socket programming in any other language like C/C++, you will love the Python `socket` module.

In this chapter, we will explore the socket module by creating a diverse range of Python scripts.

The following are the highlights of this chapter:

- Basics of sockets
- Working with TCP sockets
- Working with UDP sockets
- TCP port forwarding
- Non-blocking socket I/O
- Securing sockets with SSL/TLS
- Creating custom SSL client/server

Basics of sockets

Network programming in any programming language can begin with sockets. But what is a socket? Simply put, a network socket is a virtual end point where entities can perform inter-process communication. For example, one process sitting in a computer, exchanges data with another process sitting on the same or another computer. We typically label the first process which initiates the communication as the client and the latter one as the server.

Python has quite an easy way to start with the socket interface. In order to understand this better, let's see the big picture first. In the following figure, a flow of client/server interaction is shown. This will give you an idea of how to use the socket API.

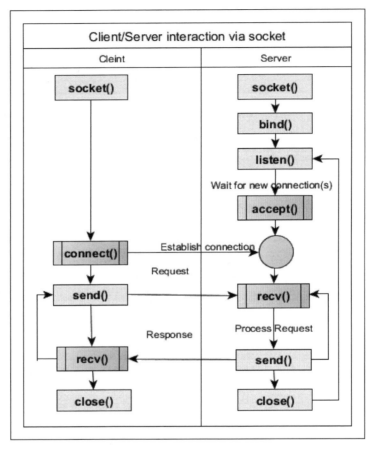

client/server interaction through socket

In the interaction between a typical client and a server, the server process has to work a bit more, as you may have thought. After creating a socket object, the server process binds that socket to a particular IP address and port. This is much like a telephone connection with an extension number. In a corporate office, after a new employee has been allocated with his desk phone, usually he or she will be assigned to a new extension number. So, if anybody makes a phone call to this employee, the connection can be established using his phone number and extension. After the successful binding, the server process will start listening for a new client connection. For a valid client session, the server process can accept the request of the client process. At this point, we can say that the connection between the server and the client has been established.

Then the client/server enters into the request/response loop. The client process sends data to the server process, and the server process processes the data and returns a response to the client. When the client process finishes, it exits by closing down the connection. At that moment, the server process probably goes back to the listening state.

The above interaction between client and server is a very simplified representation of the actual reality. In practice, any production server process has multiple threads or subprocesses to handle concurrent connections from thousands of clients over respective virtual channels.

Working with TCP sockets

Creating a socket object in Python is very straightforward. You just need to import the `socket` module and call the `socket()` class:

```
from socket import*
import socket

#create a TCP socket (SOCK_STREAM)
s = socket.socket(family=AF_INET, type=SOCK_STREAM, proto=0)
print('Socket created')
```

Traditionally, the class takes plenty of parameters. Some of them are listed in the following:

- **Socket family**: This is the domain of socket, such as `AF_INET` (about 90 percent of the sockets of the Internet fall under this category) or `AF_UNIX`, which is sometimes used as well. In Python 3, you can create a Bluetooth socket using `AF_BLUETOOTH`.

- **Socket type**: Depending on your need, you need to specify the type of socket. For example, TCP and UDP-based sockets are created by specifying `SOCK_STREAM` and `SOCK_DGRAM`, respectively.

- **Protocol**: This specifies the variation of protocol within a socket family and type. Usually, it is left as zero.

For many reasons, socket operations may not be successful. For example, if you don't have permission to access a particular port as a normal user, you may not be able to bind to a socket. This is why it is a good idea to do proper error handling when creating a socket or doing some network-bound communication.

Let's try to connect a client socket to a server process. The following code is an example of TCP client socket that makes a connection to server socket:

```python
import socket
import sys

if __name__ == '__main__':

    try:
        sock = socket.socket(socket.AF_INET, socket.SOCK_STREAM)
    except socket.error as err:
        print("Failed to crate a socket")
        print("Reason: %s" %str(err))
        sys.exit();

    print('Socket created')

    target_host = input("Enter the target host name to connect: ")
    target_port = input("Enter the target port: ")

    try:
        sock.connect((target_host, int(target_port)))
        print("Socket Connected to %s on port: %s" %(target_host,
        target_port))
    sock.shutdown(2)
    except socket.error as err:
        print("Failed to connect to %s on port %s" %(target_host,
        target_port))
        print("Reason: %s" %str(err))
        sys.exit();
```

If you run the preceding TCP client, an output similar to the following will be shown:

```
# python 7_1_tcp_client_socket.py
Socket created
Enter the target host name to connect: 'www.python.org'
Enter the target port: 80
Socket Connected to www.python.org on port: 80
```

However, if socket creation has failed for some reason, such as invalid DNS, an output similar to the following will be shown:

```
# python 7_1_tcp_client_socket.py
Socket created
```

```
Enter the target host name to connect:
  www.asgdfdfdkflakslalalasdsdsds.invalid

Enter the target port: 80

Failed to connect to www.asgdfdfdkflakslalalasdsdsds.invalid on port
  80
Reason: [Errno -2] Name or service not known
```

Now, let's exchange some data with the server. The following code is an example of a simple TCP client:

```python
import socket

HOST = 'www.linux.org' # or 'localhost'
PORT = 80
BUFSIZ = 4096
ADDR = (HOST, PORT)

if __name__ == '__main__':
    client_sock = socket.socket(socket.AF_INET,
    socket.SOCK_STREAM)
    client_sock.connect(ADDR)

    while True:
        data = 'GET / HTTP/1.0\r\n\r\n'
        if not data:
            break
        client_sock.send(data.encode('utf-8'))
        data = client_sock.recv(BUFSIZ)
        if not data:
            break
        print(data.decode('utf-8'))

    client_sock.close()
```

If you look carefully, you can see that the preceding code actually created a raw HTTP client that fetches a web page from a web server. It sends an HTTP GET request to pull the home page:

```
# python 7_2_simple_tcp_client.py
HTTP/1.1 200 OK
Date: Sat, 07 Mar 2015 16:23:02 GMT
Server: Apache
Last-Modified: Mon, 17 Feb 2014 03:19:34 GMT
Accept-Ranges: bytes
```

```
Content-Length: 111
Connection: close
Content-Type: text/html


<html><head><META HTTP-EQUIV="refresh" CONTENT="0;URL=/cgi-
    sys/defaultwebpage.cgi"></head><body></body></html>
```

Inspecting the client/server communication

The interaction between the client and server through the exchange of network packets can be analyzed using any network packet capturing tool, such as Wireshark. You can configure Wireshark to filter packets by port or host. In this case, we can filter by port 80. You can get the options under the **Capture | Options** menu and type port 80 in the input box next to the **Capture Filter** option, as shown in the following screenshot:

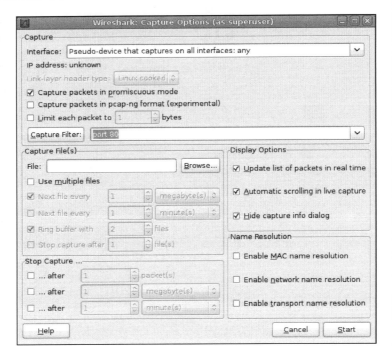

In the **Interface** option, we choose to capture packets passing through any interface. Now, if you run the preceding TCP client to connect to www.linux.org, you can see the sequence of packets exchanged in Wireshark, as shown in the following screenshot:

Source	Destination	Protocol	Info
10.0.2.15	107.170.40.56	TCP	41153 > 80 [SYN] Seq=0 Win=5840 Len=0 MSS=1460 TSV=19033303 TSER=0 WS=6
107.170.40.56	10.0.2.15	TCP	80 > 41153 [SYN, ACK] Seq=0 Ack=1 Win=65535 Len=0 MSS=1460
10.0.2.15	107.170.40.56	TCP	41153 > 80 [ACK] Seq=1 Ack=1 Win=5840 Len=0
10.0.2.15	107.170.40.56	HTTP	GET / HTTP/1.0
107.170.40.56	10.0.2.15	TCP	80 > 41153 [ACK] Seq=1 Ack=19 Win=65535 Len=0
107.170.40.56	10.0.2.15	HTTP	HTTP/1.1 200 OK (text/html)
107.170.40.56	10.0.2.15	TCP	80 > 41153 [FIN, ACK] Seq=317 Ack=19 Win=65535 Len=0
10.0.2.15	107.170.40.56	TCP	41153 > 80 [ACK] Seq=19 Ack=317 Win=6432 Len=0
10.0.2.15	107.170.40.56	HTTP	GET / HTTP/1.0
10.0.2.15	107.170.40.56	TCP	41153 > 80 [FIN, ACK] Seq=37 Ack=318 Win=6432 Len=0
107.170.40.56	10.0.2.15	TCP	80 > 41153 [ACK] Seq=318 Ack=38 Win=65535 Len=0

As you can see, the first three packets establish the TCP connection by a three-way handshake process between the client and server. We are more interested in the fourth packet that makes an HTTP GET request to the server. If you double-click the selected row, you can see the details of the HTTP request, as shown in the following screenshot:

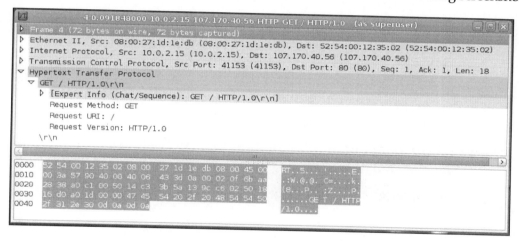

As you can see, the HTTP GET request has other components such as Request URI, version, and so on. Now you can check the HTTP response from the web server to your client. It has come after the TCP acknowledgment packet, that is, the sixth packet. Here, the server typically sends an HTTP response code (in this case 200), content length, and the data or web page content. The structure of this packet is shown in the following screenshot:

From the preceding analysis of the interaction between the client and server, you can now understand, at a basic level, what happens behind the scenes when you visit a web page using your web browser. In the next section, you will be shown how to create your own TCP server and examine the interactions between your personal TCP client and server.

TCP servers

As you understood from the very first client/server interaction diagram, the server process needs to carry out a bit of extra work. It needs to bind to a socket address and listen for incoming connections. The following code snippet shows how to create a TCP server:

```python
import socket
from time import ctime

HOST = 'localhost'
PORT = 12345
BUFSIZ = 1024
ADDR = (HOST, PORT)

if __name__ == '__main__':
    server_socket = socket.socket(socket.AF_INET,
    socket.SOCK_STREAM)
    server_socket.bind(ADDR)
    server_socket.listen(5)
    server_socket.setsockopt( socket.SOL_SOCKET,
    socket.SO_REUSEADDR, 1 )

    while True:
        print('Server waiting for connection...')
        client_sock, addr = server_socket.accept()
        print('Client connected from: ', addr)

        while True:
            data = client_sock.recv(BUFSIZ)
            if not data or data.decode('utf-8') == 'END':
                break
            print("Received from client: %s" % data.decode('utf-
            8'))
            print("Sending the server time to client: %s"
            %ctime())
            try:
                client_sock.send(bytes(ctime(), 'utf-8'))
            except KeyboardInterrupt:
                print("Exited by user")
        client_sock.close()
    server_socket.close()
```

Let's modify our previous TCP client to send arbitrary data to any server. The following is an example of an enhanced TCP client:

```python
import socket

HOST = 'localhost'
PORT = 12345
BUFSIZ = 256

if __name__ == '__main__':
    client_sock = socket.socket(socket.AF_INET,
    socket.SOCK_STREAM)
    host = input("Enter hostname [%s]: " %HOST) or HOST
    port = input("Enter port [%s]: " %PORT) or PORT

    sock_addr = (host, int(port))
    client_sock.connect(sock_addr)

    payload = 'GET TIME'
    try:
        while True:
            client_sock.send(payload.encode('utf-8'))
            data = client_sock.recv(BUFSIZ)
            print(repr(data))
            more = input("Want to send more data to server[y/n]
            :")
            if more.lower() == 'y':
                payload = input("Enter payload: ")
            else:
                break
    except KeyboardInterrupt:
        print("Exited by user")

    client_sock.close()
```

If you run the preceding TCP server in one console and the TCP client in another console, you can see the following interaction between the client and server. After running the TCP server script you will get the following output:

```
# python 7_3_tcp_server.py
Server waiting for connection...
Client connected from:  ('127.0.0.1', 59961)
```

```
Received from client: GET TIME


Sending the server time to client: Sun Mar 15 12:09:16 2015
Server waiting for connection...
```

When you will run the TCP client script on another terminal then you will get the
following output:

```
# python 7_4_tcp_client_socket_send_data.py
Enter hostname [www.linux.org]: localhost
Enter port [80]: 12345
b'Sun Mar 15 12:09:16 2015'
Want to send more data to server[y/n] :n
```

Inspecting client/server interaction

Now, once again, you can configure Wireshark to capture packets, as discussed
in the last section. But, in this case, you need to specify the port that your
server is listening on (in the preceding example it's 12345), as shown in the
following screenshot:

As we are capturing packets on a non-standard port, Wireshark doesn't decode it in the **Data** section (as shown in the middle pane of the preceding screenshot). However, you can see the decoded text on the bottom pane where the server's timestamp is shown on the right side.

Working with UDP sockets

Unlike TCP, UDP doesn't check for errors in the exchanged datagram. We can create UDP client/servers similar to the TCP client/servers. The only difference is you have to specify SOCK_DGRAM instead of SOCK_STREAM when you create the socket object.

Let us create a UDP server. Use the following code to create the UDP server:

```
from socket import socket, AF_INET, SOCK_DGRAM
maxsize = 4096

sock = socket(AF_INET,SOCK_DGRAM)
sock.bind(('',12345))
while True:
  data, addr = sock.recvfrom(maxsize)
    resp = "UDP server sending data"
  sock.sendto(resp,addr)
```

Now, you can create a UDP client to send some data to the UDP server, as shown in the following code:

```
from socket import socket, AF_INET, SOCK_DGRAM

MAX_SIZE = 4096
PORT = 12345

if __name__ == '__main__':
    sock = socket(AF_INET,SOCK_DGRAM)
    msg = "Hello UDP server"
    sock.sendto(msg.encode(),('', PORT))
    data, addr = sock.recvfrom(MAX_SIZE)
    print("Server says:")
    print(repr(data))
```

In the preceding code snippet, the UDP client sends a single line of text Hello UDP server and receives the response from the server. The following screenshot shows the request sent from the client to the server:

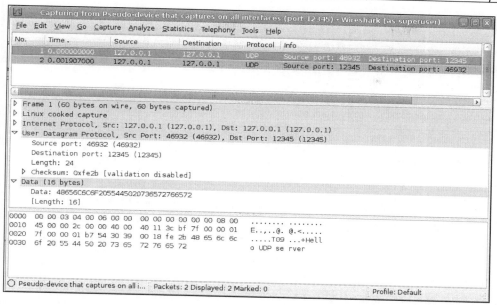

The following screenshot shows the server's response sent to the client. After inspecting UDP client/server packets, we can easily see that UDP is much simpler than TCP. It's often termed as a connectionless protocol as there is no acknowledgment or error checking involved.

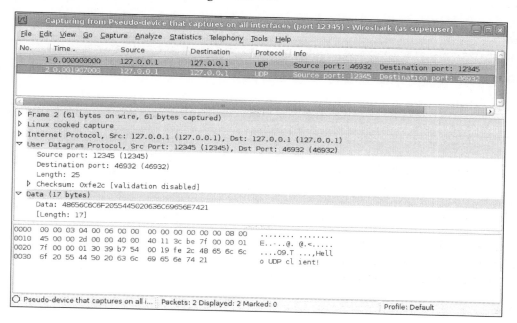

TCP port forwarding

One of the interesting experiments we can do with TCP socket programming is to set up a TCP port forwarding. This has very good use cases. Say, for example, if you are running an insecure program like FTP in a public server that doesn't have any SSL capability to do secure communication (FTP passwords can be seen clear-text over the wires). Since this server is accessible from Internet, you must not login with your password to the server without ensuring that the passwords are encrypted. One way of doing this is to use Secure FTP or SFTP. We can use a simple SSH tunnel in order to show how this approach works. So, any communication between your local FTP client and remote FTP server will happen via this encrypted channel.

Let us run the FTP program to the same SSH server host. But create an SSH tunnel from your local machine that will give you a local port number and will directly connect you to the remote FTP server daemon.

Python has a third party `sshtunnel` module that is a wrapper around the Paramiko's SSH library. The following is a code snippet of TCP port forwarding that shows how the concept can be realized:

```
import sshtunnel
from getpass import getpass

ssh_host = '192.168.56.101'
ssh_port = 22
ssh_user = 'YOUR_SSH_USERNAME'

REMOTE_HOST = '192.168.56.101'
REMOTE_PORT = 21

from sshtunnel import SSHTunnelForwarder
ssh_password = getpass('Enter YOUR_SSH_PASSWORD: ')

server = SSHTunnelForwarder(
    ssh_address=(ssh_host, ssh_port),
    ssh_username=ssh_user,
    ssh_password=ssh_password,
```

```
        remote_bind_address=(REMOTE_HOST, REMOTE_PORT))

    server.start()
    print('Connect the remote service via local port: %s'
        %server.local_bind_port)
    # work with FTP SERVICE via the `server.local_bind_port.
    try:
        while True:
            pass
    except KeyboardInterrupt:
        print("Exiting user user request.\n")
        server.stop()
```

Let us capture the packet transfer from the local machine `192.168.0.102` to the remote machine `192.168.0.101`. You will see all network traffic is encrypted. When you run the preceding script, you will get a local port number. Use the `ftp` command to connect to that local port number:

```
$ ftp <localhost> <local_bind_port>
```

If you run the preceding command, then you will get the following screenshot:

In the preceding screenshot, you cannot see any FTP traffic. As you can see, first we connect to local port `5815` (see the first three packets) and suddenly an encrypted session started with the remote host. You can continue watching the remote traffic, but there is no trace of FTP.

If you can also capture packets on your remote machine (192.168.56.101),
you could see FTP traffic, as shown in the following screenshot:

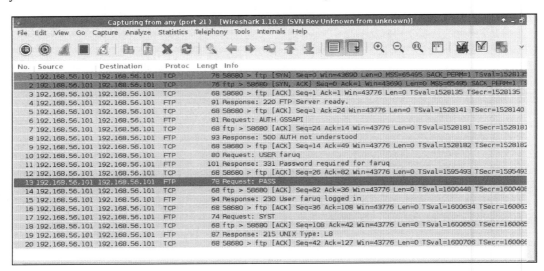

Interestingly, you can see your FTP password sent from the local machine (over SSH
tunnel) as clear-text only on your remote box, not over the network, as shown in the
following screenshot:

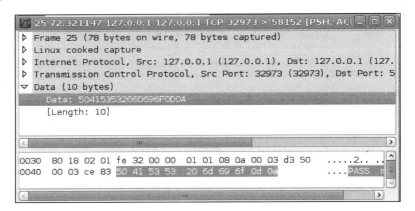

So, in this way, you can hide any sensitive network traffic in an SSL tunnel. Not only
the FTP, you can also pass remote desktop session encrypted over an SSH channel.

A non-blocking socket I/O

In this section, we will see a small example code snippet to test a non-blocking socket I/O. This is useful if you know that the synchronous blocking connection is not necessary for your program. The following is an example of non-blocking I/O:

```
import socket

if __name__ == '__main__':
    sock = socket.socket(socket.AF_INET, socket.SOCK_STREAM)
    sock.setblocking(0)
    sock.settimeout(0.5)
    sock.bind(("127.0.0.1", 0))

    socket_address =sock.getsockname()
    print("Asynchronous socket server launched on socket: %s"
    %str(socket_address))
    while(1):
        sock.listen(1)
```

This script will run a socket server and listen in a non-blocking style. This means you can connect more clients who won't be necessarily blocked for I/O.

Securing sockets with TLS/SSL

You have probably come across the discussion around secure web communication using **Secure Socket Layer (SSL)**, or more precisely **Transport Layer Security (TLS)**, which is adopted by many other high-level protocols. Let us see how we can wrap a plain sockets connection with SSL. Python has the built-in `ssl` module, which serves this purpose.

In this example, we would like to create a plain TCP socket and connect to an HTTPS enabled web server. Then, we can wrap that connection using SSL and check the various properties of the connection. For example, to check the identity of the remote web server, we can see if the hostname is same in the SSL certificate as we expect it to be. The following is an example of a secure socket-based client:

```
import socket
import ssl
from ssl import wrap_socket, CERT_NONE, PROTOCOL_TLSv1, SSLError
from ssl import SSLContext
```

```python
from ssl import HAS_SNI

from pprint import pprint

TARGET_HOST = 'www.google.com'
SSL_PORT = 443
# Use the path of CA certificate file in your system
CA_CERT_PATH = '/usr/local/lib/python3.3/dist-
  packages/requests/cacert.pem'

def ssl_wrap_socket(sock, keyfile=None, certfile=None,
  cert_reqs=None, ca_certs=None, server_hostname=None,
  ssl_version=None):

    context = SSLContext(ssl_version)
    context.verify_mode = cert_reqs

    if ca_certs:
        try:
            context.load_verify_locations(ca_certs)
        except Exception as e:
            raise SSLError(e)

    if certfile:
        context.load_cert_chain(certfile, keyfile)

    if HAS_SNI:  # OpenSSL enabled SNI
        return context.wrap_socket(sock,
        server_hostname=server_hostname)

    return context.wrap_socket(sock)

if __name__ == '__main__':
    hostname = input("Enter target host:") or TARGET_HOST
    client_sock = socket.socket(socket.AF_INET,
    socket.SOCK_STREAM)
    client_sock.connect((hostname, 443))

    ssl_socket = ssl_wrap_socket(client_sock,
    ssl_version=PROTOCOL_TLSv1,
    cert_reqs=ssl.CERT_REQUIRED,
    ca_certs=CA_CERT_PATH,
    server_hostname=hostname)

    print("Extracting remote host certificate details:")
```

```
cert = ssl_socket.getpeercert()
pprint(cert)
if not cert or ('commonName', TARGET_HOST) not in
cert['subject'][4]:
    raise Exception("Invalid SSL cert for host %s. Check if
    this is a man-in-the-middle attack!" )
ssl_socket.write('GET / \n'.encode('utf-8'))
#pprint(ssl_socket .recv(1024).split(b"\r\n"))
ssl_socket.close()
client_sock.close()
```

If you run the preceding example, you will see the details of the SSL certificate of a remote web server such as www.google.com. Here we have created a TCP socket and connected it to HTTPS port 443. Then that socket connection is wrapped into SSL packets using our ssl_wrap_socket() function. This function takes the following parameters as arguments:

- sock: TCP socket
- keyfile: SSL private key file path
- certfile: SSL public certificate path
- cert_reqs: Confirmation if certificate is required from other side to make connection and if validation test is required
- ca_certs: Public certificate authority certificate path
- server_hostname: The target remote server's hostname
- ssl_version: The intended SSL version to be used by the client

At the beginning of the SSL socket wrapping process, we have created an SSL context using the SSLContext() class. This is necessary to set up the SSL connection specific properties. Instead of using a custom context, we could also use a default context, supplied by default with the ssl module, using the create_default_context() function. You can specify whether you'd like to create client or server side sockets using a constant. The following is an example for creating a client side socket:

```
context = ssl.create_default_context(Purpose.SERVER_AUTH)
```

The SSLContext object takes the SSL version argument, that in our example is set to PROTOCOL_TLSv1, or you should use the latest version. Note that SSLv2 and SSLv3 are broken and must not be used in any production code for serious security issues.

In the preceding example, CERT_REQUIRED indicates that server certificate is necessary for the connection to continue, and this certificate will be validated later.

If the CA certificate parameter has been presented with a certificate path, the `load_verify_locations()` method is used to load the CA certificate files. This will be used to verify the peer server certificates. If you'd like to use the default certificate path on your system, you'd probably call another context method; `load_default_certs(purpose=Purpose.SERVER_AUTH)`.

When we operate on server side, usually the `load_cert_chain()` method is used to load the key and certificate file so that clients can verify the server's authenticity.

Finally, the `wrap_socket()` method is called to return an SSL wrapped socket. Note that, if OpenSSL library comes with **Server Name Indication (SNI)** support enabled, you can pass the remote server's host name while wrapping the socket. This is useful when the remote server uses different SSL certificates for different secure services using a single IP address, for example, name-based virtual hosting.

If you run the preceding SSL client code, you will see the various properties of the SSL certificate of the remote server, as shown in the following screenshot. This is used to verify the authenticity of the remote server by calling the `getpeercert()` method and comparing it with the returned hostname.

```
root@localhost:~/learnpynet/ch7
File  Edit  View  Search  Terminal  Help
[root@localhost ch7]# python 7_8_ssl_client.py
Enter target host:www.google.com
Extracting remote host certificate details:
{'issuer': ((('countryName', 'US'),),
            (('organizationName', 'Google Inc'),),
            (('commonName', 'Google Internet Authority G2'),)),
 'notAfter': 'Jun 17 00:00:00 2015 GMT',
 'notBefore': 'Mar 19 08:48:59 2015 GMT',
 'serialNumber': '3B1B6E2EB2625C04',
 'subject': ((('countryName', 'US'),),
             (('stateOrProvinceName', 'California'),),
             (('localityName', 'Mountain View'),),
             (('organizationName', 'Google Inc'),),
             (('commonName', 'www.google.com'),)),
 'subjectAltName': (('DNS', 'www.google.com'),),
 'version': 3}
[root@localhost ch7]#
```

Interestingly, if any other fake web server wants to pretend to be the Google's web server, it simply can't do that, provided that you check the SSL certificate that is signed by an accredited certificate authority, unless an accredited CA has been compromised/subverted. This form of attack to your web browser is commonly referred to as the **man in the middle (MITM)** attack.

Inspecting standard SSL client/server communication

The following screenshot shows the interaction between the SSL client and the remote server:

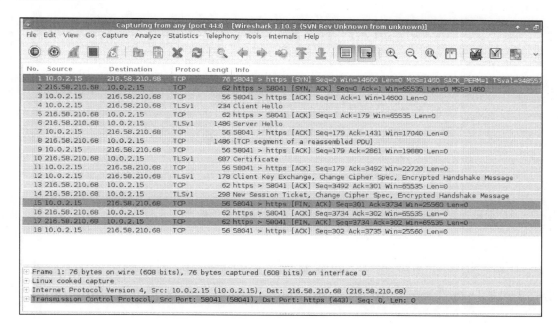

Let us examine the SSL handshake process between the client and the server. In the first step of a SSL handshake, the client sends a `Hello` message to the remote server saying what it is capable of, in terms handling key files, encrypting messages, doing message integrity checks, and so on. In the following screenshot, you can see that the client is presenting a set of 38 cipher suites to the server to choose relevant algorithms. It also sends the TLS version number 1.0 and a random number to generate a master secret for encrypting the subsequent message exchanges. This is helpful for preventing any third party to look inside the packets. The random numbers seen in the hello messages are used to generate the pre-master secret, which both ends will process further to arrive at the master secret, and then use that to generate the symmetric key.

In the second packet from server to client, the server selects the cipher suite `TLS_ECDHE_RSA_WITH_RC4_128_SHA` for the purpose of connecting to the client. This roughly means the server wants to use the RSA algorithm for key handling, RC4 for encryption, and SHA for integrity checking (hashing). This is shown in the following screenshot:

In the second phase of the SSL handshake, the server sends an SSL certificate to the client. This certificate is issued by a CA, as mentioned earlier. It contains a serial number, public key, validity period, and the details of the subject and the issuer. The following screenshot show the remote server certificate. Can you locate the server's public key inside the packet?

In the third phase of the handshake, the client exchanges a key and calculates a master secret to encrypt the messages and continue further communications. Client also sends the request to change the cipher specification that was agreed on the previous phase. It then indicates to start encrypting the message. The following screenshot shows this process:

```
 12 0.100009000 10.0.2.15 216.58.210.36 TLSv1 178 Client Key Exchange, Change Cipher Spec, Encrypted Ha  ↑  _  □  ×
 Frame 12: 178 bytes on wire (1424 bits), 178 bytes captured (1424 bits) on interface 0
 Linux cooked capture
 Internet Protocol Version 4, Src: 10.0.2.15 (10.0.2.15), Dst: 216.58.210.36 (216.58.210.36)
 Transmission Control Protocol, Src Port: 41910 (41910), Dst Port: https (443), Seq: 179, Ack: 3492, Len:
 Secure Sockets Layer
   TLSv1 Record Layer: Handshake Protocol: Client Key Exchange
       Content Type: Handshake (22)
       Version: TLS 1.0 (0x0301)
       Length: 70
     Handshake Protocol: Client Key Exchange
       Handshake Type: Client Key Exchange (16)
       Length: 66
       EC Diffie-Hellman Client Params
         Pubkey Length: 65
         pubkey: 04bdb5ef88a16bb52b2ab6f51d222ed9c398a1523e3980f3...
   TLSv1 Record Layer: Change Cipher Spec Protocol: Change Cipher Spec
       Content Type: Change Cipher Spec (20)
       Version: TLS 1.0 (0x0301)
       Length: 1
       Change Cipher Spec Message
   TLSv1 Record Layer: Handshake Protocol: Encrypted Handshake Message
       Content Type: Handshake (22)
       Version: TLS 1.0 (0x0301)
       Length: 36
       Handshake Protocol: Encrypted Handshake Message
```

In the final task of the SSL handshake process, a new session ticket is generated by the server for the client's particular session. This happens due to a TLS extension where the client advertises its support by sending an empty session ticket extension in the client Hello message. The server answers with an empty session ticket extension in its server Hello message. This session ticket mechanism enables the client to remember the whole session state, and the server becomes less engaged in maintaining a server-side session cache. The following screenshot shows an example for presenting an SSL session ticket:

```
14 0.116012000 216.58.210.36 10.0.2.15 TLSv1 298 New Session Ticket, Change Cipher Spec, Encryp↑ _ □ ×
    Protocol: TCP (6)
  ⊞ Header checksum: 0xc0bd [correct]
    Source: 216.58.210.36 (216.58.210.36)
    Destination: 10.0.2.15 (10.0.2.15)
⊞ Transmission Control Protocol, Src Port: https (443), Dst Port: 41910 (41910), Seq: 3492, Ack: ⌷
⊟ Secure Sockets Layer
  ⊟ TLSv1 Record Layer: Handshake Protocol: New Session Ticket
      Content Type: Handshake (22)
      Version: TLS 1.0 (0x0301)
      Length: 190
    ⊟ Handshake Protocol: New Session Ticket
        Handshake Type: New Session Ticket (4)
        Length: 186
      ⊟ TLS Session Ticket
          Session Ticket Lifetime Hint: 100800
          Session Ticket Length: 180
          Session Ticket: 4452449371ea698543335aa0534c98059bdd1bb339ec1acd...
  ⊟ TLSv1 Record Layer: Change Cipher Spec Protocol: Change Cipher Spec
      Content Type: Change Cipher Spec (20)
      Version: TLS 1.0 (0x0301)
      Length: 1
      Change Cipher Spec Message
  ⊟ TLSv1 Record Layer: Handshake Protocol: Encrypted Handshake Message
      Content Type: Handshake (22)
      Version: TLS 1.0 (0x0301)
      Length: 36
      Handshake Protocol: Encrypted Handshake Message
```

Creating a custom SSL client/server

So far, we have been dealing more with the SSL or TLS client. Now, let us have a look at the server side briefly. As you are already familiar with the TCP/UDP socket server creation process, let's skip that part and just concentrate on the SSL wrapping part. The following code snippet shows an example of a simple SSL server:

```python
import socket
import ssl

SSL_SERVER_PORT = 8000

if __name__ == '__main__':
    server_socket = socket.socket()
```

```
server_socket.bind(('', SSL_SERVER_PORT))
server_socket.listen(5)
print("Waiting for ssl client on port %s" %SSL_SERVER_PORT)
newsocket, fromaddr = server_socket.accept()
# Generate your server's  public certificate and private key
pairs.
ssl_conn = ssl.wrap_socket(newsocket, server_side=True,
certfile="server.crt", keyfile="server.key",
ssl_version=ssl.PROTOCOL_TLSv1)
print(ssl_conn.read())
ssl_conn.write('200 OK\r\n\r\n'.encode())
print("Served ssl client. Exiting...")
ssl_conn.close()
server_socket.close()
```

As you can see, the server socket is wrapped with the wrap_socket() method, which uses some intuitive parameters such as certfile, keyfile, and SSL version number. You can easily generate the certificate by following any step-by-step guide found on the Internet. For example, http://www.akadia.com/services/ssh_test_certificate.html suggests to generate the SSL certificate in a few steps.

Now, let's make a simplified version of a SSL client to talk with the above SSL server. The following code snippet shows an example of a simple SSL client:

```
from socket import socket
import ssl

from pprint import pprint

TARGET_HOST ='localhost'
TARGET_PORT = 8000
CA_CERT_PATH = 'server.crt'


if __name__ == '__main__':

    sock = socket()
    ssl_conn = ssl.wrap_socket(sock, cert_reqs=ssl.CERT_REQUIRED,
    ssl_version=ssl.PROTOCOL_TLSv1, ca_certs=CA_CERT_PATH)
    target_host = TARGET_HOST
    target_port = TARGET_PORT
    ssl_conn.connect((target_host, int(target_port)))
```

```
# get remote cert
cert = ssl_conn.getpeercert()
print("Checking server certificate")
pprint(cert)
if not cert or ssl.match_hostname(cert, target_host):
    raise Exception("Invalid SSL cert for host %s. Check if
    this is a man-in-the-middle attack!" %target_host )
print("Server certificate OK.\n Sending some custom request...
GET ")
ssl_conn.write('GET / \n'.encode('utf-8'))
print("Response received from server:")
print(ssl_conn.read())
ssl_conn.close()
```

Running the client/server will show output similar to the following screenshot.
Can you see any difference in comparison to our last example client/server
communication?

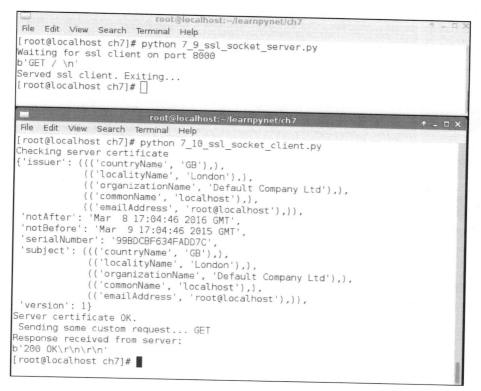

Inspecting interaction between a custom SSL client/server

Let us inspect the SSL client/server interaction once again in order to observe the differences. The first screenshot shows the entire communication sequence. In the following screenshot we can see that the server's Hello and certificate are combined in the same message.

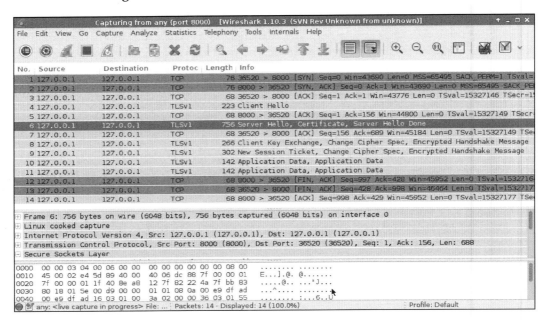

The client's **Client Hello** packet looks pretty similar to our previous SSL connection, as shown in the following screenshot:

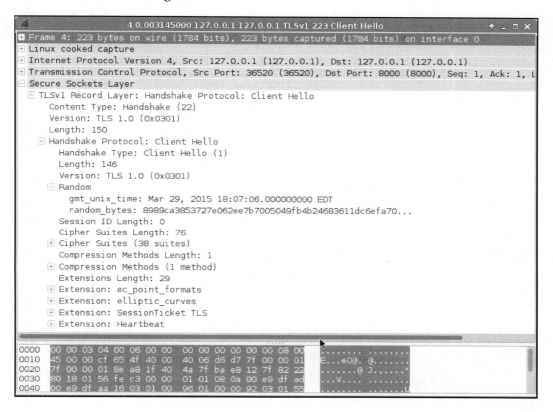

The server's **Server Hello** packet is a bit different. Can you identify the differences? The cipher specification is different that is TLS_RSA_WITH_AES_256_CBC_SHA, as shown in the following screenshot:

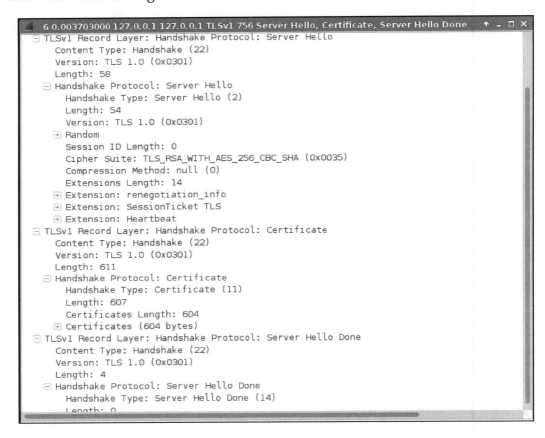

```
6 0.003703000 127.0.0.1 127.0.0.1 TLSv1 756 Server Hello, Certificate, Server Hello Done     ↑ _ □ X
TLSv1 Record Layer: Handshake Protocol: Server Hello
   Content Type: Handshake (22)
   Version: TLS 1.0 (0x0301)
   Length: 58
 Handshake Protocol: Server Hello
      Handshake Type: Server Hello (2)
      Length: 54
      Version: TLS 1.0 (0x0301)
   Random
      Session ID Length: 0
      Cipher Suite: TLS_RSA_WITH_AES_256_CBC_SHA (0x0035)
      Compression Method: null (0)
      Extensions Length: 14
   Extension: renegotiation_info
   Extension: SessionTicket TLS
   Extension: Heartbeat
TLSv1 Record Layer: Handshake Protocol: Certificate
   Content Type: Handshake (22)
   Version: TLS 1.0 (0x0301)
   Length: 611
 Handshake Protocol: Certificate
      Handshake Type: Certificate (11)
      Length: 607
      Certificates Length: 604
   Certificates (604 bytes)
TLSv1 Record Layer: Handshake Protocol: Server Hello Done
   Content Type: Handshake (22)
   Version: TLS 1.0 (0x0301)
   Length: 4
 Handshake Protocol: Server Hello Done
      Handshake Type: Server Hello Done (14)
      Length: 0
```

The **Client key exchange** packet also looks very familiar, as shown in the following screenshot:

```
    8 0.006286000 127.0.0.1 127.0.0.1 TLSv1 266 Client Key Exchange, Change Cipher Spec, Encrypted Handshake Message
⊞ Frame 8: 266 bytes on wire (2128 bits), 266 bytes captured (2128 bits) on interface 0
⊞ Linux cooked capture
⊞ Internet Protocol Version 4, Src: 127.0.0.1 (127.0.0.1), Dst: 127.0.0.1 (127.0.0.1)
⊞ Transmission Control Protocol, Src Port: 36520 (36520), Dst Port: 8000 (8000), Seq: 156, Ack: 689, Len: 198
⊟ Secure Sockets Layer
  ⊟ TLSv1 Record Layer: Handshake Protocol: Client Key Exchange
      Content Type: Handshake (22)
      Version: TLS 1.0 (0x0301)
      Length: 134
    ⊟ Handshake Protocol: Client Key Exchange
        Handshake Type: Client Key Exchange (16)
        Length: 130
      ⊟ RSA Encrypted PreMaster Secret
          Encrypted PreMaster length: 128
          Encrypted PreMaster: 8c6e0664610e73f8a12048f26592adb085a4a26abcb59738...
  ⊟ TLSv1 Record Layer: Change Cipher Spec Protocol: Change Cipher Spec
      Content Type: Change Cipher Spec (20)
      Version: TLS 1.0 (0x0301)
      Length: 1
      Change Cipher Spec Message
  ⊟ TLSv1 Record Layer: Handshake Protocol: Encrypted Handshake Message
      Content Type: Handshake (22)
      Version: TLS 1.0 (0x0301)
      Length: 48
      Handshake Protocol: Encrypted Handshake Message
```

The following screenshot shows the **New Session Ticket** packet offered in this connection:

```
    9 0.009807000 127.0.0.1 127.0.0.1 TLSv1 302 New Session Ticket, Change Cipher Spec, Encrypted Handshake Message
⊞ Frame 9: 302 bytes on wire (2416 bits), 302 bytes captured (2416 bits) on interface 0
⊞ Linux cooked capture
⊞ Internet Protocol Version 4, Src: 127.0.0.1 (127.0.0.1), Dst: 127.0.0.1 (127.0.0.1)
⊞ Transmission Control Protocol, Src Port: 8000 (8000), Dst Port: 36520 (36520), Seq: 689, Ack: 354, Len: 234
⊟ Secure Sockets Layer
  ⊟ TLSv1 Record Layer: Handshake Protocol: New Session Ticket
      Content Type: Handshake (22)
      Version: TLS 1.0 (0x0301)
      Length: 170
    ⊟ Handshake Protocol: New Session Ticket
        Handshake Type: New Session Ticket (4)
        Length: 166
      ⊟ TLS Session Ticket
          Session Ticket Lifetime Hint: 7200
          Session Ticket Length: 160
          Session Ticket: c9faa63ba044c4c02e571ebd24240a8e56eaee9624a5548e...
  ⊟ TLSv1 Record Layer: Change Cipher Spec Protocol: Change Cipher Spec
      Content Type: Change Cipher Spec (20)
      Version: TLS 1.0 (0x0301)
      Length: 1
      Change Cipher Spec Message
  ⊟ TLSv1 Record Layer: Handshake Protocol: Encrypted Handshake Message
      Content Type: Handshake (22)
      Version: TLS 1.0 (0x0301)
      Length: 48
      Handshake Protocol: Encrypted Handshake Message
```

Now let's have a look at the application data. Is that encrypted? For the captured packet, it looks like garbage. The following screenshot shows the encrypted message that hides the real data. This is what we want to achieve using SSL/TLS.

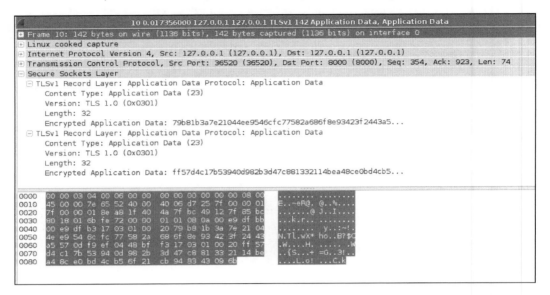

Summary

In this chapter, we discussed basic TCP/IP socket programming using Python's `socket` and `ssl` module. We demonstrated how simple TCP sockets can be wrapped with TLS and used to carry encrypted data. We also found the ways to validate the authenticity of a remote server using SSL certificates. Some other minor issues around socket programming, such as non-blocking socket I/O were also presented. The detailed packet analysis in each section helps us to understand what happens under the hood in our socket programming exercises.

In the next chapter, we will learn about the socket server design, particularly the popular multithreaded and event-driven approaches will be touched upon.

8
Client and Server Applications

In the previous chapter, we looked at exchanging data between devices by using the sockets interface. In this chapter, we're going to use sockets to build network applications. Sockets follow one of the main models of computer networking, that is, the **client/server** model. We'll look at this with a focus on structuring server applications. We'll cover the following topics:

- Designing a simple protocol
- Building an echo server and client
- Building a chat server and client
- Multithreaded and event-driven server architectures
- The `eventlet` and `asyncio` libraries

The examples in this chapter are best run on Linux or a Unix operating system. The Windows sockets implementation has some idiosyncrasies, and these can create some error conditions, which we will not be covering here. Note that Windows does not support the `poll` interface that we'll use in one example. If you do use Windows, then you'll probably need to use *ctrl + break* to kill these processes in the console, rather than using *ctrl - c* because Python in a Windows command prompt doesn't respond to *ctrl – c* when it's blocking on a socket send or receive, which will be quite often in this chapter! (and if, like me, you're unfortunate enough to try testing these on a Windows laptop without a *break* key, then be prepared to get very familiar with the Windows Task Manager's **End task** button).

Client and server

The basic setup in the client/server model is one device, the server that runs a service and patiently waits for clients to connect and make requests to the service. A 24-hour grocery shop may be a real world analogy. The shop waits for customers to come in and when they do, they request certain products, purchase them and leave. The shop might advertise itself so people know where to find it, but the actual transactions happen while the customers are visiting the shop.

A typical computing example is a web server. The server listens on a TCP port for clients that need its web pages. When a client, for example a web browser, requires a web page that the server hosts, it connects to the server and then makes a request for that page. The server replies with the content of the page and then the client disconnects. The server advertises itself by having a hostname, which the clients can use to discover the IP address so that they can connect to it.

In both of these situations, it is the client that initiates any interaction – the server is purely responsive to that interaction. So, the needs of the programs that run on the client and server are quite different.

Client programs are typically oriented towards the interface between the user and the service. They retrieve and display the service, and allow the user to interact with it. Server programs are written to stay running for indefinite periods of time, to be stable, to efficiently deliver the service to the clients that are requesting it, and to potentially handle a large number of simultaneous connections with a minimal impact on the experience of any one client.

In this chapter, we will look at this model by writing a simple echo server and client, and then upgrading it to a chat server, which can handle a session with multiple clients. The `socket` module in Python perfectly suits this task.

An echo protocol

Before we write our first client and server programs, we need to decide how they are going to interact with each other, that is we need to design a protocol for their communication.

Our echo server should listen until a client connects and sends a bytes string, then we want it to echo that string back to the client. We only need a few basic rules for doing this. These rules are as follows:

1. Communication will take place over TCP.
2. The client will initiate an echo session by creating a socket connection to the server.
3. The server will accept the connection and listen for the client to send a bytes string.
4. The client will send a bytes string to the server.
5. Once it sends the bytes string, the client will listen for a reply from the server
6. When it receives the bytes string from the client, the server will send the bytes string back to the client.
7. When the client has received the bytes string from the server, it will close its socket to end the session.

These steps are straightforward enough. The missing element here is how the server and the client will know when a complete message has been sent. Remember that an application sees a TCP connection as an endless stream of bytes, so we need to decide what in that byte stream will signal the end of a message.

Framing

This problem is called **framing**, and there are several approaches that we can take to handle it. The main ones are described here:

1. Make it a protocol rule that only one message will be sent per connection, and once a message has been sent, the sender will immediately close the socket.
2. Use fixed length messages. The receiver will read the number of bytes and know that they have the whole message.
3. Prefix the message with the length of the message. The receiver will read the length of the message from the stream first, then it will read the indicated number of bytes to get the rest of the message.
4. Use special character delimiters for indicating the end of a message. The receiver will scan the incoming stream for a delimiter, and the message comprises everything up to the delimiter.

Option 1 is a good choice for very simple protocols. It's easy to implement and it doesn't require any special handling of the received stream. However, it requires the setting up and tearing down of a socket for every message, and this can impact performance when a server is handling many messages at once.

Option 2 is again simple to implement, but it only makes efficient use of the network when our data comes in neat, fixed-length blocks. For example in a chat server the message lengths are variable, so we will have to use a special character, such as the null byte, to pad messages to the block size. This only works where we know for sure that the padding character will never appear in the actual message data. There is also the additional issue of how to handle messages longer than the block length.

Option 3 is usually considered as one of the best approaches. Although it can be more complex to code than the other options, the implementations are still reasonably straightforward, and it makes efficient use of bandwidth. The overhead imposed by including the length of each message is usually minimal as compared to the message length. It also avoids the need for any additional processing of the received data, which may be needed by certain implementations of option 4.

Option 4 is the most bandwidth-efficient option, and is a good choice when we know that only a limited set of characters, such as the ASCII alphanumeric characters, will be used in messages. If this is the case, then we can choose a delimiter character, such as the null byte, which will never appear in the message data, and then the received data can be easily broken into messages as this character is encountered. Implementations are usually simpler than option 3. Although it is possible to employ this method for arbitrary data, that is, where the delimiter could also appear as a valid character in a message, this requires the use of character escaping, which needs an additional round of processing of the data. Hence in these situations, it's usually simpler to use length-prefixing.

For our echo and chat applications, we'll be using the UTF-8 character set to send messages. The null byte isn't used in any character in UTF-8 except for the null byte itself, so it makes a good delimiter. Thus, we'll be using method 4 with the null byte as the delimiter to frame our messages.

So, our rule number 8 will become:

> *Messages will be encoded in the UTF-8 character set for transmission, and they will be terminated by the null byte.*

Now, let's write our echo programs.

A simple echo server

As we work through this chapter, we'll find ourselves reusing several pieces of code, so to save ourselves from repetition, we'll set up a module with useful functions that we can reuse as we go along. Create a file called `tincanchat.py` and save the following code in it:

```python
import socket

HOST = ''
PORT = 4040

def create_listen_socket(host, port):
    """ Setup the sockets our server will receive connection
    requests on """
    sock = socket.socket(socket.AF_INET, socket.SOCK_STREAM)
    sock.setsockopt(socket.SOL_SOCKET, socket.SO_REUSEADDR, 1)
    sock.bind((host, port))
    sock.listen(100)
    return sock

def recv_msg(sock):
    """ Wait for data to arrive on the socket, then parse into
    messages using b'\0' as message delimiter """
    data = bytearray()
    msg = ''
    # Repeatedly read 4096 bytes off the socket, storing the bytes
    # in data until we see a delimiter
    while not msg:
        recvd = sock.recv(4096)
        if not recvd:
            # Socket has been closed prematurely
            raise ConnectionError()
        data = data + recvd
        if b'\0' in recvd:
            # we know from our protocol rules that we only send
            # one message per connection, so b'\0' will always be
            # the last character
            msg = data.rstrip(b'\0')
    msg = msg.decode('utf-8')
    return msg
```

```
def prep_msg(msg):
    """ Prepare a string to be sent as a message """
    msg += '\0'
    return msg.encode('utf-8')

def send_msg(sock, msg):
    """ Send a string over a socket, preparing it first """
    data = prep_msg(msg)
    sock.sendall(data)
```

First we define a default interface and a port number to listen on. The empty `' '` interface, specified in the HOST variable, tells `socket.bind()` to listen on all available interfaces. If you want to restrict access to just your machine, then change the value of the HOST variable at the beginning of the code to `127.0.0.1`.

We'll be using `create_listen_socket()` to set up our server listening connections. This code is the same for several of our server programs, so it makes sense to reuse it.

The `recv_msg()` function will be used by our echo server and client for receiving messages from a socket. In our echo protocol, there isn't anything that our programs may need to do while they're waiting to receive a message, so this function just calls `socket.recv()` in a loop until it has received the whole message. As per our framing rule, it will check the accumulated data on each iteration to see if it has received a null byte, and if so, then it will return the received data, stripping off the null byte and decoding it from UTF-8.

The `send_msg()` and `prep_msg()` functions work together for framing and sending a message. We've separated the null byte termination and the UTF-8 encoding into `prep_msg()` because we will use them in isolation later on.

Handling the received data

Note that we're drawing ourselves a careful line with these send and receive functions as regards string encoding. Python 3 strings are Unicode, while the data that we receive over the network is bytes. The last thing that we want to be doing is handling a mixture of these in the rest of our program code, so we're going to carefully encode and decode the data at the boundary of our program, where the data enters and leaves the network. This will ensure that any functions in the rest of our code can assume that they'll be working with Python strings, which will later on make things much easier for us.

Of course, not all the data that we may want to send or receive over a network will be text. For example, images, compressed files, and music, can't be decoded to a Unicode string, so a different kind of handling is needed. Usually this will involve loading the data into a class, such as a **Python Image Library (PIL)** image for example, if we are going to manipulate the object in some way.

There are basic checks that could be done here on the received data, before performing full processing on it, to quickly flag any problems with the data. Some examples of such checks are as follows:

- Checking the length of the received data
- Checking the first few bytes of a file for a magic number to confirm a file type
- Checking values of higher level protocol headers, such as the Host header in an HTTP request

This kind of checking will allow our application to fail fast if there is an obvious problem.

The server itself

Now, let's write our echo server. Open a new file called 1.1-echo-server-uni.py and save the following code in it:

```
import tincanchat

HOST = tincanchat.HOST
PORT = tincanchat.PORT


def handle_client(sock, addr):
    """ Receive data from the client via sock and echo it back """
    try:
        msg = tincanchat.recv_msg(sock)  # Blocks until received
                                         # complete message
        print('{}: {}'.format(addr, msg))
        tincanchat.send_msg(sock, msg)  # Blocks until sent
    except (ConnectionError, BrokenPipeError):
        print('Socket error')
    finally:
        print('Closed connection to {}'.format(addr))
        sock.close()
```

```
if __name__ == '__main__':
    listen_sock = tincanchat.create_listen_socket(HOST, PORT)
    addr = listen_sock.getsockname()
    print('Listening on {}'.format(addr))

    while True:
        client_sock, addr = listen_sock.accept()
        print('Connection from {}'.format(addr))
        handle_client(client_sock, addr)
```

This is about as simple as a server can get! First, we set up our listening socket with the `create_listen_socket()` call. Second, we enter our main loop, where we listen forever for incoming connections from clients, blocking on `listen_sock.accept()`. When a client connection comes in, we invoke the `handle_client()` function, which handles the client as per our protocol. We've created a separate function for this code, partly to keep the main loop tidy, and partly because we'll want to reuse this set of operations in later programs.

That's our server, now we just need to make a client to talk to it.

A simple echo client

Create a file called `1.2-echo_client-uni.py` and save the following code in it:

```
import sys, socket
import tincanchat

HOST = sys.argv[-1] if len(sys.argv) > 1 else '127.0.0.1'
PORT = tincanchat.PORT

if __name__ == '__main__':
    while True:
        try:
            sock = socket.socket(socket.AF_INET,
                                 socket.SOCK_STREAM)
            sock.connect((HOST, PORT))
            print('\nConnected to {}:{}'.format(HOST, PORT))
            print("Type message, enter to send, 'q' to quit")
            msg = input()
            if msg == 'q': break
            tincanchat.send_msg(sock, msg)  # Blocks until sent
            print('Sent message: {}'.format(msg))
```

```
                    msg = tincanchat.recv_msg(sock)   # Block until
                                                       # received complete
                                                       # message
                print('Received echo: ' + msg)
            except ConnectionError:
                print('Socket error')
                break
            finally:
                sock.close()
                print('Closed connection to server\n')
```

If we're running our server on a different machine from the one on which we are running the client, then we can supply the IP address or the hostname of the server as a command line argument to the client program. If we don't, then it will default to trying to connect to the localhost.

The third and forth lines of the code check the command line arguments for a server address. Once we've determined which server to connect to, we enter our main loop, which loops forever until we kill the client by entering q as a message. Within the main loop, we first create a connection to the server. Second, we prompt the user to enter the message to send and then we send the message using the tincanchat. send_msg() function. We then wait for the server's reply. Once we get the reply, we print it and then we close the connection as per our protocol.

Give our client and server a try. Run the server in a terminal by using the following command:

$ python 1.1-echo_server-uni.py
Listening on ('0.0.0.0', 4040)

In another terminal, run the client and note that you will need to specify the server if you need to connect to another computer, as shown here:

$ python 1.2-echo_client.py 192.168.0.7
Type message, enter to send, 'q' to quit

Running the terminals side by side is a good idea, because you can simultaneously see how the programs behave.

Type a few messages into the client and see how the server picks them up and sends them back. Disconnecting with the client should also prompt a notification on the server.

Concurrent I/O

If you're adventurous, then you may have tried connecting to our server using more than one client at once. If you tried sending messages from both of them, then you'd have seen that it does not work as we might have hoped. If you haven't tried this, then give it a go.

A working echo session on the client should look like this:

```
Type message, enter to send. 'q' to quit
hello world
Sent message: hello world
Received echo: hello world
Closed connection to server
```

However, when trying to send a message by using a second connected client, we'll see something like this:

```
Type message, enter to send. 'q' to quit
hello world
Sent message: hello world
```

The client will hang when the message is sent, and it won't get an echo reply. You may also notice that if we send a message by using the first connected client, then the second client will get its response. So, what's going on here?

The problem is that the server can only listen for the messages from one client at a time. As soon as the first client connects, the server blocks at the socket.recv() call in tincanchat.recv_msg(), waiting for the first client to send a message. The server isn't able to receive messages from other clients while this is happening and so, when another client sends a message, that client blocks too, waiting for the server to send a reply.

This is a slightly contrived example. The problem in this case could easily be fixed in the client end by asking the user for an input before establishing a connection to the server. However in our full chat service, the client will need to be able to listen for messages from the server while simultaneously waiting for user input. This is not possible in our present procedural setup.

There are two solutions to this problem. We can either use more than one thread or process, or use **non-blocking** sockets along with an **event-driven** architecture. We're going to look at both of these approaches, starting with **multithreading**.

Multithreading and multiprocessing

Python has APIs that allow us to write both multithreading and multiprocessing applications. The principle behind multithreading and multiprocessing is simply to take copies of our code and run them in additional threads or processes. The operating system automatically schedules the threads and processes across available CPU cores to provide fair processing time allocation to all the threads and processes. This effectively allows a program to simultaneously run multiple operations. In addition, when a thread or process blocks, for example, when waiting for IO, the thread or process can be de-prioritized by the OS, and the CPU cores can be allocated to other threads or processes that have actual computation to do.

Here is an overview of how threads and processes relate to each other:

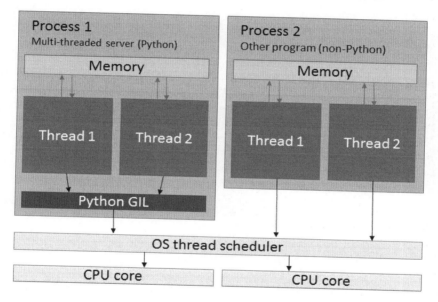

Threads exist within processes. A process can contain multiple threads but it always contains at least one thread, sometimes called the **main thread**. Threads within the same process share memory, so data transfer between threads is just a case of referencing the shared objects. Processes do not share memory, so other interfaces, such as files, sockets, or specially allocated areas of shared memory, must be used for transferring data between processes.

When threads have operations to execute, they ask the operating system thread scheduler to allocate them some time on a CPU, and the scheduler allocates the waiting threads to CPU cores based on various parameters, which vary from OS to OS. Threads in the same process may run on separate CPU cores at the same time.

Although two processes have been displayed in the preceding diagram, multiprocessing is not going on here, since the processes belong to different applications. The second process is displayed to illustrate a key difference between Python threading and threading in most other programs. This difference is the presence of the GIL.

Threading and the GIL

The CPython interpreter (the standard version of Python available for download from www.python.org) contains something called the **Global Interpreter Lock** (**GIL**). The GIL exists to ensure that only a single thread in a Python process can run at a time, even if multiple CPU cores are present. The reason for having the GIL is that it makes the underlying C code of the Python interpreter much easier to write and maintain. The drawback of this is that Python programs using multithreading cannot take advantage of multiple cores for parallel computation.

This is a cause of much contention; however, for us this is not so much of a problem. Even with the GIL present, threads that are blocking on I/O are still de-prioritized by the OS and put into the background, so threads that do have computational work to do can run instead. The following figure is a simplified illustration of this:

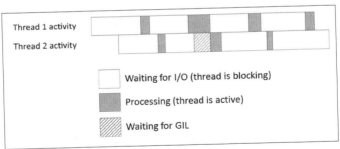

The **Waiting for GIL** state is where a thread has sent or received some data and so is ready to come out of the blocking state, but another thread has the GIL, so the ready thread is forced to wait. In many network applications, including our echo and chat servers, the time spent waiting on I/O is much higher than the time spent processing data. As long as we don't have a very large number of connections (a situation we'll discuss later on when we come to event driven architectures), thread contention caused by the GIL is relatively low, and hence threading is still a suitable architecture for these network server applications.

With this in mind, we're going to use multithreading rather than multiprocessing in our echo server. The shared data model will simplify the code that we'll need for allowing our chat clients to exchange messages with each other, and because we're I/O bound, we don't need processes for parallel computation. Another reason for not using processes in this case is that processes are more "heavyweight" in terms of the OS resources, so creating a new process takes longer than creating a new thread. Processes also use more memory.

One thing to note is that if you need to perform an intensive computation in your network server application (maybe you need to compress a large file before sending it over the network), then you should investigate methods for running this in a separate process. Because of quirks in the implementation of the GIL, having even a single computationally intensive thread in a mainly I/O bound process when multiple CPU cores are available can severely impact the performance of all the I/O bound threads. For more details, go through the David Beazley presentations linked to in the following information box:

Processes and threads are different beasts, and if you're not clear on the distinctions, it's worthwhile to read up. A good starting point is the Wikipedia article on threads, which can be found at `http://en.wikipedia.org/wiki/Thread_(computing)`.

A good overview of the topic is given in *Chapter 4* of Benjamin Erb's thesis, which is available at `http://berb.github.io/diploma-thesis/community/`.

Additional information on the GIL, including the reasoning behind keeping it in Python can be found in the official Python documentation at `https://wiki.python.org/moin/GlobalInterpreterLock`.

You can also read more on this topic in Nick Coghlan's Python 3 Q&A, which can be found at `http://python-notes.curiousefficiency.org/en/latest/python3/questions_and_answers.html#but-but-surely-fixing-the-gil-is-more-important-than-fixing-unicode`.

Finally, David Beazley has done some fascinating research on the performance of the GIL on multi-core systems. Two presentations of importance are available online. They give a good technical background, which is relevant to this chapter. These can be found at `http://pyvideo.org/video/353/pycon-2010--understanding-the-python-gil---82` and at `https://www.youtube.com/watch?v=5jbG7UKT114`.

A multithreaded echo server

A benefit of the multithreading approach is that the OS handles the thread switches for us, which means we can continue to write our program in a procedural style. Hence we only need to make small adjustments to our server program to make it multithreaded, and thus, capable of handling multiple clients simultaneously.

Create a new file called `1.3-echo_server-multi.py` and add the following code to it:

```python
import threading
import tincanchat

HOST = tincanchat.HOST
PORT = tincanchat.PORT

def handle_client(sock, addr):
    """ Receive one message and echo it back to client, then close
        socket """
    try:
        msg = tincanchat.recv_msg(sock)  # blocks until received
                                         # complete message
        msg = '{}: {}'.format(addr, msg)
        print(msg)
        tincanchat.send_msg(sock, msg)   # blocks until sent
    except (ConnectionError, BrokenPipeError):
        print('Socket error')
    finally:
        print('Closed connection to {}'.format(addr))
        sock.close()

if __name__ == '__main__':
    listen_sock = tincanchat.create_listen_socket(HOST, PORT)
    addr = listen_sock.getsockname()
    print('Listening on {}'.format(addr))

    while True:
        client_sock,addr = listen_sock.accept()
        # Thread will run function handle_client() autonomously
        # and concurrently to this while loop
        thread = threading.Thread(target=handle_client,
                                  args=[client_sock, addr],
                                  daemon=True)
        thread.start()
        print('Connection from {}'.format(addr))
```

You can see that we've just imported an extra module and modified our main loop to run our `handle_client()` function in separate threads, rather than running it in the main thread. For each client that connects, we create a new thread that just runs the `handle_client()` function. When the thread blocks on a receive or send, the OS checks the other threads to see if they have come out of a blocking state, and if any have, then it switches to one of them.

Notice that we have set the `daemon` argument in the thread constructor call to `True`. This will allow the program to exit if we hit *ctrl - c* without us having to explicitly close all of our threads first.

If you try this echo server with multiple clients, then you'll see that a second client that connects and sends a message will immediately get a response.

Designing a chat server

We've got a working echo server and it can handle multiple clients simultaneously, so we're pretty close to having a functional chat client. However, our server needs to broadcast the messages it receives to all the connected clients. Sounds simple, but there are two problems that we need to overcome to make this happen.

First, our protocol needs an overhaul. If we think about what needs to happen from a client's point of view, then we can no longer rely on the simple work flow:

client connect > client send > server send > client disconnect.

Clients can now potentially receive messages at any time, and not just when they send a message to the server themselves.

Second, we need to modify our server to send messages to all of the connected clients. As we are using multiple threads to handle our clients, this means that we need to set up communication between the threads. With this, we're dipping our toe into the world of concurrent programming, and it should be approached with care and forethought. While the shared state of threads is useful, it is also deceptive in its simplicity. Having multiple threads of control asynchronously accessing and changing the same resources is a perfect breeding ground for race conditions and subtle deadlock bugs. While a full discussion on concurrent programming is well beyond the scope of this text, we'll cover some simple principles, which can help preserve your sanity.

A chat protocol

The main purpose of our protocol update will be to specify that clients must be able to accept all messages that are sent to them, whenever they are sent.

In theory, one solution for this would be for our client itself to set up a listening socket, so that the server can connect to it whenever it has a new message to deliver. In the real world, this solution will rarely be applicable. Clients are almost always protected by some kind of firewall, which prevents any new inbound connections from connecting to the client. In order for our server to make a connection to a port on our client, we would need to ensure that any intervening firewalls are configured to allow our server to connect. This requirement would make our software much less appealing to most users since there are already chat solutions which don't require this.

If we can't assume that the server can connect to the client, then we need to meet our requirement by only using the client-initiated connection to the server. There are two ways in which we can do this. First, we can have our clients run in a disconnected state by default, then have them periodically connect to the server, download any waiting messages, and then disconnect again. Alternatively, we can have our clients connect to the server and then leave the connection open. They can then continuously listen on the connection and handle new messages sent by the server in one thread, while accepting user input and sending messages over the same connection in another thread.

You may recognize these scenarios as the **pull** and **push** options that are available in some e-mail clients. They are called pull and push because of how the operations appear to the client. The client either pulls data from the server, or the server pushes data to the client.

There are pros and cons to using either of the two approaches, and the decision depends on an application's needs. Pull results in a lower load on the server, but higher latency for the client in receiving messages. While this is fine for many applications, such as e-mail, in a chat server we usually expect immediate updates. While we could poll very frequently, this imposes unneeded load on the client, server, and network as the connections are repeatedly set up and torn down.

Push is better suited for a chat server. As the connection remains open continuously the amount of network traffic is limited to the initial connection setup, and the messages themselves. Also, the client gets new messages from the server almost immediately.

So, we'll use a push approach, and we will now write our chat protocol as follows:

1. Communication will be conducted over TCP.
2. The client will initiate a chat session by creating a socket connection to the server.
3. The server will accept the connection, listen for any messages from the client, and accept them.
4. The client will listen on the connection for any messages from the server, and accept them.
5. The server will send any messages from the client to all the other connected clients.
6. Messages will be encoded in the UTF-8 character set for transmission, and they will be terminated by the null byte.

Handling data on persistent connections

A new problem which our persistent connection approach raises is that we can no longer assume that our `socket.recv()` call will contain data from only one message. In our echo server, because of how we have defined the protocol, we know that as soon as we see a null byte, the message that we have received is complete, and that the sender won't be sending anything further. That is, everything we read in the last `socket.recv()` call is a part of that message.

In our new setup, we'll be reusing the same connection to send an indefinite number of messages, and these won't be synchronized with the chunks of data that we will pull from each `socket.recv()`. Hence, it's quite possible that the data from one `recv()` call will contain data from multiple messages. For example, if we send the following:

```
caerphilly,
illchester,
brie
```

Then on the wire they will look like this:

```
caerphilly\0illchester\0brie\0
```

Due to the vagaries of network transmission though, a set of successive `recv()` calls may receive them as:

```
recv 1: caerphil
recv 2: ly\0illches
recv 3: ter\0brie\0
```

Notice that `recv 1` and `recv 2`, when taken together contain a complete message, but they also contain the beginning of the next message. Clearly, we need to update our parsing. One option is to read data from the socket one byte at a time, that is, use `recv(1)`, and check every byte to see if it's a null byte. This is a dismally inefficient way to use a network socket though. We want to read as much data in our call to `recv()` as we can. Instead, when we encounter an incomplete message we can cache the extraneous bytes and use them when we next call `recv()`. Lets do this, add these functions to the `tincanchat.py` file:

```python
def parse_recvd_data(data):
    """ Break up raw received data into messages, delimited
        by null byte """
    parts = data.split(b'\0')
    msgs = parts[:-1]
    rest = parts[-1]
    return (msgs, rest)


def recv_msgs(sock, data=bytes()):
    """ Receive data and break into complete messages on null byte
        delimiter. Block until at least one message received, then
        return received messages """
    msgs = []
    while not msgs:
        recvd = sock.recv(4096)
        if not recvd:
            raise ConnectionError()
        data = data + recvd
        (msgs, rest) = parse_recvd_data(data)
    msgs = [msg.decode('utf-8') for msg in msgs]
    return (msgs, rest)
```

From now on, we'll be using `recv_msgs()` wherever we were using `recv_msg()` before. So, what are we doing here? Starting with a quick scan through `recv_msgs()`, you can see that it's similar to `recv_msg()`. We make repeated calls to `recv()` and accumulate the received data as before, but now we will be using `parse_recvd_data()` to parse it, with the expectation that it may contain multiple messages. When `parse_recvd_data()` finds one or more complete messages in the received data, it splits them into a list and returns them, and if there is anything left after the last complete message, then it additionally returns this using the `rest` variable. The `recv_msgs()` function then decodes the messages from UTF-8, and returns them and the `rest` variable.

The `rest` value is important because we will feed it back to `recv_msgs()` next time we call it, and it will be prefixed to the data from the `recv()` calls. In this way, the leftover data from the last `recv_msgs()` call won't be lost.

So, in our preceding example, parsing the messages would take place as shown here:

recv_msgs call	data **argument**	recv **result**	**Accumulated** data	msgs	rest
1	-	'caerphil'	'caerphil'	[]	b''
1	-	'ly\0illches'	'caerphilly\0illches'	['caerphilly']	'illches'
2	'illches'	'ter\0brie\0'	'illchester\0brie\0'	['illchester', 'brie']	b''

Here, we can see that the first `recv_msgs()` call doesn't return after its first iteration. It loops again because msgs is still empty. This is why the `recv_msgs` call numbers are 1, 1, and 2.

A multithreaded chat server

So let's put this to use and write our chat server. Make a new file called `2.1-chat_server-multithread.py` and put the following code in it:

```
import threading, queue
import tincanchat

HOST = tincanchat.HOST
PORT = tincanchat.PORT

send_queues = {}
lock = threading.Lock()

def handle_client_recv(sock, addr):
    """ Receive messages from client and broadcast them to
        other clients until client disconnects """
    rest = bytes()
    while True:
        try:
            (msgs, rest) = tincanchat.recv_msgs(sock, rest)
        except (EOFError, ConnectionError):
            handle_disconnect(sock, addr)
            break
```

```
        for msg in msgs:
            msg = '{}: {}'.format(addr, msg)
            print(msg)
            broadcast_msg(msg)

def handle_client_send(sock, q, addr):
    """ Monitor queue for new messages, send them to client as
        they arrive """
    while True:
        msg = q.get()
        if msg == None: break
        try:
            tincanchat.send_msg(sock, msg)
        except (ConnectionError, BrokenPipe):
            handle_disconnect(sock, addr)
            break

def broadcast_msg(msg):
    """ Add message to each connected client's send queue """
    with lock:
        for q in send_queues.values():
            q.put(msg)

def handle_disconnect(sock, addr):
    """ Ensure queue is cleaned up and socket closed when a client
        disconnects """
    fd = sock.fileno()
    with lock:
        # Get send queue for this client
        q = send_queues.get(fd, None)
    # If we find a queue then this disconnect has not yet
    # been handled
    if q:
        q.put(None)
        del send_queues[fd]
        addr = sock.getpeername()
        print('Client {} disconnected'.format(addr))
        sock.close()

if __name__ == '__main__':
    listen_sock = tincanchat.create_listen_socket(HOST, PORT)
    addr = listen_sock.getsockname()
    print('Listening on {}'.format(addr))
```

```
while True:
    client_sock,addr = listen_sock.accept()
    q = queue.Queue()
    with lock:
        send_queues[client_sock.fileno()] = q
    recv_thread = threading.Thread(target=handle_client_recv,
                                   args=[client_sock, addr],
                                   daemon=True)
    send_thread = threading.Thread(target=handle_client_send,
                                   args=[client_sock, q,
                                         addr],
                                   daemon=True)
    recv_thread.start()
    send_thread.start()
    print('Connection from {}'.format(addr))
```

We're now using two threads per client. One thread handles the messages received and the other thread handles the task of sending messages. The idea here is to break out each place a block might happen into its own thread. This will give us the lowest latency for each client, but it does come at the cost of system resources. We're reducing the potential number of clients that we may be able to handle simultaneously. There are other models that we could use, such as having a single thread for each client which receives messages and then sends them itself to all the connected clients, but I've chosen to optimize for latency.

To facilitate the separate threads, we've broken the receiving code and the sending code into the `handle_client_recv()` function and `handle_client_send()` function respectively.

Our `handle_client_recv` threads are tasked with receiving messages from the clients, and our `handle_client_send` threads are tasked with sending messages to the clients, but how do the received messages get from the receive threads to the send threads? This is where the `queue`, `send_queue`, `dict` and `lock` objects come in.

Queues

A `Queue` is a **first-in first-out (FIFO)** pipe. You add items to it by using the `put()` method, and pull them out by using the `get()` method. The important thing about `Queue` objects is that they are completely **thread safe**. Objects in Python are generally not thread safe unless it is explicitly specified in their documentation. Being thread safe means that operations on the object are guaranteed to be **atomic**, that is, they will always complete without any chance of another thread getting to that object and doing something unexpected to it.

Hang on, you might ask, earlier, didn't you say that because of the GIL the OS is running only one Python thread per process at any given moment in time? If that's so, then how could two threads perform an operation on an object simultaneously? Well, this is a fair question. Most operations in Python are, in fact, made up of many operations at the OS level, and it is at the OS level that threads are scheduled. A thread could start an operation on an object—say by appending an item to a `list`—and when the thread gets halfway through its OS level operations the OS could switch to another thread, which also starts appending to the same `list`. Since `list` objects provide no warranty of their behavior when abused like this by threads (they're not thread safe), anything could happen next, and it's unlikely to be a useful outcome. This situation can be called a **race condition**.

Thread safe objects remove this possibility, so they should absolutely be preferred for sharing state among threads.

Getting back to our server, the other useful behavior of `Queues` is that if `get()` is called on an empty `Queue`, then it will block until something is added to the `Queue`. We take advantage of this in our send threads. Notice, how we go into an infinite loop, with the first operation being a `get()` method call on a `Queue`. The thread will block there and patiently wait until something is added to its `Queue`. And, you've probably guessed it, our receive threads add the messages to the queues.

We create a `Queue` object for each send thread as it's being created and then we store the queues in the `send_queues` dict. For our receive threads to broadcast new messages, they just need to add the message to each `Queue` in `send_queues`, which we do in the `broadcast_msgs()` function. Our waiting send threads will then unblock, pick the message out of their `Queue` and then send it to their client.

We've also added a `handle_disconnect()` function, which gets called whenever a client disconnects or a socket error occurs. This function ensures that queues associated with closed connections are cleaned up, and that the socket is closed properly from the server end.

Locks

Contrast our use of the `Queues` object with our use of `send_queues`. `Dict` objects are not thread safe, and unfortunately there isn't a thread safe associative array type in Python. Since we need to share this `dict`, we need to take extra precautions whenever we access it, and this is where the `Lock` comes in. `Lock` objects are a type of **synchronization primitive**. These are special objects built with functionality to help manage our threads and ensure that they don't trip over each others' accesses.

A `Lock` is either locked or unlocked. A thread can lock a thread by either calling `acquire()` on it, or as in our program, using it as a context manager. If a thread has acquired a lock and another thread also tries to acquire the lock, then the second thread will block on the `acquire()` call until the first thread releases the lock or exits the context. There is no limit on the number of threads that can try to acquire a lock at once – all but the first will block. By wrapping all the accesses to a non-thread safe object with a lock, we can ensure that no two threads operate on the object at the same time.

So, every time we add or remove something from `send_queues`, we wrap it in a `Lock` context. Notice that we're also protecting `send_queues` when we iterate over it. Even though we're not changing it, we want to be sure that it doesn't get modified while we're working with it.

Although we're being careful and using locks and thread safe primitives, we're not protected against all possible thread related pitfalls. Since the thread synchronization mechanisms themselves block, it's still quite possible to create deadlocks, where two threads are simultaneously blocking on objects locked by the other thread. The best approach to managing thread communication is to keep all the accesses to your shared state restricted to as small an area of your code as you can. In the case of this server, this module could be reworked as a class providing a minimum number of public methods. It could also be documented such that it discourages the changing of any internal state. This will keep this chunk of threading strictly confined to this class.

A multithreaded chat client

Now that we have a new, all receiving and broadcasting chat server, we just need a client to go with it. We have mentioned before that we will hit a problem with our procedural client when trying to listen for both network data and user input at the same time. Well, now that we have some idea of how to employ threads, we can have a go at addressing this. Create a new text file called `2.2-chat_client-multithread.py` and save the following code in it:

```
import sys, socket, threading
import tincanchat

HOST = sys.argv[-1] if len(sys.argv) > 1 else '127.0.0.1'
PORT = tincanchat.PORT

def handle_input(sock):
    """ Prompt user for message and send it to server """
    print("Type messages, enter to send. 'q' to quit")
```

```
        while True:
            msg = input()   # Blocks
            if msg == 'q':
                sock.shutdown(socket.SHUT_RDWR)
                sock.close()
                break
            try:
                tincanchat.send_msg(sock, msg)   # Blocks until sent
            except (BrokenPipeError, ConnectionError):
                break

if __name__ == '__main__':
    sock = socket.socket(socket.AF_INET, socket.SOCK_STREAM)
    sock.connect((HOST, PORT))
    print('Connected to {}:{}'.format(HOST, PORT))

    # Create thread for handling user input and message sending
    thread = threading.Thread(target=handle_input,
                              args=[sock],
                              daemon=True)
    thread.start()
    rest = bytes()
    addr = sock.getsockname()
    # Loop indefinitely to receive messages from server
    while True:
        try:
            # blocks
            (msgs, rest) = tincanchat.recv_msgs(sock, rest)
            for msg in msgs:
                print(msg)
        except ConnectionError:
            print('Connection to server closed')
            sock.close()
            break
```

We've updated our client to honor our new chat protocol by creating a new thread to handle user input and send messages, while handling receiving messages in the main thread. This allows the client to deal with the user input and receive the messages at the same time.

Note that there's no shared state here, so we didn't have to get clever with Queues or synchronization primitives.

Let's give our new programs a try. Fire up the multithreaded chat server, and then launch at least two clients. If you can, run them in terminals such that you can watch all of them at once. Now, try and send some messages from the clients and see how they are sent to all of the other clients.

Event-driven servers

For many purposes threads are great, especially because we can still program in the familiar procedural, blocking-IO style. But they suffer from the drawback that they struggle when managing large numbers of connections simultaneously, because they are required to maintain a thread for each connection. Each thread consumes memory, and switching between threads incurs a type of CPU overhead called **context switching**. Although these aren't a problem for small numbers of threads, they can impact performance when there are many threads to manage. Multiprocessing suffers from similar problems.

An alternative to threading and multiprocessing is using the **event-driven** model. In this model, instead of having the OS automatically switch between active threads or processes for us, we use a single thread which registers blocking objects, such as sockets, with the OS. When these objects become ready to leave the blocking state, for example a socket receives some data, the OS notifies our program; our program can then access these objects in non-blocking mode, since it knows that they are in a state that is ready for immediate use. Calls made to objects in non-blocking mode always return immediately. We structure our application around a loop, where we wait for the OS to notify us of activity on our blocking objects, then we handle that activity, and then we go back to waiting. This loop is called the **event loop**.

This approach provides comparable performance to threading and multiprocessing, but without the memory or context switching overheads, and hence allows for greater scaling on the same hardware. The challenge of engineering applications that can efficiently handle very large numbers of simultaneous connections has historically been called the **c10k problem**, referring to the handling of ten-thousand concurrent connections in a single thread. With the help of event-driven architectures, this problem was solved, though the term is still often used to refer to the challenges of scaling when it comes to handling many concurrent connections.

On modern hardware it's actually possible to handle ten-thousand concurrent connections using a multithreading approach as well, see this Stack Overflow question for some numbers `https://stackoverflow.com/questions/17593699/tcp-ip-solving-the-c10k-with-the-thread-per-client-approach`.

The modern challenge is the "c10m problem", that is, ten million concurrent connections. Solving this involves some drastic software and even operating system architecture changes. Although this is unlikely to be manageable with Python any time soon, an interesting (though unfortunately incomplete) general introduction to the topic can be found at `http://c10m.robertgraham.com/p/blog-page.html`.

The following diagram shows the relationship of processes and threads in an event-driven server:

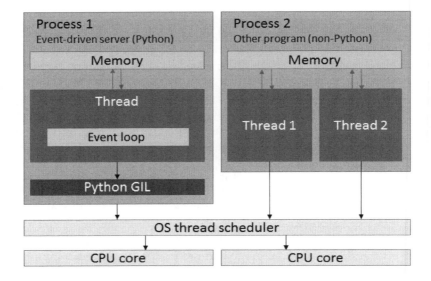

Although the GIL and the OS thread scheduler are shown here for completeness, in the case of an event-driven server, they have no impact on performance because the server only uses a single thread. The scheduling of I/O handling is done by the application.

A low-level event-driven chat server

So the event-driven architecture has a few great benefits, the catch is that for a low-level implementation, we need to write our code in a completely different style. Let's write an event-driven chat server to illustrate this.

Note that this example will not at all work on Windows as Windows lacks the `poll` interface which we will be employing here. There is an older interface, called `select`, which Windows does support, however it is slower and more complicated to work with. The event-driven frameworks that we look at later do automatically switch to `select` for us though, if we're running on Windows.

There is a higher performance alternative to `poll` called `epoll`, available on Linux operating systems, however it also more complicated to use, so for simplicity we'll stick with `poll` here. Again, the frameworks we discuss later automatically take advantage of `epoll` if it is available.

Finally, counter-intuitively, Python's `poll` interface lives in a module called `select`, hence we will import `select` in our program.

Create a file called `3.1-chat_server-poll.py` and save the following code in it:

```python
import select
import tincanchat
from types import SimpleNamespace
from collections import deque

HOST = tincanchat.HOST
PORT = tincanchat.PORT
clients = {}

def create_client(sock):
    """ Return an object representing a client """
    return SimpleNamespace(
            sock=sock,
            rest=bytes(),
            send_queue=deque())

def broadcast_msg(msg):
    """ Add message to all connected clients' queues """
    data = tincanchat.prep_msg(msg)
    for client in clients.values():
        client.send_queue.append(data)
        poll.register(client.sock, select.POLLOUT)
```

```
if __name__ == '__main__':
    listen_sock = tincanchat.create_listen_socket(HOST, PORT)
    poll = select.poll()
    poll.register(listen_sock, select.POLLIN)
    addr = listen_sock.getsockname()
    print('Listening on {}'.format(addr))

    # This is the event loop. Loop indefinitely, processing events
    # on all sockets when they occur
    while True:
        # Iterate over all sockets with events
        for fd, event in poll.poll():
            # clear-up a closed socket
            if event & (select.POLLHUP |
                        select.POLLERR |
                        select.POLLNVAL):
                poll.unregister(fd)
                del clients[fd]

            # Accept new connection, add client to clients dict
            elif fd == listen_sock.fileno():
                client_sock,addr = listen_sock.accept()
                client_sock.setblocking(False)
                fd = client_sock.fileno()
                clients[fd] = create_client(client_sock)
                poll.register(fd, select.POLLIN)
                print('Connection from {}'.format(addr))

            # Handle received data on socket
            elif event & select.POLLIN:
                client = clients[fd]
                addr = client.sock.getpeername()
                recvd = client.sock.recv(4096)
                if not recvd:
                    # the client state will get cleaned up in the
                    # next iteration of the event loop, as close()
                    # sets the socket to POLLNVAL
                    client.sock.close()
                    print('Client {} disconnected'.format(addr))
                    continue
                data = client.rest + recvd
                (msgs, client.rest) = \
```

```
                        tincanchat.parse_recvd_data(data)
            # If we have any messages, broadcast them to all
            # clients
            for msg in msgs:
                msg = '{}: {}'.format(addr, msg)
                print(msg)
                broadcast_msg(msg)

        # Send message to ready client
        elif event & select.POLLOUT:
            client = clients[fd]
            data = client.send_queue.popleft()
            sent = client.sock.send(data)
            if sent < len(data):
                client.sends.appendleft(data[sent:])
            if not client.send_queue:
                poll.modify(client.sock, select.POLLIN)
```

The crux of this program is the `poll` object, which we create at the start of execution. This is an interface for the kernel's poll service, which lets us register sockets for the OS to watch and notify us when they are ready for us work with them.

We register a socket by calling the `poll.register()` method, passing the socket as an argument along with the type of activity that we want the kernel to watch out for. There are several conditions which we can monitor by specifying various `select.POLL*` constants. We're using `POLLIN` and `POLLOUT` in this program to watch out for when a socket is ready to receive and send data respectively. Accepting a new incoming connection on our listening socket will be counted as a read.

Once a socket is registered with `poll`, the OS will watch it and record when the socket is ready to carry out the activity that we requested. When we call `poll.poll()`, it returns a list of all the sockets that have become ready for us to work with. For each socket, it also returns an `event` flag, which indicates the state of the socket. We can use this event flag to tell whether we can read from (`POLLIN` event) or write to the socket (`POLLOUT` event), or whether an error has occurred (`POLLHUP`, `POLLERR`, `POLLNVAL` events).

To make use of this, we enter our event loop, repeatedly calling `poll.poll()`, iterating through the ready objects it returns and operating on them as per their event flags.

Because we're only running in a single thread, we don't need any of the synchronization mechanisms which we had to employ in the multithreaded server. We're just using a regular `dict` to keep track of our clients. If you've not come across it before, the `SimpleNamespace` object that we use in the `create_client()` function is just a new idiom for creating an empty object with a `__dict__` (this is needed because `Object` instances don't have a `__dict__` so they won't accept arbitrary attributes). Previously, we may have used the following to give us an object which we can assign arbitrary attributes to:

```
class Client:
  pass
client = Client()
```

Python version 3.3 and later versions give us the new, more explicit `SimpleNamespace` object.

We can run our multithreaded client against this server. The server is still using the same network protocol, and the architecture of the two programs won't affect the communication. Give it a try and verify if it works as expected.

This style of programming, employing `poll` and non-blocking sockets, is often referred to as **non-blocking** and **asynchronous,** since we use sockets in non-blocking mode, and the thread of control handles I/O reactively, as it needs to happen, rather than locking to a single I/O channel until it's done. However, you should note that our program isn't completely non-blocking, since it still blocks on the `poll.poll()` call. This is pretty much inevitable in an I/O bound system because when nothing's happening, you've got to wait for the I/O activity somewhere.

Frameworks

As you can see, writing servers using these lower level threading and `poll` APIs can be quite involved, especially considering that various things which would be expected in a production system, such as logging and comprehensive error handling, haven't been included in our examples due to brevity.

Many people have hit these problems before us, and several libraries and frameworks are available for taking some of the leg work out of writing the network servers.

An eventlet-based chat server

The `eventlet` library provides a high-level API for event-driven programming, but it does so in a style that mimics the procedural, blocking-IO style that we used in our multithreaded servers. The upshot is that we can effectively take our multithreaded chat server code, make a few minor modifications to it to use `eventlet` instead, and immediately gain the benefits of the event-driven model!

The `eventlet` library is available in PyPi, and it can be installed with `pip`, as shown here:

```
$ pip install eventlet
Downloading/unpacking eventlet
```

 The `eventlet` library automatically falls back to `select` if `poll` is not available, so it will run properly on Windows.

Once it's installed, create a new file called `4.1-chat_server-eventlet.py` and save the following code in it:

```python
import eventlet
import eventlet.queue as queue
import tincanchat

HOST = tincanchat.HOST
PORT = tincanchat.PORT
send_queues = {}

def handle_client_recv(sock, addr):
    """ Receive messages from client and broadcast them to
        other clients until client disconnects """
    rest = bytes()
    while True:
        try:
            (msgs, rest) = tincanchat.recv_msgs(sock)
        except (EOFError, ConnectionError):
            handle_disconnect(sock, addr)
            break
        for msg in msgs:
            msg = '{}: {}'.format(addr, msg)
            print(msg)
            broadcast_msg(msg)
```

```python
def handle_client_send(sock, q, addr):
    """ Monitor queue for new messages, send them to client as
        they arrive """
    while True:
        msg = q.get()
        if msg == None: break
        try:
            tincanchat.send_msg(sock, msg)
        except (ConnectionError, BrokenPipe):
            handle_disconnect(sock, addr)
            break


def broadcast_msg(msg):
    """ Add message to each connected client's send queue """
    for q in send_queues.values():
        q.put(msg)


def handle_disconnect(sock, addr):
    """ Ensure queue is cleaned up and socket closed when a client
        disconnects """
    fd = sock.fileno()
    # Get send queue for this client
    q = send_queues.get(fd, None)
    # If we find a queue then this disconnect has not yet
    # been handled
    if q:
        q.put(None)
        del send_queues[fd]
        addr = sock.getpeername()
        print('Client {} disconnected'.format(addr))
        sock.close()


if __name__ == '__main__':
    server = eventlet.listen((HOST, PORT))
    addr = server.getsockname()
    print('Listening on {}'.format(addr))

    while True:
        client_sock,addr = server.accept()
        q = queue.Queue()
        send_queues[client_sock.fileno()] = q
        eventlet.spawn_n(handle_client_recv,
                         client_sock,
                         addr)
```

```
eventlet.spawn_n(handle_client_send,
                 client_sock,
                 q,
                 addr)
print('Connection from {}'.format(addr))
```

We can test this with our multithreaded client to ensure that it works as expected.

As you can see, it's pretty much identical to our multithreaded server, with a few changes made so as to use `eventlet`. Notice that we've removed the synchronization code and the `lock` around `send_queues`. We're still using queues, although they're the `eventlet` library's queues, because we want to retain the blocking behavior of `Queue.get()`.

 There are more examples of using eventlet for programming on the eventlet site at `http://eventlet.net/doc/examples.html`.

An asyncio-based chat server

The `asyncio` Standard Library module is new in Python 3.4 and it is an effort at bringing some standardization around asynchronous I/O into the Standard Library. The `asyncio` library uses a co-routine based style of programming. It provides a powerful loop class, which our programs can submit prepared tasks, called co-routines, to, for asynchronous execution. The event loop handles the scheduling of the tasks and optimization of performance around blocking I/O calls.

It has built-in support for socket-based networking, which makes building a basic server a straightforward task. Let's see how this can be done. Create a new file called `5.1-chat_server-asyncio.py` and save the following code in it:

```
import asyncio
import tincanchat

HOST = tincanchat.HOST
PORT = tincanchat.PORT
clients = []

class ChatServerProtocol(asyncio.Protocol):
    """ Each instance of class represents a client and the socket
        connection to it. """
```

```python
    def connection_made(self, transport):
        """ Called on instantiation, when new client connects """
            self.transport = transport
        self.addr = transport.get_extra_info('peername')
        self._rest = b''
        clients.append(self)
        print('Connection from {}'.format(self.addr))

    def data_received(self, data):
        """ Handle data as it's received. Broadcast complete
        messages to all other clients """
        data = self._rest + data
        (msgs, rest) = tincanchat.parse_recvd_data(data)
        self._rest = rest
        for msg in msgs:
            msg = msg.decode('utf-8')
            msg = '{}: {}'.format(self.addr, msg)
            print(msg)
            msg = tincanchat.prep_msg(msg)
            for client in clients:
                client.transport.write(msg)   # <-- non-blocking

    def connection_lost(self, ex):
        """ Called on client disconnect. Clean up client state """
        print('Client {} disconnected'.format(self.addr))
        clients.remove(self)

if __name__ == '__main__':
    loop = asyncio.get_event_loop()
    # Create server and initialize on the event loop
    coroutine = loop.create_server(ChatServerProtocol,
                                    host=HOST,
                                    port=PORT)
    server = loop.run_until_complete(coroutine)
    # print listening socket info
    for socket in server.sockets:
        addr = socket.getsockname()
        print('Listening on {}'.format(addr))
    # Run the loop to process client connections
    loop.run_forever()
```

Again, we can test this with our multithreaded client to make sure that it works as we expect it to.

Let's step through the code, as it's quite different from our previous servers. We begin by defining our server behavior in a subclass of the `asyncio.Protocol` abstract class. We're required to override the three methods `connection_made()`, `data_received()`, and `connection_lost()`. By using this class we can instantiate a new server scheduled on the event loop, which will listen on a socket and behave according to the contents of these three methods. We perform this instantiation in the main section further down with the `loop.create_server()` call.

The `connection_made()` method is called when a new client connects to our socket, which is equivalent to `socket.accept()` receiving a connection. The `transport` argument that it receives is a writable stream object, that is, it is an `asyncio.WriteTransport` instance. We will use this to write data to the socket, so we hang on to it by assigning it to the `self.transport` attribute. We also grab the client's host and port by using `transport.get_extra_info('peername')`. This is the transport's equivalent of `socket.getpeername()`. We then set up a `rest` attribute to hold the leftover data from `tincanchat.parse_recvd_data()` calls, and then we add our instance to the global `clients` list so that the other clients can broadcast to it.

The `data_received()` method is where the action happens. This function is called every time the `Protocol` instance's socket receives any data. This is equivalent to `poll.poll()` returning a `POLLIN` event, and then us performing a `recv()` on the socket. When called, this method is passed the data that is received from the socket as the `data` argument, which we then parse using `tincanchat.parse_recvd_data()`, as we have done before.

We then iterate over any received messages, and for each one, send it to every client in the `clients` list by calling the `write()` method on the clients' transport objects. The important thing to note here is that the `Transport.write()` call is non-blocking and so returns immediately. The send just gets submitted to the event loop, to be scheduled for completion soon. Hence the broadcast itself completes quickly.

The `connection_lost()` method is called when the client disconnects or the connection is lost, which is equivalent to a `socket.recv()` returning an empty result, or a `ConnectionError`. Here, we just remove the client from the `clients` global list.

In the main module code we acquire an event loop, and then create an instance of our `Protocol` server. The call to `loop.run_until_complete()` runs the initialization phase of our server on the event loop, setting up the listening socket. Then we call `loop.run_forever()`, which starts our server listening for incoming connections.

More on frameworks

I've broken from our usual procedural form and used an object-oriented approach in the last example for two reasons. First, although it is possible to write a purely procedural style server with `asyncio`, it requires a deeper understanding of co-routines than what we were able to provide here. If you're curious, then you can go through an example co-routine style echo server, which is in the `asyncio` documentation at `https://docs.python.org/3/library/asyncio-stream.html#asyncio-tcp-echo-server-streams`.

The second reason is that this kind of class-based approach is generally a more manageable model to follow in a full system.

There is in fact a new module called `selectors` in Python 3.4, which provides an API for quickly building an object-oriented server based on the IO primitives in the `select` module (including `poll`). The documentation and an example can be seen at `https://docs.python.org/3.4/library/selectors.html`.

There are other third-party event-driven frameworks available, popular ones are Tornado (`www.tornadoweb.org`) and circuits (`https://github.com/circuits/circuits`). Both are worth investigating for comparison, if you intend to choose a framework for a project.

Moreover, no discussion of Python asynchronous I/O would be complete without a mention of the Twisted framework. Until Python 3, this has been the go to solution for any serious asynchronous I/O work. It is an event-driven engine, with support for a large number of network protocols, good performance, and a large and active community. Unfortunately, it hasn't finished the jump to Python 3 yet (a view of the migration progress can be seen at `https://rawgit.com/mythmon/twisted-py3-graph/master/index.html`). Since we're focused squarely on Python 3 in this book, we decided to not include a detailed treatment of it. However, once it does get there, Python 3 will have another very powerful asynchronous framework, which will be well worth investigating for your projects.

Taking our servers forward

There are a number of things that we can do to improve our servers. For multithreaded systems, it's common to have a mechanism for capping the number of threads in use at any one time. This can be done by keeping a count of the active threads and immediately closing any new incoming connections from clients while it's above a threshold.

For all our servers, we would also want to add a logging mechanism. I strongly recommend the standard library `logging` module for this, the documentation for this is complete and full of good examples. The basic tutorial is a good place to start if you've not used it before, and it can be found at `https://docs.python.org/3/howto/logging.html#logging-basic-tutorial`.

We also want to handle errors more comprehensively. Since the intention is that our server should be long running with minimal intervention, we want to make sure that nothing less than a critical exception causes the process to exit. We also want to make sure that errors that occur when handling one client do not affect other connected clients.

Finally there are some basic features of chat programs that it may be fun to add: letting users enter a name, which would be shown beside their messages on the other clients; adding chat rooms; and adding TLS encryption to the socket connections to provide privacy and security.

Summary

We looked at how to develop network protocols while considering aspects such as the connection sequence, framing of the data on the wire, and the impact these choices will have on the architecture of the client and server programs.

We worked through different architectures for network servers and clients, demonstrating the differences between the multithreaded and event-driven models by writing a simple echo server and upgrading it to a multi-client chat server. We discussed performance issues around threaded and event-driven architectures. Finally, we looked at the `eventlet` and `asyncio` frameworks, which can greatly simplify the process of writing servers when using an event-driven approach.

In the next and final chapter of this book, we will look at bringing several threads of this book together for writing server-side web applications.

Applications for the Web **9**

In *Chapter 2, HTTP and Working with the Web*, we explored the HTTP protocol—the primary protocol used by the World Wide Web—and we learned how to use Python as an HTTP client. In *Chapter 3, APIs in Action*, we expanded on this and looked at ways to consume web APIs. In this chapter, we'll be turning our focus around and looking at how we can use Python to build applications that serve responses to HTTP requests.

In this chapter, we'll cover the following:

- Python web frameworks
- A Python web application
- Hosting Python and WSGI

I should note up front that hosting modern web applications is a very large topic, and a complete treatment is well beyond the scope of this book, where we're focusing on applying Python code to network problems. Topics such as database access, selecting and configuring load balancers and reverse-proxies, containerization, and the system administration techniques needed to keep the whole show up and running won't be covered here. There are many great resources online though that can give you a start, and we'll try to mention as many as we can where relevant, as we go along.

Having said that, the technologies listed above aren't a requirement for creating and serving Python-based web applications, they're simply what a service comes to require as it reaches scale. As we'll see, there are options for easily manageable small-scale application hosting too.

What's in a web server?

To understand how we can employ Python in responding to HTTP requests, we need to know a bit about what typically needs to occur in order to respond to a request, and what tools and patterns already exist to do this.

A basic HTTP request and response might look like this:

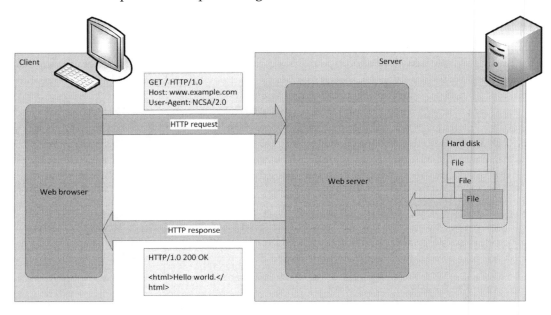

Here our web client sends an HTTP request to a server, where a web server program interprets the request, creates a suitable HTTP response, and sends it back. In this case, the response body is simply the contents of an HTML file read from, with the response headers added by the web server program.

The web server is responsible for the entire process of responding to the client's request. The basic steps it needs to perform are:

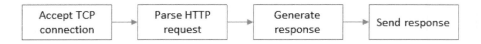

First the web server program needs to accept the TCP connection attempt by the client. It then receives the HTTP request from the client over the TCP connection. The server needs to keep the TCP connection open while it generates the HTTP response, and it uses the connection to send the response back to the client. What the server does with the connection after that depends on the HTTP version in use and the value of a possible Connection header in the request (see the RFC for full details at `http://tools.ietf.org/html/rfc7230#section-6.3`).

Once the web server has received the request, it parses it, then generates the response. When the requested URL maps to a valid resource on the server, the server will respond with the resource at that URL. The resource could be a file on disk (so-called **static content**), as shown in the diagram of a basic HTTP request and response from before, it could be an HTTP redirect, or it could be a dynamically generated HTML page. If something goes wrong, or the URL is not valid, then instead the response will include a status code in the 4xx or 5xx range. Once the response is prepared, the server sends it back to the client over the TCP connection.

In the early days of the Web, when almost all requested resources consisted of static files read from disk, web servers could be written in a single language and could easily handle all four steps shown in the preceding image. However, as more and more dynamic content came into demand, such as shopping baskets and database-driven resources such as blogs, wikis, and social media, it was quickly found that hard-coding these functionalities into the web server itself was impractical. Instead, facilities were built into web servers to allow the invocation of external code as part of the page generation process.

Hence, web servers could be written in a fast language such as C and could deal with the low-level TCP connections, initial parsing and validating of requests, and handling static content, but then could invoke external code to handle page generation duties when a dynamic response was needed.

This external code is what we commonly refer to when we talk about web applications. So the response process duties can be split, as shown in the following figure:

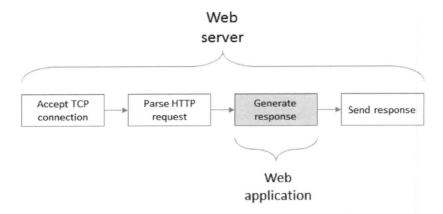

Web applications can be written in any language that the web server is able to invoke, providing great flexibility and allowing higher level languages to be used. This can drastically reduce the time it takes to develop a new web service. These days there is a great range of languages that can be used to write web applications, and Python is no exception.

Python and the Web

Using some of the techniques discussed in this book, in particular *Chapter 8, Client and Server Applications*, it is possible to use Python to write a full web server that handles all four of the steps of handling an HTTP request that we listed in the previous section. There are several actively developed web servers already in existence written in pure Python, including Gunicorn (http://gunicorn.org), and CherryPy (http://www.cherrypy.org). There is even a very basic HTTP server in the standard library http.server module.

Writing a full HTTP server is not a trivial task and a detailed treatment is well beyond the scope of this book. It is also not a very common requirement nowadays, primarily due to the prevalence of excellent web servers that are already ready to deploy. If you do feel the need to have a crack at this challenge though, I would start with looking through the source code of the web servers mentioned earlier, looking in more detail at the frameworks listed in *Chapter 8, Client and Server Applications*, and reading the full HTTP specifications in the relevant RFCs. You may also want to read the WSGI specifications, discussed in the WSGI section later on, so as to allow the server to act as a host for other Python web applications.

The much stronger requirement is to build a web service application to generate some dynamic content, and to get it up and running quickly. In this situation, Python provides us with some excellent options in the form of web frameworks.

Web frameworks

A web framework is a layer that sits between the web server and our Python code, which provides abstractions and streamlined APIs to perform many of the common operations of interpreting HTTP requests and generating responses. Ideally, it is also structured so that it guides us into employing well-tested patterns for good web development. Frameworks for Python web applications are usually written in Python, and can be considered part of the web application.

The basic services a framework provides are:

- Abstraction of HTTP requests and responses
- Management of the URL space (routing)
- Separation of Python code and markup (templating)

There are many Python web frameworks in use today, and here's a non-exhaustive list of some popular ones, in no particular order:

- Django (www.djangoproject.com)
- CherryPy (www.cherrypy.org)
- Flask (flask.pocoo.org)
- Tornado (www.tornadoweb.org)
- TurboGears (www.turbogears.org)
- Pyramid (www.pylonsproject.org)

 An up-to-date list of frameworks is maintained at http://wiki.python.org/moin/WebPrameworks and http://docs.python-guide.org/en/latest/scenarios/web/#frameworks.

There are so many frameworks because there are many approaches that can be taken to the tasks they perform, and many different opinions about what tasks they should even perform.

Some frameworks provide the minimum to quickly build a simple web application. These are often called **microframeworks**, the most popular here being Armin Ronacher's excellent Flask. Although they may not include the functionality of some of the heavyweight frameworks, what they do, they generally do very well, and provide hooks to allow easy extension for more complex tasks. This allows a fully customizable approach to web application development.

Other frameworks take a much more batteries-included stance, providing for all the common needs of modern web applications. The major contender here is Django, which includes everything from templating to form management and database abstraction, and even a complete out-of-the-box web-based database admin interface. TurboGears provides similar functionality by integrating a core microframework with several established packages for the other features.

Yet other frameworks provide features such as supporting web applications with an event-driven architecture, such as Tornado, and CherryPy. Both of these also feature their own built-in production quality web servers.

Choosing a framework can be a tricky decision, and there is no right answer. We're going to take a quick look at one of today's most popular frameworks to get an idea of the services a framework can offer, then discuss how you might approach choosing one.

Flask – a microframework

To get a taste of working with a Python web framework, we're going to write a small app with Flask. We've chosen Flask because it provides a lean interface, giving us the features we need while getting out of the way and letting us code. Also, it doesn't require any significant preconfiguration, all we need to do is install it, like this:

```
>>> pip install flask
Downloading/unpacking flask
```

Flask can also be downloaded from the project's homepage at http://flask.pocoo.org. Note that to run Flask under Python 3, you will need Python 3.3 or higher.

Now create a project directory, and within the directory create a text file called tinyflaskapp.py. Our app is going to allow us to browse the docstrings for the Python built-in functions. Enter this into tinyflaskapp.py:

```
from flask import Flask, abort
app = Flask(__name__)
app.debug = True

objs = __builtins__.__dict__.items()
```

```
        docstrings = {name.lower(): obj.__doc__ for name, obj in objs if
                  name[0].islower() and hasattr(obj, '__name__')}

    @app.route('/')
    def index():
        link_template = '<a href="/functions/{}">{}</a></br>'
        links = []
        for func in sorted(docstrings):
            link = link_template.format(func, func)
            links.append(link)
        links_output = '\n'.join(links)
        return '<h1>Python builtins docstrings</h1>\n' + links_output

    @app.route('/functions/<func_name>')
    def show_docstring(func_name):
        func_name = func_name.lower()
        if func_name in docstrings:
            output = '<h1>{}</h1>\n'.format(func_name)
            output += '<pre>{}</pre>'.format(docstrings[func_name])
            return output
        else:
            abort(404)


    if __name__ == '__main__':
        app.run()
```

This code can be found in this book's source code download for this chapter within the 1-init folder.

Flask includes a development web server, so to try out our application all we need to do is run the following command:

```
$ python3.4 tinyflaskapp.py
 * Running on http://127.0.0.1:5000/ (Press CTRL+C to quit)
 * Restarting with stat
```

We can see that the Flask server tells us the IP address and port it's listening on. Connect to the URL it displays (in the preceding example this is http://127.0.0.1:5000/) now in a web browser, and you should see a page with a list of Python built-in functions. Clicking on one should display a page showing the function name and its docstring.

If you want to run the server on another interface or port, you can change the app.run() call, for example, to app.run(host='0.0.0.0', port=5001).

Let's go through our code. From the top, we create our Flask app by creating a `Flask` instance, in this case giving it the name of our main module. We then set debug mode to active, which provides nice tracebacks in the browser when something goes wrong, and also sets the development server to automatically reload code changes without needing a restart. Note that debug mode should never be left active in a production app! This is because the debugger has an interactive element, which allows code to be executed on the server. By default, debug is off, so all we need to do is delete the `app.config.debug` line when we put the app into production.

Next we filter the built-in function objects out of the globals and extract their docstrings for later use. Now we have the main section of the app, and we encounter the first of Flask's superpowers: URL routing. The heart of a Flask app is a set of functions, usually called **views**, that handle requests for various parts of our URL space—`index()` and `show_docstring()` are such functions. You will see both are preceded by a Flask decorator function, `app.route()`. This tells Flask which parts of our URL space the decorated function should handle. That is, when a request comes in with a URL that matches a pattern in an `app.route()` decorator, the function with the matching decorator is called to handle the request. View functions must return a response that Flask can return to the client, but more on that in a moment.

The URL pattern for our `index()` function is just the site root, `'/'`, meaning that only requests for the root will be handled by `index()`.

In `index()`, we just compile our output HTML as a string—first our list of links to the functions' pages, then a header—and then we return the string. Flask takes the string and creates a response out of it, using the string as the response body and adding a few HTTP headers. In particular, for `str` return values, it sets `Content-Type` to `text/html`.

The `show_docstrings()` view does a similar thing—it returns the name of the built-in function we're viewing in an HTML header tag, plus the docstring wrapped in a `<pre>` tag (to preserve new lines and whitespace).

The interesting part is the `app.route('/functions/<func_name>')` call. Here we're declaring that our functions' pages will live in the `functions` directory, and we're capturing the name of the requested function using the `<func_name>` segment. Flask captures the section of the URL in angle brackets and makes it available to our view. We pull it into the view namespace by declaring the `func_name` argument for `show_docstring()`.

In the view, we check that the name supplied is valid by seeing whether it appears in the `docstrings` dict. If it's okay, we build and return the corresponding HTML. If it's not okay, then we return a `404 Not Found` response to the client by calling Flask's `abort()` function. This function raises a Flask `HTTPException`, which if not handled by our application, will cause Flask to generate an error page and return it to the client with the corresponding status code (in this case 404). This is a good way to fail fast when we encounter bad requests.

Templating

You can see from our preceding views that even when cheekily omitting the usual HTML formalities such as `<DOCTYPE>` and the `<html>` tag to save complexity, constructing HTML in Python code is clunky. It's difficult to get a feel for the overall page, and it's impossible for designers with no Python knowledge to work on the page design. Also, mixing the generation of the presentation code with the application logic makes both harder to test.

Pretty much all web frameworks solve this problem by employing the template idiom. Since the bulk of the HTML is static, the question arises: Why keep it in the application code at all? With templates, we extract the HTML entirely into separate files. These then comprise HTML code, with the inclusion of some special placeholder and logic markup to allow dynamic elements to be inserted.

Flask uses another Armin Ronacher creation, the *Jinja2* templating engine, for this task. Let's adapt our application to use templates. In your project folder, create a folder called `templates`. In there, create three new text files, `base.html`, `index.html`, and `docstring.html`. Fill them out as follows:

The `base.html` file will be like this:

```
<!DOCTYPE html>
<html>
<head>
    <title>Python Builtins Docstrings</title>
</head>
<body>
{% block body %}{% endblock %}
</body>
</html>
```

The `index.html` file will be like this:

```
{% extends "base.html" %}
{% block body %}
    <h1>Python Builtins Docstrings</h1>
    <div>
    {% for func in funcs %}
        <div class="menuitem link">
            <a href="/functions/{{ func }}">{{ func }}</a>
        </div>
    {% endfor %}
    </table>
{% endblock %}
```

The `docstring.html` file will be like this:

```
{% extends 'base.html' %}
{% block body %}
    <h1>{{ func_name }}</h1>
    <pre>{{ doc }}</pre>
    <p><a href="/">Home</a></p>
{% endblock %}
```

Add `render_template` to the `from flask import...` line at the top of `tinyflaskapp.py`, then modify your views to look like this:

```
@app.route('/')
def index():
    return render_template('index.html', funcs=sorted(docstrings))

@app.route('/functions/<func_name>')
def show_docstring(func_name):
    func_name = func_name.lower()
    if func_name in docstrings:
        return render_template('docstring.html',
                               func_name=func_name,
                               doc=docstrings[func_name])
    else:
        abort(404)
```

This code can be found in the `2-templates` folder of this chapter's source code.

Notice how the views become much simpler, and the HTML is much more readable now? Instead of composing a return string by hand, our views simply call `render_template()` and return the result.

So what does `render_template()` do? Well, it looks in the `templates` folder for the file supplied as the first argument, reads it, runs any processing instructions in the file, then returns the processed HTML as a string. Any keyword arguments supplied to `render_template()` are passed to the template and become available to its processing instructions.

Looking at the templates, we can see they are mostly HTML, but with some extra instructions for Flask, contained in `{{ }}` and `{% %}` tags. The `{{ }}` instructions simply substitute the value of the named variable into that point of the HTML. So for example the `{{ func_name }}` in `docstrings.html` substitutes the value of the `func_name` value we passed to `render_template()`.

The `{% %}` instructions contain logic and flow control. For example, the `{% for func in funcs %}` instruction in `index.html` loops over values in `funcs` and repeats the contained HTML for each value.

Finally, you may have spotted that templates allow **inheritance**. This is provided by the `{% block %}` and `{% extends %}` instructions. In `base.html` we declare some shared boilerplate HTML, then in the `<body>` tag we just have a `{% block body %}` instruction. In `index.html` and `docstring.html`, we don't include the boilerplate HTML; instead we extend `base.html`, meaning that these templates will fill the block instructions declared in `base.html`. In both `index.html` and `docstring.html`, we declare a `body` block, the contents of which Flask inserts into the HTML in `base.html`, replacing the matching `{% block body %}` there. Inheritance allows the reuse of common code, and it can cascade through as many levels as needed.

There is a lot more functionality available in Jinja2 template instructions; check out the template designer documentation for a full list at `http://jinja.pocoo.org/docs/dev/templates/`.

Other templating engines

Jinja2 is certainly not the only templating package in existence; you can find a maintained list of Python templating engines at `https://wiki.python.org/moin/Templating`.

Like frameworks, different engines exist because of differing philosophies on what makes a good engine. Some feel that logic and presentation should be absolutely separate and that flow control and expressions should never be available in templates, providing only value substitution mechanisms. Others take the opposite tack and allow full Python expressions within template markup. Others, such as Jinja2, take a middleground approach. And some engines use different schemes altogether, such as XML-based templates or declaring logic via special HTML tag attributes.

There isn't a "right" approach; it's best to experiment with a few and see what works best for you. Where a framework has its own engine though, like Django, or is tightly integrated with an existing engine, like Flask, you'll usually have a smoother run sticking with what they supply, if you can.

Adding some style

At the moment, our pages look a little plain. Let's add some style. We'll do this by including a static CSS document, but the same approach can be used to include images and other static content. The code for this section can be found in the 3-style folder in this chapter's source code.

First create a new static folder in your project folder, and in there create a new text file called style.css. Save the following to it:

```
body          { font-family: Sans-Serif; background: white; }
h1            { color: #38b; }
pre           { margin: 0px; font-size: 1.2em; }
.menuitem     { float: left; margin: 1px 1px 0px 0px; }
.link         { width: 100px; padding: 5px 25px; background: #eee; }
.link a       { text-decoration: none; color: #555; }
.link a:hover { font-weight: bold; color: #38b; }
```

Next update the <head> section of your base.html file to look like this:

```
<head>
    <title>Python Builtins Docstrings</title>
    <link rel="stylesheet" href="{{ url_for('static', filename='style.
css') }}"/>
</head>
```

Note the third and forth lines in the preceding code—that is the <link> tag—should be a single line in your code. Try your web application in the browser again and notice that it looks (hopefully) a little more up to date.

Here we've just added a stylesheet to our boilerplate HTML in base.html, adding a <link> tag pointing to our static/style.css file. We use Flask's url_for() function for this. The url_for() function returns paths to named parts of our URL space. In this case, it's the special static folder, which by default Flask looks for in the root of our web application. Another thing we can use url_for() for is to get the paths of our view functions, for example, url_for('index') would return /.

You can put images and other resources in the `static` folder, and reference them in the same way.

A note on security

If you're new to web programming, then I strongly recommend you read up on two common types of security flaw in web applications. Both are fairly easily avoided but can have serious consequences if not addressed.

XSS

The first is **Cross-Site Scripting (XSS)**. This is where an attacker injects malicious script code into a site's HTML, causing a user's browser to carry out operations in the security context of that site without the user's knowledge. A typical vector is user submitted info being redisplayed to users without proper sanitization or escaping.

For example, one method is to trick users into visiting URLs containing carefully crafted GET parameters. As we saw in *Chapter 2, HTTP and Working with the Web*, these parameters can be used by web servers to generate pages, and sometimes their content is included in the HTML of the response page itself. If the server is not careful to replace special characters in the URL parameters with their HTML escape codes when displayed, an attacker can put executable code, for example Javascript, into URL parameters and actually have it executed when that URL is visited. If they can trick a victim into visiting that URL, that code will be executed in the user's browser, enabling the attacker to potentially perform any action the user could.

The basic XSS prevention is to ensure that any input received from outside the web application is escaped properly when returned to the client. Flask is very helpful in this regard since it activates Jinja2's auto-escaping feature by default, meaning that anything we render via template is automatically protected. Not all frameworks have this feature though, and some that do need it to be manually set. Also, this only applies in situations where your user-generated content can't include markup. In situations like a wiki that allows some markup in user-generated content, you need to take much greater care—see the source code download for this chapter in the 5-search folder for an example of this. You should always make sure you check out your framework's documentation.

CSRF

The second form of attack is the **Cross-Site Request Forgery (CSRF)**. In this attack, a site is tricked into carrying out actions in the security context of a user, without the user's knowledge or consent. Frequently this is initiated by an XSS attack that causes a user's browser to perform an operation on the target site while the user is logged in. It should be noted that this can affect sites even when a user isn't actively browsing them; sites often clear cookie authentication tokens only when a user explicitly logs out, and hence from the site and browser's point of view, any request coming from the browser even after the user has stopped browsing a site—if they haven't logged out—will be as if the user is still logged in.

One technique to help prevent CSRF attacks is to make potentially abusable operations, such as submitting forms, require a one-time nonce value that is only known to the server and the client. CRSF attacks often take the form of a pre-composed HTTP request, mimicking a user submitting a form or similar. However, if every time a server sends a form to a client it includes a different nonce value, then the attacker has no way of including this in the pre-composed request, and hence the attack attempt can be detected and rejected. This technique is less effective against XSS initiated attacks, and attacks where an attacker is eavesdropping the HTTP traffic of a browsing session. The former is difficult to completely protect against, and the best solution is to ensure XSS vulnerabilities are not present in the first place. The latter can be mitigated using HTTPS rather than HTTP. See the OWASP pages linked to below for further information.

Different frameworks have different approaches to providing nonce-based CSRF protection. Flask doesn't have this functionality built in, but it is very easy to add something, for example:

```python
@app.before_request
def csrf_protect():
    if request.method == "POST":
        token = session.pop('_csrf_token', None)
        if not token or token != request.form.get('_csrf_token'):
            abort(403)


def generate_csrf_token():
    if '_csrf_token' not in session:
        session['_csrf_token'] = some_random_string()
    return session['_csrf_token']

app.jinja_env.globals['csrf_token'] = generate_csrf_token
```

Then in templates with forms, just do the following:

```
<form method="post" action="<whatever>">
    <input name="_csrf_token" type="hidden" value="{{ csrf_token()
}}">
```

This is from the Flask site: `http://flask.pocoo.org/snippets/3/`. Although this contains some Flask functionality, we haven't covered, including sessions and the `@app.before_request()` decorator, you just need to include the above code in your app, and make sure you include a `_csrf_token` hidden input in every form. An alternative approach is to use the Flask-WTF plugin that provides integration with the `WTForms` package, which has built-in CSRF protection.

Django on the other hand has built-in protection, though you need to enable and use it. Other frameworks vary. Always check your chosen framework's documentation.

> There is more information on XSS and CSRF on the Flask and Django sites:
> - `http://flask.pocoo.org/docs/latest/security/`
> - `https://docs.djangoproject.com/en/1.7/topics/security/`
>
> Also on the OWASP site, there is a repository of all sorts of computer security related information:
> - `https://www.owasp.org/index.php/XSS`
> - `https://www.owasp.org/index.php/CSRF`

Finishing up with frameworks

That's as far as we're going to take our dip into Flask, here. There are some examples of further adaptations to our application in the downloadable source code of this chapter, notably form submission, accessing form values in the request, and sessions. The Flask tutorial covers many of these elements in some detail, and is well worth checking out `http://flask.pocoo.org/docs/0.10/tutorial/`.

So that's a taste of what a very basic Python web application can look like. There are obviously as many ways to write the same app as there are frameworks though, so how do you choose a framework?

Firstly, it helps to have a clear idea of what you're looking to achieve with your application. Do you require database interaction? If so, a more integrated solution like Django may be quicker to get started with. Will you need a web-based data entry or administration interface? Again if so, Django has this out of the box.

Next you can look at your environment. Are there already preferred packages in your organization for operations you might want to perform, such as database access or unit testing? If so, do any frameworks already use these? If not then a microframework might be a better option, plugging in your required packages. Do you have a preferred operating system or web server for hosting, and which frameworks support these? Does your hosting restrict you in terms of Python version, database technology, or similar? Also, if you have web designers, do you have time to get them up to speed on a complex templating language, or must it be kept simple?

Answers to these questions can help you narrow down your choices. Then, researching the frameworks, asking people who are using them, and trying out a few likely looking ones will get you where you need to go.

Having said that, for a general web application that needs some user form submission and database access, you can't really go wrong with Django. It really is "batteries included", its database model is elegant, and its out-of-the box database administration and data entry interface is very powerful and can be a huge timesaver. And for simpler applications such as APIs, Flask is also a great choice, coupled with SQLAlchemy if database access is needed.

As I mentioned before, there's no right answer, but there's a lot to be learned by exploring what's available and seeing the different approaches that the frameworks take.

Of course, once we've got our web application, we need a way to host it. We're going to look at some options now.

Hosting Python web applications

As we discussed at the beginning of this chapter, in order to run a Python web application, we need a web server to host it. There are many web servers in existence today, and you will very likely have heard of several. Popular examples are Apache, nginx (pronounced *engine-x*), lhttpd (pronounced *lighty*), and Microsoft's **Internet Information Services (IIS)**.

There is a lot of terminology around web servers and various mechanisms they can use to invoke Python web applications. We're going to take a very brief tour of the history of web applications to help explain some of these concepts.

CGI

In the early days of the Web, web servers would mostly only be required to send clients HTML pages, or the occasional image file. As in the earlier figure of a HTTP request journey, these static resources would live on the hard disk of the server, and the web server's main task would be to accept socket connections from clients, map the URL of a request to a local file, and send the file back over the socket as an HTTP response.

However, with the rise of the need for dynamic content, web servers were given the ability to generate pages by invoking external programs and scripts, which we today call web applications. Web applications originally took the form of scripts or compiled executables that lived on disk next to the regular static content as part of the published web tree. The web server would be configured so that when a client requested these web application files, instead of just reading the file and returning it, the web server would launch a new operating system process and execute the file, returning the result as the requested HTML web page.

If we update our HTTP request's journey from our earlier image, our request's journey would now look something like this:

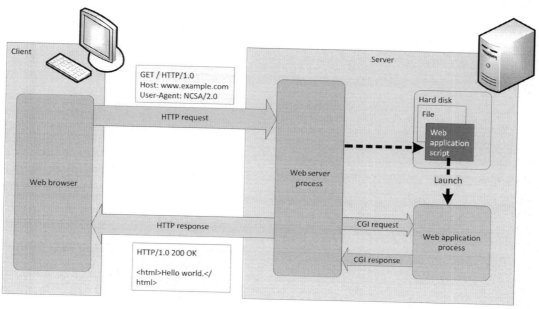

There obviously needs to be some kind of protocol for the web server and the web application to pass the HTTP request and the returned HTML page between them. The earliest mechanism for this was called the **Common Gateway Interface (CGI)**. The web server would decompose the request into environment variables, which it would add to the environment of the handler program when it was invoked, and pass the body of the request, if there was one, to the program via its standard input. The program would then simply pipe the HTTP response it generated to its standard output, which the web server would catch and return to the client.

Due to performance issues however, CGI is slowly falling out of favor these days, and writing a Python CGI application is something that should be avoided if at all possible.

Recycling for a better world

CGI works, but the major drawback is that a new process has to be launched for each request. Launching processes is expensive in terms of operating system resources, and so this approach is very inefficient. Alternatives have been developed.

Two approaches became common. The first was to make web servers launch and maintain multiple processes at startup, ready to accept new connections— a technique known as **pre-forking**. With this technique, there is still a one-process-per- client relationship, but the processes are already created when a new client connects, improving response time. Also the processes can be reused instead of being re-created anew with each connection.

Alongside this, web servers were made extensible and bindings were created to different languages so that the web application could be embedded within the web server processes themselves. The most commonly seen examples of these are the various language modules for the Apache web server for languages such as PHP and Perl.

With pre-forking and web application embedding, our request's journey might look like this:

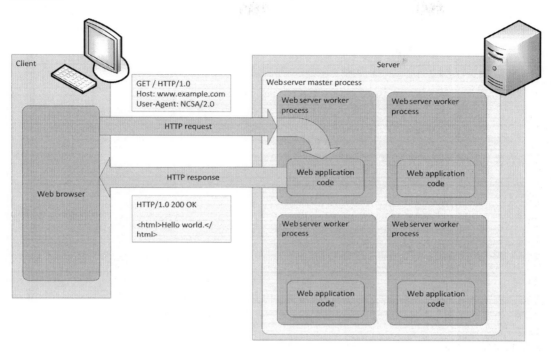

Here, the request is transformed by the language binding code, and the request our web application sees depends on the design of the binding itself. This approach to managing a web application works fairly well for general web loads, and remains a popular way to host web applications today. Modern browsers usually also offer multithreaded variants, where each process can handle requests using multiple threads, one for each client connection, further improving efficiency.

The second approach to solving CGI's performance problems was to hand off the management of the web application processes completely to a separate system. The separate system would pre-fork and maintain a pool of processes running the web application code. Like web server pre-forking, these could be reused for each client connection. New protocols were developed to allow the web server to pass requests to the external processes, the most notable being FastCGI and SCGI. In this situation, our journey would be:

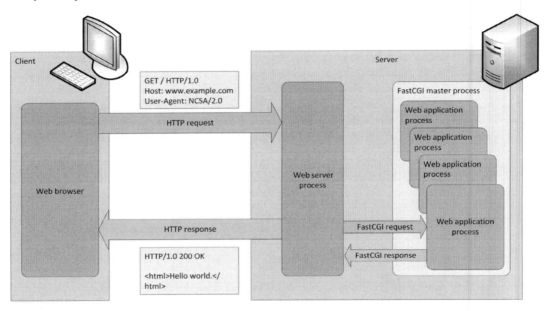

Again, how the request is transformed and presented to the web application depends on the protocol used.

Although in practice this is somewhat more complex to configure, it has advantages over embedding a copy of the application code in pre-forked web server processes. Primarily, the web application process pool can be managed independently of the web server process pool, allowing more efficient tuning of both.

Event-driven servers

Web client numbers continued to grow though, and the need arose for servers to be able to handle very large numbers of simultaneous client connections, numbers that proved problematic using the multiprocessing approaches. This spurred the development of event-driven web servers, such as *nginx* and *lighttpd*, which can handle many thousands of simultaneous connections in a single process. These servers also leverage preforking, maintaining a number of event-driven processes in line with the number of CPU cores in a machine, and hence making sure the server's resources are fully utilized while also receiving the benefits of the event-driven architecture.

WSGI

Python web applications were originally written against these early integration protocols: CGI, FastCGI, and a now mostly defunct mod_python Apache module. This proved troublesome though since Python web applications were tied to the protocol or server they had been written for. Moving them to a different server or protocol required some reworking of the application code.

This problem was solved with PEP 333, which defined the **Web Services Gateway Interface (WSGI)** protocol. This established a common calling convention for web servers to invoke web application code, similar to CGI. When web servers and web applications both support WSGI, servers and applications can be exchanged with ease. WSGI support has been added to many modern web servers and is nowadays the main method of hosting Python applications on the Web. It was updated for Python 3 in PEP 3333.

Many of the web frameworks we discussed earlier support WSGI behind the scenes to communicate with their hosting web servers, Flask and Django included. This is another big benefit to using such a framework — you get full WSGI compatibility for free.

There are two ways a web server can use WSGI to host a web application. Firstly it can directly support hosting WSGI applications. Pure Python servers such as Gunicorn follow this approach, and they make serving Python web applications very easy. This is becoming a very popular way to host Python web applications.

The second approach is for a non-Python server to use an adapter plugin, such as Apache's `mod_wsgi`, or the `mod_wsgi` plugin for nginx.

The exception to the WSGI revolution is event-driven servers. WSGI doesn't include a mechanism to allow a web application to pass control back to the calling process, hence there is no benefit to using an event-driven server with a blocking-IO style WSGI web application because as soon as the application blocks, for example, for database access, it will block the whole web server process.

Hence, most event-driven frameworks include a production-ready web server—making the web application itself event-driven and embedding it in the web server process is really the only way to host it. To host web applications with these frameworks, check out the framework's documentation.

Hosting in practice

So how does this all work in practice? Well as we saw with Flask, many frameworks come with their own built-in development web servers. However, these are not recommended for use in a production environment as they're generally not designed to be used where security and scalability are important.

Currently, probably the quickest way to host a Python web application with a production quality server is with the Gunicorn server. Using our Flask application from earlier, we can get it up and running using just a few steps. First we install Gunicorn:

```
$ pip install gunicorn
```

Next we need to slightly modify our Flask app so that it's use of `__builtins__` works correctly under Gunicorn. In your `tinyflaskapp.py` file, find the line:

```
objs = __builtins__.__dict__.items()
```

Change it to:

```
objs = __builtins__.items()
```

Now we can run Gunicorn. From within your Flask application project folder, run the following command:

```
$ gunicorn --bind 0.0.0.0:5000 tinyflaskapp:app
```

This will launch the Gunicorn web server, listening on port 5000 on all available interfaces and serving our Flask application. If we now visit it in a web browser via `http://127.0.0.1:5000`, we should see our documentation index page. There are instructions to daemonize Gunicorn, so that it runs in the background and starts and stops automatically with the system, available in the documentation pages at `http://gunicorn-docs.readthedocs.org/en/latest/deploy.html#monitoring`.

Gunicorn uses the pre-fork process model described earlier. You can set the number of processes (Gunicorn calls them workers) using the -w command line option. The 'Design' section of the documentation contains details on determining the best number of workers to use, though a good place to start is (2 x $num_cores) + 1, where $num_cores is the number of CPU cores available to Gunicorn.

Gunicorn offers two standard worker types: sync and async. The sync type provides strictly one-worker-per-client-connection behavior, the async type uses eventlet (see *Chapter 8, Client and Server Applications*, for details and installation instructions for this library) to provide an event-based worker, which can handle multiple connections. The sync type is only recommended if you are using Gunicorn behind a reverse proxy (see below), as using the sync type to serve directly to the Internet leaves your application vulnerable to Denial of Service attacks (see the Design section of the documentation for more details). If you are not using a reverse proxy, the async type should be used instead. The worker type is set on the command line using the -k option.

One effective way to improve performance and scale further is to employ a fast, event-driven web server, such as nginx, as a **reverse proxy** in front of your Gunicorn instance. A reverse proxy acts as a first line server for incoming web requests. It directly responds to any requests it can determine are erroneous, and can also be configured to serve static content in place of our Gunicorn instance. However, it is also configured to forward any requests that do require dynamic content to our Gunicorn instance so our Python web application can handle them. In this way, we get the performance benefits of nginx to deal with the bulk of our web traffic, and Gunicorn and our web application can focus on delivering just the dynamic pages.

 Detailed instructions on configuring this reverse proxy configuration can be found on the Gunicorn pages at http://gunicorn-docs.readthedocs.org/en/latest/deploy.html#nginx-configuration.

If you're more comfortable with Apache, then another effective hosting method is Apache with the mod_wsgi module. This takes a little more configuring, and full instructions can be found at: https://code.google.com/p/modwsgi/. mod_wsgi defaults to running applications in embedded mode, where the web application is hosted in each Apache process, and which results in a setup like the preceding pre-forking example. Alternatively it provides a daemon mode, where mod_wsgi manages a pool of processes external to Apache, similar to the earlier FastCGI example. Daemon mode is in fact recommended for stability and memory performance. See the mod_wsgi quick configuration documentation for instructions on this configuration, it can be found at: https://code.google.com/p/modwsgi/wiki/QuickConfigurationGuide.

Summary

We've taken a whistle-stop tour of putting Python applications on the Web. We got an overview of web application architectures and their relationship to web servers. We looked at the utility of Python web frameworks, noting how they give us tools and structure to write better web applications more quickly, and help us integrate our applications with web servers.

We wrote a tiny application in the Flask web framework, we saw how it can help us elegantly manage our URL space, and how templating engines can help us cleanly manage the seperation of application logic and HTML. We also highlighted a couple of common potential security vulnerabilities— XSS and CSRF— and looked at some basic mitigation techniques.

Finally, we discussed web hosting architectures and the various methods that can be used to deploy Python web applications to the Web. In particular, WSGI is the standard protocol of web server/web application interaction, and Gunicorn can be used for rapid deployment and scaled with an nginx reverse proxy. Apache with mod_wsgi is also an effective hosting approach.

We've covered a lot of ground in this book, and there's still plenty more exploring to be done. We hope this book has given you a taste of what's possible and an appetite for discovering more, and that this is just the start of your adventures in network programming with Python.

Working with Wireshark

When developing network applications, it's often useful to be able to see exactly what's being transmitted over the network. Maybe something weird is going on with your framing, you're trying to discover the user agent for your browser, or you want to see what's happening in the IP protocol or lower layers. We can employ a class of tools called **packet sniffers** to do this.

Packet sniffers

Packet sniffers are designed to capture all the network traffic that enters and leaves a computer, allowing us to see the full, raw contents of all packets that our programs send and receive, and all the headers and payloads of all the protocols on the stack.

We're going to take a quick look at one of these applications. It not only provides us with a very useful debugging tool for network programming, it also gives you a direct view of the structure of network traffic and gives you a better feel for the concepts of layering and encapsulation.

A small word of caution before we begin though; if you're using a computer on a network you do not own, such as at your place of work or study, you should get permission from your network administrator before running a packet sniffer. On networks that use network hubs rather than switches, sniffers may capture data destined for computers other than your own. Also, running a packet sniffer may be against your network's usage policy. Even if it's not, packet sniffers are powerful network monitoring tools and administrators generally like to be aware of when they're being used.

If this turns out to be difficult, don't panic! This book doesn't rely on having access to a packet sniffer at any point; we just think that you'll find them handy while programming for networks.

Wireshark

The program that we're going to take a look at is called **Wireshark**. It's an open source packet sniffer with support for interpreting a vast range of network protocols.

Installation

For Windows and Linux, Wireshark can be downloaded from `http://www.wireshark.org`. On Debian, Ubuntu, RHEL, CentOS, and Fedora it's available as the `wireshark` package.

You'll need to have root or administrator access in order to install this. On Windows, make sure that you install or update the `WinPcap` library if it asks you to do so, and also allow it to start the `WinPcap` driver at boot time when prompted.

On Debian and Ubuntu, you will need to configure Wireshark to allow regular users to run captures. Run the following command:

```
$ sudo dpkg-reconfigure wireshark-common
```

Say `Yes` to `Should non-superusers be able to capture packets?` Note that this doesn't automatically allow all non-super users to use Wireshark, they still need to be added to the `wireshark` group. Do this now for your own user, for example:

```
$ sudo usermod -aG wireshark myuser
```

You may need to log out and log in again for this to take effect, or possibly even reboot. For other Linux distributions, check their documentation, or there are instructions on the Wireshark wiki for assigning these rights at `http://wiki.wireshark.org/CaptureSetup/CapturePrivileges`.

If you run into trouble at any point, you can get further help regarding the installation on the wiki at `http://wiki.wireshark.org/CaptureSetup`.

Once configured, on Linux, just run `wireshark` in an X session to start the graphical interface.

Capturing some packets

Once you have Wireshark installed and running, you'll see a window that looks like this:

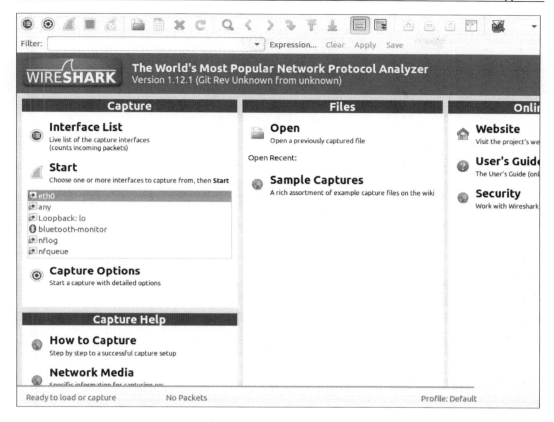

Packet sniffing usually works in two steps: first, we run a traffic capture session, and then we analyze the captured traffic. During a capture, Wireshark asks the operating system for a copy of all the network traffic it processes, which Wireshark then keeps in a buffer for us to analyze. Wireshark provides us with tools that let us filter the captured data so that we can work on only the data streams we want, and drill into each packet in order to take a look at the header data and the payloads.

So first, we need to select the interfaces on which we want to capture the traffic. We can see that there's a list of interfaces below the **Start** button. Wireshark captures all the network traffic that passes over all the interfaces that we select; this usually means that we end up capturing a lot of data that we're not actually interested in. In order to reduce this noise, it's best to capture as few interfaces as possible, ideally just one.

We're going to use the first RFC downloader, from *Chapter 1*, *Network Programming and Python*, RFC_downloader.py, to generate some network traffic to analyze. Since this program communicates with a host on the Internet, we want to capture the network interface that provides our Internet connection.

If you're not sure which interface is your Internet interface, then click on the **Interface List** button above the **Start** button to bring up the window, as shown in the following screenshot:

On the right-side of the dialog box, you can see the live counts of the number of packets that have passed through each of the interfaces, since we opened the window. You can generate some Internet traffic by browsing a website if there's not much happening. The interface with the fastest rising packet count will be the Internet interface (ignore the any interface on Linux). Make a note of the interface's name and close the window.

Network interfaces can capture packets in one of two modes: promiscuous mode and non-promiscuous mode. In promiscuous mode, the interface will pass all traffic that it receives on to the sniffer, even if it is traffic that is not destined for our computer. In non-promiscuous mode, the interface filters out any traffic that is not for our computer. Unless you have a very specific reason to, it's usually best to run in non-promiscuous mode, as this reduces the amount of extraneous traffic we need to filter manually. Wireshark enables promiscuous mode by default. To disable, go into **Capture | Options...** and ensure 'Use promiscuous mode on all interfaces' is unticked. Then check the 'Prom Mode' column in the interfaces list at the top of the options window, and ensure it's says disabled for the interfaces you're capturing on. When done, close the options window to return to the main screen.

Select your Internet interface from the interface list, which is below the **Start** button on the main screen, and click on **Start** to begin a capture. After a moment or two, we should see some packets coming in:

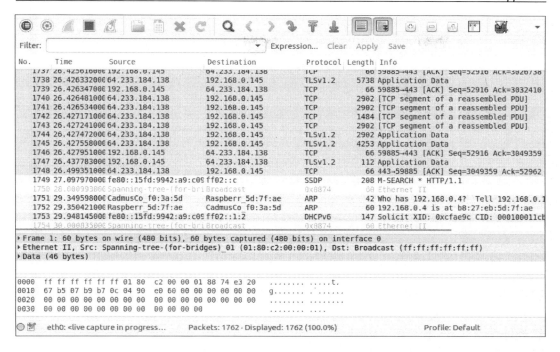

While Wireshark is capturing packets, let's generate some traffic that we're interested in analyzing. Run the `RFC_downloader.py` RFC downloader program in a terminal to download RFC 2324:

```
$ python3 RFC_downloader.py 2324

...

Network Working Group                                    L. Masinter
Request for Comments: 2324                            1 April 1998
Category: Informational

...
```

Once the download has run, return to Wireshark and stop the capture by clicking on the **Stop** button in the toolbar. If something goes awry with the capture, don't worry, we can try it again; just stop the capture, then click on the **Start a new live capture** button in the toolbar, and don't save changes to the previous capture when prompted. When it's running, run `RFC_downloader.py` again. Once you have a capture that contains the RFC downloader traffic, let's take a closer look at it.

As shown in the preceding screenshot, the Wireshark capture screen is broken into three sections. The top section lists the captured packets, one packet per row, and provides basic information for each packet, such as the source and destination addresses, and the name of the highest layer protocol for which the packet contains data.

The middle section contains a breakdown of the protocols present in the selected packet. The top line is equivalent to layer 1 in the network stack, with subsequent lines corresponding to the higher layers.

The bottom section contains a raw listing of the entire captured packet. This is broken into three main vertical areas. The numbers in the first column on the left-hand side are the byte offsets in hex of the start of the line from the beginning of the packet. The middle section consists of two columns of 8 hexadecimal numbers each; this section shows each byte in the packet as a hexadecimal integer. The section on the right-hand side, consisting of two columns of ASCII characters, is the ASCII representation of the bytes in the packet. Dots are used here, where a byte value maps to a nonprintable character.

Filtering

Let's see if we can find the packets that our downloader program has generated. There's probably a fair amount of extra network data in the capture, so first, we need to filter this out.

Wireshark lets us filter using any property of any of the protocols it supports. To filter, we use the filter box that is under the toolbar. Wireshark has a complete filter language, which you can investigate with the help system. For now, we're just going to do a few basic queries to find our packets. Type http in the filter box, and click on the **Apply** button. This restricts the displayed packets to just those that involve the HTTP protocol, as shown in the following screenshot:

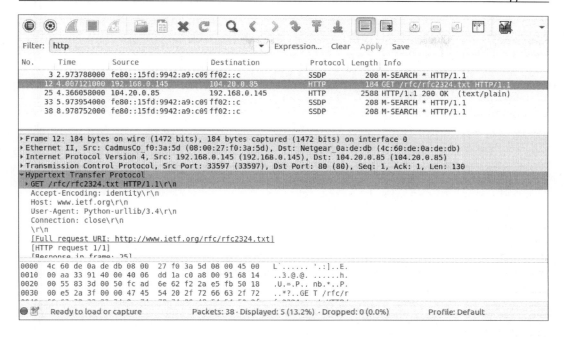

Even if the only HTTP traffic that you deliberately generated during the capture session was through the downloader program, it's possible that we'll see more HTTP packets than just those. This is because some programs, such as file cloud storage clients, communicate with their services in the background quite frequently through HTTP. Also, Wireshark currently identifies SSDP protocol packets as HTTP, since SSDP is derived from HTTP.

Not a problem though, we can refine our filter. The unique identifying feature of our downloader packets is the server that we communicated with, www.ietf.org. If we take a look at the packet list, you can see that the source and destination addresses of the captured packets are IP addresses, so before we write our new filter, we need to find out the IP address of www.ietf.org.

Retrieving the IP address of a hostname is called **name resolution**, and this is exactly the task that DNS was designed for. There are several mechanisms that we can use to interact with DNS. On Linux and Windows, we can use the `nslookup` command-line tool. Run the following command:

```
$ nslookup www.ietf.org
Server:         127.0.1.1
Address:        127.0.1.1#53


Non Authoritative answer:
www.ietf.org    canonical name = www.ietf.org.cdn.cloudflare-
                                dnssec.net.
Name:   www.ietf.org.cdn.cloudflare-dnssec.net
Address: 104.20.1.85
Name:   www.ietf.org.cdn.cloudflare-dnssec.net
Address: 104.20.0.85
```

The output indicates that `www.ietf.org` is actually hosted at two IP addresses: `104.20.1.85` and `104.20.0.85`. This is becoming increasingly frequent as more websites deploy load balancing and content delivery networks to spread the workload across servers.

A quick glance at our captured HTTP packets list will probably allow us to see which server we ended up connecting to. In the preceding example, it's `104.20.0.85`. However, to make sure, we can filter for both the IP addresses.

Note that `nslookup` may return different IP addresses than those shown in the preceding example. Web services can change IP addresses of their servers for various reasons.

So now, we can filter for `www.ietf.org`. Using the IP addresses you just resolved, enter this new query in the filter box:

```
http and (ip.addr == 104.20.1.85 or ip.addr == 104.20.0.85)
```

Click on the **Apply** button again. This query adds the extra condition that, as well as involving the HTTP protocol, packets must have an IP source or destination address of either `104.20.1.85` or `104.20.0.85`.

The `ip.addr` syntax is a typical example of filtering on a property of a protocol. There are many more. For example, if we want to filter by just the source address rather than both the source and destination addresses, we can use the following command:

```
http and (ip.src == 104.20.1.85 or ip.src == 104.20.0.85)
```

To explore all the available protocols and their properties, click on the **Expression...** button to the right of the filter box. In the left-hand pane of the window that appears, we can see all the protocols listed, and we can expand one by clicking on the corresponding triangle or **+** symbol, which will show its properties. In this window, IP is listed as `IPv4`.

Inspecting packets

Getting back to our RFC downloader packets, let's close the expression window if it's open, and turn our attention to the main window. After applying the `http and (ip.addr == 104.20.1.85 or ip.addr == 104.20.0.85)` filter, we should see two packets listed in the top section of the screen:

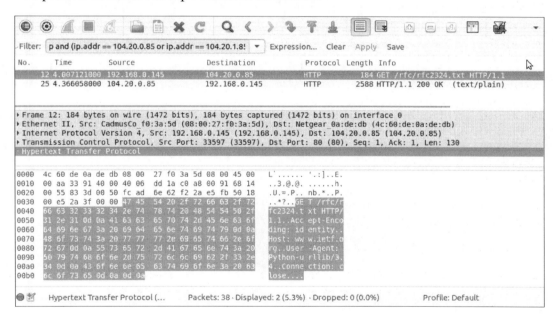

The first is the HTTP request that `urlopen()` sent to the server, and the second is the server's HTTP response.

Click on the first packet to select it, and turn your attention to the middle section of the window. We can see five lines of information. Each corresponds to a layer in the network stack and the protocol that is being used in this layer. While keeping an eye on the raw listing of the packets in the bottom section of the screen, click on the different lines in the middle section. You'll see that different areas of the raw packet listing get highlighted. The highlighted areas are the sections of the raw packet that are relevant for the protocol that you clicked on. For the first layer (the line beginning in **Frame**), it highlights the whole packet, since the whole packet is what's sent over the wire. For the last layer, **Hypertext Transfer Protocol**, it highlights the section of the packet that is the HTTP request, as shown in the preceding example. For the layers in between, it just highlights the header for that protocol's encapsulated packet.

We can drill into the header data for each encapsulated packet by clicking on the triangle or **+** symbols to the left of each protocol line in the middle section. If we do this for the **Hypertext Transfer Protocol** line, we get something like this:

```
▶ Frame 15: 184 bytes on wire (1472 bits), 184 bytes captured (1472 bits) on interface 0
▶ Ethernet II, Src: CadmusCo_f0:3a:5d (08:00:27:f0:3a:5d), Dst: Netgear_0a:de:db (4c:60:de:0a:de:db)
▶ Internet Protocol Version 4, Src: 192.168.0.145 (192.168.0.145), Dst: 104.20.1.85 (104.20.1.85)
▶ Transmission Control Protocol, Src Port: 42515 (42515), Dst Port: 80 (80), Seq: 1, Ack: 1, Len: 130
▼ Hypertext Transfer Protocol
  ▶ GET /rfc/rfc2324.txt HTTP/1.1\r\n
    Accept-Encoding: identity\r\n
    Host: www.ietf.org\r\n
    User-Agent: Python-urllib/3.4\r\n
    Connection: close\r\n
    \r\n
    [Full request URI: http://www.ietf.org/rfc/rfc2324.txt]
    [HTTP request 1/1]
```

The HTTP headers in our request have been interpreted by Wireshark and broken out to make them more readable. You can explore the other protocols' data in the same way.

Let's inspect the second packet that we captured, the HTTP response. Click on it now in the top section of the window:

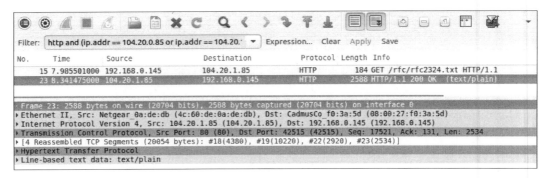

You'll notice some extra lines for this packet in the middle section. The line that refers to reassembled TCP segments indicates that the HTTP response was actually large enough to be broken across four TCP packets. Wireshark recognized this and reassembled the full HTTP packet by combining the relevant TCP packets, so when we click on the **Hypertext Transport Protocol** line, we see the whole HTTP packet.

> If you don't see this, you may need to switch it on in the options menu. Go to **Edit | Preferences...** to bring up the preference window, then expand **Protocols** in the list on the left-hand side of the screen, and scroll down and find **HTTP**. Make sure that both the options that mention spanning multiple TCP segments are checked.

Finally, the **Line-based text data** line shows us the response content media type (described in *Chapter 2, HTTP and Working with the Web*), and expanding the line shows us the text data of the body of the response.

A versatile tool

As you'll probably notice from browsing the menus, Wireshark is a very feature-rich network analyzer, and we've barely even scratched the surface of its full capabilities. I encourage you to keep it handy as you work with this book, and do use it wherever you'd like to take a closer look at the data being sent or received over the network.

Index

template designer documentation
   URL 257
templating 255-257
threading 220, 221
threads 219
thread safe 229
TLS (Transport Layer Security)
   about 117, 193
   e-mail, sending with 117-120
Tornado
   URL 251
Transmission Control Protocol (TCP) 13-15
TurboGears
   URL 251
Twitter API
   about 90
   authentication 91
   final touches 98
   rate limits 96, 97
   reply, sending 97, 98
   tweets, polling for 94
   tweets, processing 95, 96
   Twitter world clock 91
   URL 90
Twitter streaming APIs
   about 99
   alternative oAuth flows 99, 100

U

UDP sockets
   working with 188, 189
UdpTransportTarget() parameter 145
upstream 7
urllib package 29
URLs
   about 48, 49
   absolute URL 49
   in summary 54
   path URLs 49, 50
   query string 51, 52
   relative URLs 49, 50
   URL encoding 52-54
user agents
   about 42, 43
   URL 108

User Datagram Protocol (UDP)
   about 13, 14
   versus TCP 16

V

views 254

W

web API 65
web framework
   about 251
   basic services 251
webmaster
   about 107
   Robots.txt file 108
   user agent, selecting 108
web server 248-250
Web Services Gateway Interface (WSGI)
   protocol 267, 268
Wireshark
   about 272
   filtering 276-278
   installing 272
   packets, capturing 272-276
   packets, inspecting 279-281
   URL 272
   URL, for wiki 272
   versatile tool 281

X

XML API
   about 66
   approaches 66
   ElementTree 67, 68
XML parsing, Amazon S3 API 82
XSS (Cross-Site Scripting)
   about 259
   URL 261

Thank you for buying
Learning Python Network Programming

About Packt Publishing

Packt, pronounced 'packed', published its first book, *Mastering phpMyAdmin for Effective MySQL Management*, in April 2004, and subsequently continued to specialize in publishing highly focused books on specific technologies and solutions.

Our books and publications share the experiences of your fellow IT professionals in adapting and customizing today's systems, applications, and frameworks. Our solution-based books give you the knowledge and power to customize the software and technologies you're using to get the job done. Packt books are more specific and less general than the IT books you have seen in the past. Our unique business model allows us to bring you more focused information, giving you more of what you need to know, and less of what you don't.

Packt is a modern yet unique publishing company that focuses on producing quality, cutting-edge books for communities of developers, administrators, and newbies alike. For more information, please visit our website at www.packtpub.com.

About Packt Open Source

In 2010, Packt launched two new brands, Packt Open Source and Packt Enterprise, in order to continue its focus on specialization. This book is part of the Packt Open Source brand, home to books published on software built around open source licenses, and offering information to anybody from advanced developers to budding web designers. The Open Source brand also runs Packt's Open Source Royalty Scheme, by which Packt gives a royalty to each open source project about whose software a book is sold.

Writing for Packt

We welcome all inquiries from people who are interested in authoring. Book proposals should be sent to author@packtpub.com. If your book idea is still at an early stage and you would like to discuss it first before writing a formal book proposal, then please contact us; one of our commissioning editors will get in touch with you.

We're not just looking for published authors; if you have strong technical skills but no writing experience, our experienced editors can help you develop a writing career, or simply get some additional reward for your expertise.

Python Network Programming Cookbook

ISBN: 978-1-84951-346-3   Paperback: 234 pages

Over 70 detailed recipes to develop practical solutions for a wide range of real-world network programming tasks

1. Demonstrates how to write various besopke client/server networking applications using standard and popular third-party Python libraries.

2. Learn how to develop client programs for networking protocols such as HTTP/HTTPS, SMTP, POP3, FTP, CGI, XML-RPC, SOAP and REST.

Functional Python Programming

ISBN: 978-1-78439-699-2   Paperback: 360 pages

Create succinct and expressive implementations with functional programming in Python

1. Implement common functional programming design patterns and techniques in Python.

2. Learn how to choose between imperative and functional approaches based on expressiveness, clarity, and performance.

Please check **www.PacktPub.com** for information on our titles

Mastering Object-oriented Python

ISBN: 978-1-78328-097-1   Paperback: 634 pages

Grasp the intricacies of object-oriented programming in Python in order to efficiently build powerful real-world applications

1. An object-oriented approach to Python web development gives you a much more fully-realised experience of the language. The flexibility and power of Python, combined with the improvements in design, coding and software maintenance that object-oriented programming allows, is built to respond to the challenges of increasingly more complex and data-intensive application development, making difficult tasks much more manageable.

Parallel Programming with Python

ISBN: 978-1-78328-839-7   Paperback: 128 pages

Develop efficient parallel systems using the robust Python environment

1. Demonstrates the concepts of Python parallel programming.

2. Boosts your Python computing capabilities.

3. Contains easy-to-understand explanations and plenty of examples.

Please check **www.PacktPub.com** for information on our titles